BALLOTS AND BETRAYALS

BALLOTS AND BETRAYALS

She has to defeat the man she loves

Jayanta G Borpujari

First published by NU VOICE PRESS 2024
An imprint of Hubhawks Pvt. Ltd
www.nuvoicepress.com

ISBN: 978-81-970218-6-2

Typeset by Saanvi Graphics, Noida

Published by Nu Voice Press

For Munmun, the love of my life
&
Rohin, Nihit—my crowning jewels

ACKNOWLEDGEMENT

Thanks for picking up this book. The discerning readers' patronage defines the success of an author's work.

I am grateful to my elder sisters, Juri and Jaya, for their encouragement and constructive feedback during this project. I regret making Juriba read the unpolished first draft with so many gaps. But she believed in the story. Her enthusiasm spurred me to reshape and refine this narration. A special thanks to Rohin for his quick copyedit support at a short notice.

I am indebted to everyone who reached out to me with rich tributes for my debut novel *Beyond the Blinding Sun*. They inspired me to continue this journey as a writer.

My deep appreciation to the HubHawks team for their professional work and dedication to this project. They have done amazing work to bring out this book so quickly.

Politics has never been as divided, bitter, and hostile as in recent years. *Ballots and Betrayals* is a love story in the time of intense politics. Readers on either side of the fault line, as well as the fence-sitters, will identify with the events in this story. The characters, the electioneering, the conspiracies, the heartaches, and the triumphs will feel live, relevant, and hard-hitting.

Happy reading!

Jayanta Gopal Borpujari

1

It was one of his cherished Saturday evenings.

He stared into his empty Waterford Crystal whiskey glass. Resisting a strong yearning for a refill, he closed his eyes and rocked the chair slowly. Mozart's Fifth Symphony soothed his nerves while the cleverly-placed table lamps' diffused light further mellowed the atmosphere.

Robin Garg loved his peaceful solitude. After the week's breathless days and sleepless nights, he thought he owed it to himself. Eyes shut, head thrown back, legs stretched—he savoured these peaceful moments.

But it was not destined to be just another Saturday evening.

Dinner was laid and the dishes were covered with cloches. The instructions were clear. On Saturday evenings, the housekeeper was to leave the spread on the dining table and retire for the night. He would have dinner whenever he wished, occasionally using the microwave oven to reheat the food, and leave the dirty plates in the kitchen sink. At times he opted not to eat at all and surrendered to his cravings. It could be more music—Mozart or Beethoven or Bach—a book, or the pleasure of doing absolutely nothing. No more, and no less, than two large pegs of his favourite single malt.

Robin started his professional career in Bangalore. The beautiful Garden City grew on him. He made it the base for all of his business and social service initiatives. Ritu loved the city too. They wanted, from Bangalore, to expand their business network to cover the entire country. Moving out of Garden City was never an option.

However, destiny had other designs. Robin had to leave his much-loved comfort zone and escape to the national capital after a terrible incident turned his life upside down. He had lost what he loved the most! He watched his world crash in front of him like a paralysed man watching a powerful tsunami and ever since, carried painful guilt that he should have done better to save her. Devastated, he lost his will to live. But he fought back. True to his character, he rediscovered his self-confidence and started working harder than ever. He moved fast to recover everything—his influence, popularity, and a ruthless commitment to getting whatever he set out to get. But for his painful loneliness, he was back on the top of his world.

Robin appointed a group of renowned architects, construction contractors and interior decorators to build a two-storied villa in New Delhi's Dwarka on a plot he had bought long back. He missed Ritu, well aware that the journey of constructing a home would have been so enjoyable with her around. It turned out to be a lovely house, and he took pride in the significant effort he had put to construct it. It was his own creation.

House number twenty-nine was not the biggest in the colony, but it was the most appealing one. A five-foot-high barbed-wire fence covered with deftly-trimmed Giant Thujas gave the property a homey look. The electronically-controlled gate opened to a driveway that turned right and led to a garage for three cars. Two parking spaces were in use while the middle slot remained unoccupied. Robin never allowed anyone to park there. He instructed his house help to clean that space every day with extra care. Once, he found a trash can in that space. The hapless cleaner got sacked that very day. He would never compromise on what mattered most to him.

The lush green lawns on the other side of the driveway led to a bed of colourful flowers: rose, marigold, daisy, lily, and many others. A paved track from the turn of the driveway led to the doorsteps of the main house. Past a small veranda, an imposing teakwood front door with intricate carvings added to the overall elegant facade. A classic calling bell hung prominently on the door. The calligraphic plaque to the right side of the door read 'Ritu and Robin'. This nameplate was the most precious possession Robin had carried back from Bangalore. "Don't even try to rush me on this. I *will* take my time in getting it right," shot back Ritu when Robin had urged her to hurry up while finalising the design.

The door opened to a well-appointed hall that had two distinct parts. The left part was to accommodate large gatherings. The off-white leather sofas on the right could seat up to fifteen people at a time. A glass-top centre table boasted beautiful silver artifacts. Three standing lamps, two antique table lamps, and the downlights, all placed to perfection, gave the room a pleasingly sophisticated look. Two large crystal chandeliers, one looking down on the left side carpet and the other over the glass table, were used only during large banquets. Nevertheless, they added significant glamour to the interiors even when not in use. The walls were ornate with choice collections—the most notable of which were a handcrafted Persian carpet with an intriguing play of colours and a superb reproduction of the distinctive masterpiece *Water Lily Pond* by Claude Monet.

"I feel her presence all around this house, all the time! I know Ritu would have set it up just the way I have. She has been my inspiration throughout this journey," Robin once told a friend.

The small extension to the hall at the far end on the right side provided just enough space for two cosy chairs with a small tea table. The window over the table opened out to a pretty garden. A study lamp stood out from the floor like a crane. Robin loved to have his morning tea sitting on the chair on the left. On rare occasions, he sat there in the evenings as well, looking out of the window aimlessly, for long. No one was allowed to approach him at such times.

Robin never sat on the chair on the right. Neither did he allow anyone to do so. The chair, dusted and polished every day, was totally out of bounds. All regular visitors to the house knew of this custom. Robin never explained why and no one ever asked. Everyone guessed; most were right.

He was in his study in an encore of his typical Saturday evenings. Given the audio-visuals, the room was used like a recreation room. Robin used this comfortable private retreat located in one corner of the ground floor to shed off the stress from his hectic weekly schedule. He was in a state of mental inertia, lost in Mozart's world. Malcolm Gladwell's *Outliers* rested on his knees, open but upside down.

He had left the cell phone in his bedroom upstairs in silent mode. It was a mistake. He knew they might call him tonight on his cell phone. There was a landline extension next to the music system. But it rarely rang even on weekdays.

Robin pondered having dinner but decided against it. The previous week had been very hard with a series of meetings—strategy to public relations, data mining to speech writing and fundraising to budget control. He knew he must unwind now as much as he could to be ready for the punishing schedule ahead. He would not have relaxed Saturday evenings like this for some time to come, irrespective of which candidate got the high command's blessings. He was hopeful of being nominated by the ruling Nationalist Party of Patriots (NPP) for the West Delhi parliamentary seat by-election. The party had not finalised the candidate yet. But he and his core supporters wanted to have a head start with the campaign process. They had been working for weeks as if he already had the nomination. He knew there was formidable competition for the ticket, and the old stalwarts were doing all they could to deny him a chance. He was comparatively new, still seen as an outsider by many party seniors. A few veteran party leaders thought that would be his undoing. But others, including the party's high command, considered that his strength.

In these lonely moments when his untethered mind basked in peace, Robin wondered if all of this running around was worth anything. He had risen to dizzying heights of fame and prosperity through hard work, struggle, and sacrifice, and had lost a lot in the process including the most precious jewel of his life. In a relentless chase for growth, wealth, power, and fame, he had lost what he wanted the most. Why should he even bother anymore?

He pushed his chair further back, pressed his eyelids hard in an attempt to purge unwanted images and tried to flow with the music.

To hell with everything else. The world can wait. Let me enjoy my blessed Saturday evening! Meanwhile, yet another twist to his eventful life was waiting round the corner. Yet unaware, Robin was in bliss.

2

Purnima Bajaj Bhatt tossed around in bed late into the night. After an eventful week, she looked forward to some quality sleep this Saturday evening. As someone who usually fell asleep minutes after retiring to bed, Purnima did not know how to handle this unfamiliar challenge. She stayed true to her normal sleeping posture for a while, then half-heartedly turned to her right, lay still with her back on the bed, buried her face in the pillow, and returned to her favoured left again in frustration. She pressed her eyelids hard and swore not to let them loose till elusive sleep rescued her from her misery. Exhausted with the day's gruelling schedule and drained by the extraordinary recent developments, she desperately needed a night of sound sleep. When she accepted what was uncharacteristic of her—not out of conviction, but due to persistent pressure from people she couldn't easily refuse—she knew hard days lay ahead. She had never been comfortable with politics.

Given her social standing, her professional pre-eminence, and years of laudable social work, Purnima was very popular in the city. The masses loved her dedication, generosity, amiable personality, and commitment to social justice and development. She was also a regular invitee to hi-society events in the city. The elites of politics, academia, business, and bureaucracy, all wanted to rub shoulders with her.

When Dr Harsh Malhotra, the President of the United National Democratic Party (UNDP) Delhi Unit, initially requested her to fight the by-election on a UNDP ticket, Purnima laughed it off. "You cannot be serious about this, Malhotra *saab*. I have nothing to do with politics. I do not know anything about it, nor do I wish to. So, thank you; I am truly honoured. But I will not be able to accept this kind offer."

Harsh Malhotra had smiled and replied, "Well, I see your point. But representing our celebrated party is an honour in itself. We have had many instances when political neophytes joined us with serious apprehensions and ultimately ended up making huge contributions towards our dream of an inclusive, secular, and democratic country. Today, the country needs people like you as never before. We have witnessed severe assaults on our national ethos in recent years; watched concerted efforts made to shake the very foundation on which our nation stands. The reckless centralisation of power, the politicisation of public institutions, scant respect for the minorities and the marginalised, disregard for public opinion, I can go on! These are now the norm rather than the exceptions. There are efforts being made to rewrite our history to suit one narrative. These are the times we need people like you to join mainstream politics and make a difference. We know you have clean, bright and secular credentials. West Delhi is our stronghold. We won it last time when we did very badly elsewhere. You *will* win this contest with us and you will do a great job as a parliamentarian. Please consider our offer."

Purnima thought for a while and replied, "I am truly honoured that you have considered me to be worthy of this. But, please, thank you, but no thanks. Please be so kind, Malhotra *saab*, as to appreciate *my* perspective. I am happy with my professional and social work; I hardly have time for anything else. On top of it, as I said, I do not have any interest in active politics. My sincere thanks to all concerned. But it's best we do not discuss this issue again."

Harsh Malhotra smiled and chose to not persist at that time. But, not being a person to give up easily, he put intense pressure on her subsequently. He used respected politicians, professional seniors and even one of her mentors whom she could barely refuse. The think tank in the party believed that there could be no better candidate than Purnima for this constituency. Given her unique bonding with the electorate, clean image, and commendable philanthropy, she seemed to be unbeatable if she agreed to join the fray.

Ultimately, she gave in to the persuasion and agreed to accept the UNDP nomination for the West Delhi constituency. The party's remarkable success in seizing this prestigious parliamentary seat in the previous election against the backdrop of an electoral debacle confounded the pundits. The NPP returned to power with an imposing majority in the lower house of the Parliament but lost one of their safest constituencies. It was no secret that NPP would deploy all their resources to win back the seat. The UNDP leadership was confident that Durjoy Kumar would be the NPP candidate. The two-time member of Parliament, still smarting from a loss in his backyard, was expected to go all out to restore his pride. UNDP had to be innovative. They had to challenge Durjoy Kumar with a surprise candidate, someone without political baggage, a candidate whose past would provide no latitude for smear campaigns. They believed Purnima Bajaj Bhatt was their best bet.

Purnima Bajaj Bhatt, known to the public as Purnima Bhatt, was one of the most celebrated physicians in Delhi. She had completed her MD from All India Institute of Medical Sciences (AIIMS) with top honours and joined them as a faculty member. After twelve years of dedicated service to the institute, blessed with love and admiration from her patients, Purnima took early retirement to follow her passion and serve the poor and needy. She wanted to give back something to the society that gave her much love, and attain peace and happiness that she could not find in her routine job.

Purnima had spent her childhood in different parts of the country, packing her bags every three or four years as her father moved cities with his transferrable Central Government job. However, Bangalore had a special place in her heart. She had lived in the city from the seventh standard till the end of her higher secondary education, a rare long stint in one place. Those formative early years—the years of puberty and revolt, crushes and heartbreaks, starry-eyed dreams and nightmares, the drive to excel and urge to escape—had given Bangalore a special status in her heart.

The Central School in Victoria Layout, the middle-income group housing colony in Austin Town, leisurely weekend walks down Brigade Road, delicious late evening treats in Mahatma Gandhi Road's Lakeview ice-cream parlour, her best friend Shazia—these beautiful memories always warmed her heart. However, nothing else ruled her heart as *he* did. Two decades had passed since, but his images remained in her mind as sharp as ever. She was too young to understand love but old enough to develop a crush on the young man staying one block away from her. His fair complexion, medium height, athletic body, dark hair, bright smiling eyes, reluctant moustache, inviting lips, warmth, wit, his casual soft touch, just everything about him mesmerised her in her early teens. He ruled her heart throughout adolescence and stayed true as she grew up.

Purnima did not understand why she looked forward to his visits every evening. She had no clue why she felt so shy when he came home. She wanted to talk to him for hours but could not face him even for a few minutes at one go. Every time the young man came home, the maid called out for her. Purnima always ran out of her room to greet the young man only to fade out like a late afternoon sunflower soon after exchanging pleasantries. Each time she retired hurriedly to her room with some excuse. Often, he followed her to the room and teased her, pinched her cheeks with a joke, fondly stroked her hair, asked her about school, her friends, and exams. He never asked her things that she would have loved him to ask. She never managed to say words that she would have loved to say. She failed to understand herself in those years. By the time she understood, it was too late!

The young man was in an early stage of his professional career. He was transferred to Lucknow a year and a few months before Purnima was to sit for her twelfth standard board examination. They kept in touch through letters for over a year. Her letters narrated silly incidents in school and reported the latest delicacies served by her mother, who incidentally, was a great cook. His letters delivered sermons on the importance of studying hard, along with a few restrained words of personal care and affection. Time took a toll on their communication. Busy in their respective worlds, they lost contact over time.

Purnima could never forget the young man. But she did not look for him. It was tempting to rationalise this because of the two failed relationships of her life, one with a fellow student in Guwahati Medical College and the other with a senior doctor in AIIMS. But that would be far from the truth. The first relationship had not lasted more than a few months. The second, an affair with her senior colleague Dr Satish Bhatt, had survived a few months of intense romance followed by months of turbulent marriage. They had lived separately for a year before completing the divorce formalities. The young man from Bangalore survived these tribulations, tucked safely in a corner of her heart.

Purnima often wondered why she failed to get over a relationship that did not exist. Each time she thought of reaching out to him, she asked herself why he had never bothered to get in touch with her. If he did not care, why should she?

Ever since she had agreed to contest the election, she was very busy with various political commitments. She cancelled consultation appointments and skipped other social service obligations. It was sure to get much worse until the elections were over. Although no formal announcements had been made yet, she had no doubts what was in store once the nomination was made public.

When her journalist friend Radha Saluja invited her for lunch earlier that afternoon, Purnima had no choice but to agree. It was never easy to turn down an invite from her best friend. They had a great time together as always. Between main course and dessert, Radha said something that was innocuous enough, hardly more than lunchtime gossip, but which she did not know would unleash a tempest in her friend's life.

"I must tell you this. I attended a dinner last evening hosted by an uncle of mine, Amol Sharma. Not sure if I have talked to you about him before, a *really* sweet gentleman! They are a nice family, all of them. It was their silver anniversary. They had invited many bigwigs."

"Good for you," said Purnima. "Would have been more useful if you covered the page three stuff, though."

"Wait! I want to tell you about this guy—handsome, rich, and a hell of a gentleman! I had a one-on-one chat with him for nearly half an hour. He was so impressive, I tell you. Somewhere in between the chat, I nearly wished I were not married!" said Radha with a giggle. "But I remembered *you*. You *should* meet this guy. I'm telling you, you must."

"Radha, please don't go there again."

"My dear, I am not asking you to marry him! What rubbish! I think he is a great guy. Good to make a friend. He is a very successful businessman, well connected with people who matter in this city."

Radha took out a small piece of paper from her handbag and kept it flat on the table. Then, she picked up Purnima's cell phone, took its photo and returned the phone to its place.

"That's the name. It's his handwriting. Don't judge him by his awful handwriting! You know what, when I asked him, he happily gave his contact details, and I gave mine. Of course, I don't expect you to call an unknown man. If you say yes, I shall do the necessary. Meanwhile, keep the contact details handy. You do need some change of scene, honey, with all this muck about politics and elections!" said Radha with her typical naughty smile.

For the next few minutes, she described the man, his profession, his background, where all he had been, etc. She stopped only after suspecting that she had lost Purnima's attention somewhere in between.

Purnima had laughed off Radha's non-stop account of the man and her handsome tribute to him without paying any serious attention. She knew Radha loved her. She also knew that Radha was on a constant match-making drive, driven by a belief that Purnima was not happy as a single lady. It was not the first time Radha had tried to play cupid.

Back home, stretched out on her sofa, she looked at the image on her phone casually, laughing at the sweet stupidity of her dear friend. When she read the name, it sounded very familiar! Radha's words then came back to her, describing the man's looks, background, profession *et al*. She could not believe it. *Was it him? Could it be?*

Slipping into bed, she tried hard to un-remember the name. But of course, she could not. Tossing around in bed, she returned to her teenage days. Bangalore—Austin town and the neighbourhood, the absolute charmer, his beautiful words, the blushes, the restless evenings, and the sleepless nights—everything returned to ambush her and deny her the sleep she desperately desired.

Was destiny giving her yet another chance to rise above her self-harming pride? Was he indeed the same man? She decided to not hold on to her silly vanity again. She knew she had to act. First of all, she must make sure he was the same man.

She got up, switched on the table lamp, and looked at the image again. She felt the handwriting softly with the tips of her fingers, held it close to her heart and then felt the name again before looking at the telephone number.

After some hesitation, she picked up the receiver with a nervous hand. Out of the two numbers written, she had to choose one. For no apparent reason, she chose the second one. An eight-digit number; it had to be his residential telephone.

3

It was quite late for a weekend evening. Usually by now, Praveen Lakhotia would have locked the offices and retired to his modest lodging at the far right of the compound. But it was not a routine weekend. The by-election was only a few weeks away. The nomination papers had to be filed no later than the Monday the week after. Hence, Praveen *bhai* was in the kitchen chasing away mosquitoes. But his ears were glued to the calling bell just in case his seniors were looking for him for tea, coffee or any other errands.

The old single-storied building in Central Delhi's Prithviraj Road boasted the NPP's now ubiquitous symbol prominently on its boundary wall. It was an irrefutable powerhouse for one of the most populous nations on earth. Ever since NPP stormed into power eight years ago with an absolute majority in the lower house of the Parliament, their national headquarters had become the most important building in the country. When the party returned to power with a brute majority three years back for their second term, the NPP command centre wielded unprecedented influence.

The party had an ambitious vision for the country. It was not only about ruling a nation of a billion-plus people; it was about changing the way citizens live, eat, think, and raise their children. The leaders wanted to undo 'the wrongs done to the country over decades'; they wanted to change social dynamics, alter popular perception of history and hopefully rewrite the past! The ruling elite wanted to promote an ideology that they held dear but had never been able to propagate. However, their undue haste had alienated citizens who were not charmed by their vision.

Senior party functionaries were engaged in a critical meeting. The discussions were so intense that none of the participants had thought about asking Praveen *bhai* for refreshments. Their candidate for the West Delhi parliamentary constituency had to be finalised, a decision they had deferred due to several difficulties. The selection of a candidate for the lower house of the Parliament was never easy due to multiple challenges. They had to weigh in on the abilities of the key contenders, accommodate pressure lobbies, consider caste equations, and assess the profiles of their likely opponents. A resolution on the West Delhi ticket was more complicated than usual. The constituency had always been an NPP stronghold ever since it was carved out of the Outer Delhi and South Delhi constituencies. However, it had returned a UNDP candidate in the last election. Only UNDP, the dominant national party since independence, had offered some resistance to NPP's meteoric rise to power in recent years.

"Gentlemen, we do not have much time. A decision has to be made now, right now, in this meeting," roared Manoj Seth, the NPP national president. The high-powered committee had been deliberating the nomination in a conference room in the left wing of the building.

The contrast between the left wing and the rest of the office was glaring. The large hall behind the front door, accessible to anyone who entered the compound, had upholstered sofa sets on its right side and rows of cushioned chairs with small tables on the left. The NPP's logo, portraits of their supreme leader and of the party president, and a wall clock decorated the wall behind the reception desk. The right-side wall had a huge oil painting depicting the Mahabharata's iconic moment—Sri Krishna urging a dejected Arjuna to rise to his karma. The right-side door led to a corridor with rooms of various sizes meant for the party workers' meetings, sundry work or general socialising. The door facing the entrance opened out to two dining halls—a large one for the workers and the smaller exclusive setting for the party leaders—besides a kitchen, two stores and toilets.

The electronically controlled left-wing door was accessible only to a privileged few. Most party workers never got to see this restricted side of the building which was meant only for the current office bearers and very senior members. That door opened to two meeting rooms and exclusive offices for the president and senior general secretaries. The offices were well-furnished with leather sofas, teakwood furniture, satin curtains, fine-knotted carpets, crystal flower vases, and bone chinaware. The last room in this wing had yet another security door. It was accessible to only three persons at the top of the party hierarchy apart from the two IT experts. Grapevine had it that the room hosted a sophisticated data centre.

The West Delhi parliamentary seat had fallen vacant due to the sudden demise of the sitting UNDP parliamentarian. NPP was determined to wrest it back at any cost. The party's veteran leader, who lost the last election but had won from the constituency twice earlier, was equally keen to salvage his pride by winning the seat for the third time. If denied a ticket, he was likely to revolt against the party and fight the election as an independent.

The candidate rumoured to be the frontrunner for the NPP ticket had no grassroots experience. Besides, the committee had no clue as to the likely UNDP candidate.

"Imposing an outsider is something, I am afraid, may not go well with our rank and file. I know some of them are not very happy with Kumar *saab*. But, once we nominate someone likely to be seen as an interloper, they may fall back on the usual son-of-the-soil wagon. I think we should seriously consider Gupta *ji*. He has been working in this constituency for many years, going back twenty years to his days as a Municipal Councillor," said Suresh Ahluwalia, President of the Delhi unit of NPP.

Manoj Seth shot back, "We have been through this argument before, haven't we, Suresh *bhai*? If we keep repeating ourselves, we shall not decide for another week and the nomination date shall be over. We shall do this on merits, on the ability of the candidate to win this seat for us. It is your job to handle and convince the ranks."

"Shall we take a poll and see which candidate is preferred by a majority?" asked another member.

Manoj Seth thought for a while and said, "Sure, we can do that. I need to make a call before that. Excuse me for a minute."

The party president hurried out of the room, talked to someone in a hushed but reverent tone for a few minutes and returned to the meeting room. He settled his bulky figure into the chair and locked eyes for brief seconds with each person in turn. As his silence stressed everyone in the room, he shuffled in his seat to be more comfortable, rested his clasped hands on the table and stared at the distant wall without uttering a word.

After a few anxious minutes, they heard him say in an imposing voice. "We have a decision here." He put a circle around a name on the piece of paper with the shortlisted candidates and continued, "You may take up further necessary actions from here. I guess that starts with informing the candidate."

The paper passed hands. Everyone was baffled by the sudden turn of events. Some were happy, and some were very unhappy with the choice made. But everyone was dismayed with the way the decision was taken and conveyed. Before anyone could react, if at all anyone would have, the national president got up and left the room, mumbling a perfunctory goodbye to all.

Everyone knew that discussions were over. The senior party leaders were unhappy that such theatres of egalitarian consultations followed by unilateral decisions had become a norm in the party ever since this president had taken charge. They all preferred a vote to choose the candidate. But the long discussions culminated in a decision that was imposed after a secretive call. None of them had any doubt about who the national president had called.

As the rest of the committee members left the meeting room without a word, Suresh Ahluwalia did not get up from his chair. Like many others in the party, he was fed up with the president's dictatorial style. But he knew it was better to stay quiet. He knew that the only response to a word of dissent would be his swift removal from the position of state president. As a shrewd politician with years of experience under his belt, he was not going to let imprudence rob him of the powers he enjoyed. He believed times would change. He had learnt the hard way that patience, perseverance, and a great degree of insensitivity were the hallmarks of a successful politician.

He now had the responsibility of announcing the nomination to the outside world. First, he had to inform the nominated candidate—*that haughty usurper from nowhere*! He sighed and pressed the calling bell for Praveen *bhai*. What he needed most at that time was a cup of strong coffee.

After a few sips and restless wandering, he settled back in his chair. He stared at the telephone for a while, looked away, and banged the table hard in frustration. After giving himself some time, he took a deep breath, slowly repeated it thrice and picked up the receiver.

There was no response from the called number. Suresh Ahluwalia checked if he had the candidate's landline number. He did not. Another ring to the mobile number; still no reply. He had to contact the candidate somehow; the options left were: try the landline number or go to the candidate's house himself.

He wondered what next. He had to do something he wished he didn't have to.

4

The last movement of Beethoven's Fifth Symphony had reached its finale. The relatively joyful ending had cheered Robin up. He thought the mood was just right for a switch to Mozart, but felt too lazy to walk up to his proudly-preserved, antique record player. That's when the phone rang. Hearing the ring, he cursed himself. He should have done better! When such an important call was expected tonight, it was utterly irresponsible of him to leave the cell phone upstairs. In a rare moment of nervousness, he hesitated and finally picked up the receiver with a mixed sense of enthusiasm and apprehension,

He hurriedly said, "Suresh *ji*, please tell me. Has there been a formal decision taken at the meeting?"

There was no answer from the other side.

"Hello, sorry if I made a mistake. I guess it is not Mr. Suresh Ahluwalia on the other side? Who is on the line, please?"

Still no response; Robin could hear uneasy breathing on the other side.

A few minutes earlier, Purnima had completed dialling the number and had waited breathlessly to hear the voice on the other side. Taken aback by a pointed question rather than the usual greeting, she took time to respond. She wanted to hear the voice again before speaking.

These were anxious moments for Purnima. She knew she would be embarrassed if the man was not indeed her childhood heartthrob. It was too late in the night to retreat with a simple apology. But she would be equally embarrassed if the receiver turned out to be her man. She might blush and turn speechless yet again, just like she did in her teenage years. Should she introduce herself or challenge him to identify her; should she ask for an explanation as to why he had never tried to get in touch with her or ignore the past. Should she be reserved or pour her heart out?

"This is Robin Garg. Not sure if you can hear me. Please, speak louder? I'm unable to hear you."

Purnima's heart swelled. She had found the right man. Still, she did not respond.

"Please, whoever is calling, do speak up now otherwise I shall disconnect the line."

Purnima knew there was no time to be wasted now.

"Hello!"

"Oh, good, I hear you now. May I know who is calling, please?" said Robin politely. He wanted to get over with the call as soon as possible and return to his prized privacy.

"Hi! Pardon me if I have called the wrong number at this late hour. I am looking for someone I knew very well many years back, actually decades back. My name is Purnima. Mr. Garg, were you in Bangalore many years back, like when you started your career?"

Robin paused. Purnima swallowed.

Robin replied, "Well, yes, that is correct."

Purnima pushed on, "Austin Town, was it? Were you in Austin Town in Bangalore over two decades back? You worked for Hindustan Personal Products over there and got transferred to Lucknow? Did you?"

The earnestness in her voice surprised Robin—as if a big revelation was waiting to unfold, or that he was about to be charged with a crime he had committed back then. Then suddenly—a flashback. With a shiver running down his spine, he asked, "Is this Purnima? Are you by any chance Purnima Bajaj from Bangalore?"

The caller was silent again.

Robin repeated, this time more firmly, "Is that you, Purnima? If so, you've called the correct Robin Garg. I was your neighbour in Bangalore for some time. You were a kid in school those days."

"Robin *da*, oh Robin *da*, I can't believe I'm talking to you again. Where have you been all these days? Why did you just disappear? Thank God, at least you remember someone called Purnima Bajaj!"

Robin replied with a laugh, "Are you kidding, Purnima? I never forgot you for a moment."

"Then how come you never reached out?" she quipped.

"Well, I can ask the same. If you have any answer, please let me know. We just lost touch with each other, I think. Anyway, forget the past. So nice to hear from you after ages! I'm so glad you found me and took this initiative to call. You won't believe what sweet memories of those lovely years are flooding me right now!"

Purnima replied, almost in a whisper, "I have also not forgotten those lovely days in Austin Town—your regular visits to our house, your teasing, the warm letters and so many other things. How have you been? Life has been good to you, I hope. What do you do now? And your family? Children?" Though Radha had told her he was single, she wanted to know everything directly from him—was he a bachelor, had he married and divorced, had he ever loved anyone, did he have a girlfriend now?

"Wow! You sure have a lot of questions! Why don't we meet? Like tomorrow, if possible? Let me see; I already have a busy day. On top of it, I am expecting an exciting development to come my way anytime now. That will surely drive me crazy in coming days!"

"Really? What would that be?"

"You will know, certainly, if something truly comes up. But let's not assume anything yet. In any case, this would be something to share only across the table, not on the phone. I will also not ask anything about you now. Let's catch up in person; I still remember you as a kiddo in a navy-blue skirt and a sky blue or polka-dotted white top, not to forget the ponytail," said Robin with a hearty laugh.

Purnima laughed out too, relaxed for the first time, and said, "Don't you laugh Robin *da*! I have to ask you a lot too. For starters, do you still insist on having one Cream Cracker biscuit with your morning tea?"

Robin burst out laughing. "Goodness me! You remember that, how sweet. Listen, tomorrow, as I said, is a tough day for me. However, I will escape and see you at United Coffee House in Connaught Place at 6 p.m. That is, of course, if you are free at that time."

Purnima took a while to respond. There was no doubt in her mind that she wanted to accept the invitation. She knew she would say yes but did not want to give away her overwhelming excitement. "Robin *da*, just a second, let me see." She continued after a few seconds, "Okay, I will be there. United Coffee House at six in the evening tomorrow."

"You know this place, don't you, in E Block quite close to the Rajiv Chowk metro station?"

"Yes, I do. See you tomorrow evening then. I am so excited to see you after ages! And to know what this latest interesting development is if you get to know about it tonight. I promise I will surprise you as well if all goes as planned tomorrow morning. Bye for now, Robin *da*."

"I am excited too, Purnima. It is unbelievable. Thanks again for your call; can't wait for tomorrow evening. Bye."

Once disconnected, they realised the enormity of what had just happened. Purnima crashed on the bed with her face down and wept in happiness. Robin went back to his rocking chair. Amazed by the turn of events, he stared at the ceiling and rocked his chair. He wished he could fast-forward to the next evening!

The phone rang again. Robin happily assumed Purnima had something more to say. He immediately picked it up and said with a lot of warmth in his voice, "Hey, is there anything else, Purnima?"

"Hello." The familiar male voice embarrassed Robin. "Good evening, Robin. Were you expecting someone else's call? Sorry to call this late. But I had to."

"Suresh *ji*, good evening! No issues at all; your call is welcome at any time," responded Robin.

He did not share a great rapport with the state party president. Suresh Ahluwalia believed that Robin's lateral induction to senior status in the party and his undue prominence were unnecessary and grossly unfair. He did not dispute that Robin had resources and charisma. Neither did Suresh Ahluwalia doubt Robin's popularity. But he held that the senior party leaders, who had given the better part of their lives to the party, must not be sidelined. He also believed that money and popularity did not necessarily win elections; they could never make up for a lack of political acumen and ground-level experience.

Robin was never comfortable around Suresh Ahluwalia. The state president remained highhanded and difficult despite his overtures and charm. Robin concluded that the state president resented the way he had been brought into the party by the national president without consulting anyone in the state unit and felt threatened since the national president maintained a direct line of communication with him. However, they developed a cordial working relationship.

"Let me come straight to the point, Robin. The party has confirmed its faith in you by letting you bring the West Delhi constituency back to us. Congratulations! And all the very best. We shall make formal announcements tomorrow."

"Oh, that's great news, Suresh *ji*. It is an honour. Thank you for your faith in me," said Robin knowing fully well that Suresh Ahluwalia would have tried hard to deny him the ticket.

"We are all excited about it. See you tomorrow morning in the office then."

Suresh Ahluwalia left the deserted party office. He had to catch up with much-needed sleep. Considerable challenges lay ahead for him—disgruntled hopefuls, irate supporters, critiques in the press and his strong reservations on the nominated candidate's chances.

Robin was excited beyond words. He had looked for a change. Fresh challenges, new learnings, renewed inspiration and passion—changes that would demand the best from him yet again. The routine business manoeuvres and social engagements could no longer bring him the satisfaction he craved. Further, he believed a life outside the world he had shared with Ritu might earn him sustainable happiness. It had to be something that had never been a part of their shared dreams.

After the life-altering flight spent with the president of the National Patriotic Party, he had considered politics as a possible option. With time, inspired by the sunnier side of political activism and encouraged by his pre-eminence within the party, the option of joining active politics had become more and more attractive. When an opportunity came his way after the demise of the sitting West Delhi parliamentarian, Robin went on overdrive. Starting as a novice pitted against powerful contenders, he cleverly played his cards. With the national leadership's staunch backing, he had become the top contender for the nomination only in the last few weeks.

This nomination was his crowning glory, a well-deserved reward for hard work and some excellent networking in recent years. On top of it, the sudden re-emergence of Purnima in his life had been something that he couldn't have imagined even in his wildest dreams! Robin was over the moon!

He got up from his chair and walked around, thinking about tomorrow evening with Purnima, about the busy days ahead, about the celebrations he would have on winning the elections, his first speech in the Parliament, and the possibility of even a ministry in the years to come. He considered calling a few of his close friends to share the excitement but decided against it. The world could wait as he enjoyed his last few priceless moments of solitary happiness. He walked up to his record player. It had to be Mozart's Sonata No. 17 in C to match his mood.

5

Earlier, a disappointed Suresh Ahluwalia walked listlessly out of the meeting room after everyone else had left. He was well-aware of the enormity of the job at hand. The responsibility of informing the chosen candidate, however unpleasant, was not his main trouble. His three long decades of political life had been full of intrigues and manipulations. He had embraced people who he could not tolerate for a moment, was loyal to people who he considered absolute idiots, had praised nincompoops and cozied up to political figures who had no place in civil society. He could walk up to the successful candidate and convey the news with a bouquet of warmth, praise, and sincerity in an excellent show of well-disguised skulduggery.

He worried about Durjoy Kumar, a seasoned grassroots politician, who had won twice from the same constituency earlier. He knew that Durjoy Kumar would not take this well. It was not easy to second-guess a cunning politician. However, Ahluwalia believed that Kumar would take this snub as a personal insult, as the party's betrayal of a loyal soldier, and would certainly react to protect his political base. A revolt was the most logical next step. If Durjoy Kumar fought the elections as an independent candidate, his party would suffer badly since a sizeable part of hard-core NPP supporters were his loyalists.

An upset Bhupinder Gupta, the other serious contender for the ticket, would be no less a nuisance. The party veteran had worked hard upwards through the party hierarchy to become a Vice President of the Delhi unit. Riding on his hold over the Baniya and

26

Jain community votes and the considerable influence over the upper caste electorate, he lobbied hard for the ticket. There was a strong buzz that Bhupinder Gupta would change camps and contest the by-election as the UNDP candidate if he did not get the party ticket. Suresh Ahluwalia knew that such rumours were often leaked deliberately as a pressure tactic. Nonetheless, he believed Gupta was the ideal candidate. Under the present circumstances, neither an old horse nor a brand-new face was the need of the hour.

Since he could not contact the selected candidate, he had more time to contemplate. He decided to call Durjoy Kumar first to inform him that he did not make it. His immediate reactions, however diplomatic, were likely to give a clue to his plans.

He called Durjoy Kumar from his own office.

"Kumar *saab*, sorry this is quite late. But I thought it best to call you right away."

"No problem, Suresh *ji*! Not an issue; you can call me at any time. I have been expecting this call from you. I know about your evening meeting with the party president. Come on, give me the good news now! I am all set to get this one back for the party."

"Kumar *saab*, I wanted to …"

Durjoy Kumar interrupted with a loud laugh, "Yes, I know. You would have preferred to give this news to me personally with sweets in your hand. But that's okay. There will be enough time later to share sweets. I promise there shall be a feast of sweets during our victory procession. Don't worry about anything. I have already set in motion the entire election machinery that has helped me return from this constituency twice before."

"Kumar *saab*, I have a piece of news to pass on. You are one of our party's tallest leaders, not only in Delhi but in the entire country. We need you more than we need anyone else. We can win the West Delhi parliamentary seat only with your help. We know that you will always stand by the party and guide us."

"What are you talking about? Come straight, please. You know me. I don't like to talk in a zigzag manner."

Suresh Ahluwalia said softly, "Kumar *saab*, the party considers you as our guiding spirit, as one of the leading lights at the very top of our party structure. The party shall seek and count on your support to win this by-election. The party also believes it is in its best interest to nominate a new candidate for this contest to crush any challenge UNDP may throw at us. The electorate will love a fresh new proposition, and the opposition will not have any past to play with."

"So, hang on a second… are you trying to tell me that I shall not be the NPP candidate despite having won this seat twice? Who is this new face that you believe can ensure a win?" asked an astounded Durjoy Kumar.

Ahluwalia continued in his subdued tone, "I am not in a position to tell you the name yet. But I will do so after I inform the candidate. You know that is the way our party functions. I have very high regard for you. I know that you have been expecting this ticket; probably rightly so. That's why I wanted to talk with you first."

"Is this decision final?" asked Kumar with a heavy voice.

"I am afraid yes."

"Okay then, if this is what the party does to me after lifelong dedicated service, I shall also have to make my own decision. I shall talk to my people tomorrow. Since you have given me respect by making this call, let me return the favour." After a brief silence, he continued, "You are likely to see my name on the ballot paper in any case. Thanks for the call, and good night!" He disconnected without waiting for a response.

Suresh Ahluwalia found it difficult to digest what he had just heard from a senior party leader. Although he had been apprehensive of such a threat, he could not really believe that the old warrior indeed planned to revolt. The responsibility of winning back the seat rested on his shoulders as the party president in Delhi. He dreaded the possibility of having Kumar on the ballot as a challenger. If he ultimately carried out his threat, NPP would lose a big chunk of its vote bank. He felt obliged to share this critical development with the party president.

Praveen Lakhotia had been wondering why the president had stayed back in the office so late. He considered a range of possibilities and settled for the most likely scenario—that his boss must have had a serious fight with his wife earlier in the day. Hearing the bell ring again, he ran to his boss, picked up a piece of paper with a name on it, and went straight to the records room. He quickly returned with the person's residence telephone number.

Uneasy with Kumar's prophetic words, Suresh Ahluwalia decided to talk to the party president first, well aware that the delay in informing the candidate might not go down very well with him.

"Sorry to call you so late, Manoj *bhai*. But I thought this was important."

"No worries. You informed the candidate?"

"Not yet, sorry. Can't get him on the line. I will positively do this before I go home. Meanwhile, I wanted to talk to you about something else, rather urgent."

He narrated the details of his talks with Durjoy Kumar, *verbatim*. Hearing him out patiently, Manoj Seth responded in his inimitable style, "Thanks. You leave that to me. Good night."

Suresh Ahluwalia was intrigued by the party president's composed reaction to the alarming prospects of an internal revolt in the party. But he was not surprised. The man was a shrewd manipulator and a fierce fighter with a track record of demolishing anyone who tried to stand in his way.

He stretched himself to relax his muscles, turned his neck to either side, up and down, and then clockwise and anti-clockwise.

He wanted to give himself some time before calling the nominated candidate's landline number.

Meanwhile, Durjoy Kumar paced in his bedroom. He felt betrayed as his loyalty was being traded, rather cheaply, for new blood by the arrogant party leadership. Fighting the election as an independent was an option since he had a great chance to win, given his hold on the electorate. Apart from the solid backing within the core NPP support base, many loved him but did not usually vote for him due to his party's radical ideology—they would turn to him if he fought on an independent ticket. But this option carried huge risks. It was certain that the party would expel him. After that, if he lost the elections, that would mean the end of his long political career. On the other hand, if he supported the official candidate, he would remain a senior party leader, and other opportunities would knock at his door soon.

Ultimately pride prevailed over logic. Durjoy Kumar looked for his phone to talk to his most trusted lieutenants. He had to meet with his close supporters first thing in the morning to chart the future course of action.

He had barely picked up the handset when it rang. It was the party president. Holding on to the handset, he picked up the call only after it rang for some seconds. He knew the reasons for the late-night call and was in no hurry to entertain the man.

"*Namaste*, Manoj *bhai*! You are still working this late into the night! Please tell me what I can do for you."

"Kumar *saab*, I believe Suresh *ji* talked with you a few minutes back. We have decided in the larger interests of the party without thinking about individuals. You know how much respect I and everyone else at the party have for you. You have been a great strength for the party, not only in returning from the same seat twice but also through your invaluable contributions in other party matters. The party owes its exceptional success to people like you who have made huge personal sacrifices to see the party get stronger with every election and through every crisis. We need you now like never before."

Here, Manoj Seth paused.

"Go on Manoj *bhai*, I am listening," came the cold reply.

"We have decided to field a younger candidate for the West Delhi parliamentary by-election with the future in mind. You would have noticed that we are generally not nominating candidates who are above a certain age. It is an effort to prepare the party for the challenges ahead. It does not reflect on the capabilities of our elders in any way. The party respects their strengths, values, mass appeal, and lifelong commitment to our cause. We need your full backing for the party's decision. We need your guidance and active support to ensure that we snatch this seat back from our opponents."

Durjoy Kumar intervened. "I get it. These are kind words, but I know them for what they are. I too have said such sweet things to others before. The fact remains that the party has hurt me. It has insulted me by ignoring my claim to this ticket. I have great respect for you as well. But Manoj *bhai*, these band-aids shall not heal my deep wound. I shall call for a meeting of my supporters soon after the party officially declares its candidate. I shall consult with them and take whatever steps they advise me to take."

"Please try to understand, Kumar *saab*. The party must stand united. We must seem to be united if we wish to throw these guys out of this constituency. People are intelligent. If they sense any internal discord, dissonance from stalwarts like you, we may lose this election. Please do not call for any separate meeting of your supporters."

Mr. Kumar promptly replied, "I can't promise you anything. My supporters will be very agitated. I shall have to consult with them.

If they insist, I will not hesitate to file my papers as an independent candidate."

There was a minute of silence; it felt much longer than a minute.

Manoj Seth spoke in a heavy, slow, and measured voice. "Kumar *saab*. As I said, I have a lot of respect for you. So, I do not want to say anything that will be less than respectful. The party has taken a decision, and there shall be no reconsideration. I am sorry to hear what you have just said. I hope that was nothing more than a spontaneous reaction to your understandable disappointment and, with time, you shall drop any such ideas. Let me make a few things clear. First of all, I urge you, and I believe you will accept this humble request, not to call a meeting of your supporters after we announce the nomination. Instead, I request you to publicly announce your full support for the official candidate. Please campaign to the best of your abilities in the next few weeks and help us win this seat again. If you do so and we win, you shall be nominated to the board of one of the public sector jewels. Also, you shall be one of the frontrunners when the next governor appointments are due. I think that is about six to seven months away. On the other hand, if you go ahead with the meeting and decide to file nomination papers against our party candidate, our disciplinary committee will expel you from the party with immediate effect. That will be most unfortunate."

He continued after a pause, "By the way, I heard the other day that the Central Bureau of Investigation wants to reopen the file related to the riots. It is not closed yet, just lying dormant. They insist they have compelling evidence against you. I requested the Home Minister not to open old wounds unnecessarily, and he agreed; he was very reluctant, though. On top of it, the income tax guys have found out about your two farmhouses on Mehrauli-Gurgaon Road. You should not have hidden those in your tax returns just because you registered them under someone else's names. And your last holiday in the US? I believe it was an expensive affair. We found out that the entire trip was financed by the Nipanis. The press would love that. They love big headlines, you know. Kumar *saab*, I know you are an intelligent man. As I said, I have high regard for you. Take care, Kumar *saab*. Good night!"

6

With his eyes still shut, Robin wondered why momentary urges to slow down invariably gave in to his thirst for more. Once a business colleague asked him. "Robin, what keeps you so motivated to keep working, setting higher and tougher goals for yourself, and go for them with such commitment? You don't have to do this anymore!" Robin laughed and said, "This is a question I often ask myself but get no answers. I seem to love new challenges. It is in my blood, I guess. I have come a long way from home. The momentum keeps me going, I enjoy it!"

Robin Garg's journey from a sleepy village in the North-Eastern frontiers of India to an upmarket neighbourhood in the national capital had been spectacular. He was born to poor parents in Pakamura on the outskirts of Assam's Jorhat district. His father, a primary school teacher, did not earn enough to feed his family. The paddy from the land leased out to a landless farmer and the seasonal vegetables grown in their backyard were handy in his struggles to bridge the enormous gap between his means and needs. Hoping that his son one day would break free from the confines of a remote Assamese village, he shielded Robin from his own daily struggles and never-ending wants. He went the extra mile to protect his son from their neighbours' enervated view of the world. Though he had never been beyond Jorhat town, he convinced Robin that the entire world was his playground and that he must grow up to be counted as someone in the world, that he must never settle down to a mundane life of mere survival. Living up to the dreams of a visionary father, an inspired Robin fought hard to leave his cocoon and became a role model for youngsters in his state.

The fifth rank in matriculation, second in pre-university examinations, a first-class graduate from Delhi's St. Stephens College followed by a diploma from the Indian Institute of Management, Ahmedabad (IIM-A), Robin Garg had an academic record that most people could only dream of. Truly a brilliant run! However, he would have never made it to IIM without his maternal uncle's generosity. Robin was all set to take a job immediately after graduation to support his parents. His mother's eldest brother, a wealthy businessman with diverse business interests spanning the entire state, insisted that Robin's brilliance mustn't be wasted for lack of financial support. The noble man encouraged Robin to apply for a seat in the prestigious management institute with a promise to bear all his costs for the two-year course. This changed Robin's life.

He was hired by Hindustan Personal Products Limited for their Management Training Programme and posted in Bangalore. However, five successful years in the company and endless cajoling from his seniors could not hold him back. Aiming for a bigger canvas to paint on, he set up an FMCG distribution business with one of his IIM-A friends. It was the beginning of a spectacular journey. Robin became the controlling shareholder of a large consumer products distribution company, sole owner of an IT enterprise, the minority shareholder of a television broadcasting company, and a sought-after angel investor. It was ironic that his father passed away long before he had established himself. With both parents gone, he gradually lost touch with his village.

His remarkable success made him a rich man. However, he earned mass admiration and goodwill for his NGO, Our World which worked with poor children in the age group of five to fifteen to help them develop strong and confident personalities. Robin and Ritu had started Our World together. It had a significant presence in many districts of Karnataka. Most of its success could be attributed to Ritu's enterprise and hard work. Robin changed the NGO's name after the tragic incident changed his life forever. He could never forget that miserable day when Ritu left him for good. Everything went wrong that day in Ahmedabad while he was thousands of miles away.

That was a watershed moment in his life. He had to make significant changes to his own world just to live day-by-day. For starters, he decided to leave Bangalore. The decision astonished all his friends. The city had grown on him over the years. Except for the short stint away, he had spent all his professional years in Bangalore. Resourceful, well-connected, loved, and respected, not many in his place would have contemplated moving out of the city. But it was an easy decision for him. He did not have a choice.

After the catastrophe, loneliness haunted him. Ritu's eerie presence ruled the house. Robin cleared the closet of all her clothes but the whiff of her favourite perfume lingered on. He changed the linen but the bed still retained the fascinating smell of her skin. Often, he woke up in the middle of the night and reached out to hold her. Disappointed, he felt the unrumpled pillow with his fingertips and stayed awake for hours, desolate. Her coffee mug, books, the flowers, and plants she had personally nurtured in the garden, the wall paintings bought during their various travels, the carpet she had charmed him into buying on their first visit to Turkey—every little thing that carried her unmistakable imprint talked to him in one concerted voice blaming him for not doing enough to save her.

It was impossible for him to continue a normal life in the same environment. He could not live with anything familiar any longer, not even the air he breathed! He needed a new landscape to survive.

Delhi seemed to be a decent compromise. Three years in St. Stephen's College had given him decent exposure to the capital. Besides, he could not think of any other place from where he could successfully continue running his distribution business. Decisions were made. He did not have to ask for anyone's consent. The only one who would have mattered did not exist anymore.

Though the National Distribution Network Limited had its headquarters in Bangalore, it had regional offices in various parts of the country. Its Northern Region head office in Delhi was the biggest of all the regional offices. So, Robin did not have much difficulty in shifting his headquarters to Delhi. The Bangalore setup was converted into the Southern Region's head office. The IT business was retained in Bangalore as the city continued to be an IT hub. Robin was lucky to have a trusted and efficient CEO for its operations. As for the broadcasting business based in Mumbai, he was not involved in its management due to his minority shareholding. Angel investor initiatives, of course, stayed with him. For this, his base did not matter.

Robin's biggest challenge—and a painful heartbreak—was to shift the NGO operations out of Bangalore. The NGO had done a commendable job with underprivileged children in various districts around Bangalore. It was primarily Ritu's venture. Driven by a passion to give something back to society, she researched various support organisations in the region to find that most of them either provided financial and material support or imparted classroom-style education. A firm believer in self-confidence and positivity as the fundamental building blocks for ultimate success, she wanted to help the kids develop their personalities. So, she launched Our World.

Robin had taken a personal interest in it from a nascent stage. He spent a significant amount of time travelling to distant villages in Karnataka before adopting Ramnagara and Mandya districts for the launch. Later, they expanded their programme to Tumkur and Kolar districts. He found great happiness in watching the children improve. He saw shy and nervous girls, initially scared even to say *namaskara*, deliver extempore speeches confidently for three long minutes. He saw children in total despair walk with their heads high with remarkable self-confidence. He found a sense of purpose, achievement, peace, and fulfilment in Our World's success, something that he did not find in his sprawling business empire.

Robin downsized Our World in Bangalore and asked one of his trusted local lieutenants to manage the same. He moved operations to NCR with plans to go into remote villages in Haryana and Western Uttar Pradesh. He knew that it would initially be a challenge to earn the villagers' trust, and he would have to repeat what he had done in Ramnagara and Mandya. Ritu's disarming smile would not be there this time.

Shifting his base was not as difficult as he had feared. Some of his old college friends, well-settled in Delhi by then in government jobs, business, or private corporations, were of great help. The fact that the National Distribution Network Limited had a recognised regional office in Delhi made things easier. Once the lead business adjusted well to the change, the rest fell in place. Robin's reputation and wealth followed him to Delhi. It was not much of a challenge to enter the social circles in the capital. Soon Robin was on top of a growing business enterprise, part of a swelling social circle with considerable clout, and leading a successful and influential NGO, with significant resources.

It was all going as per plan till he took the life-changing flight. It was still fresh in his mind.

Robin boarded a Jet Airways flight to New Delhi on his way back from a routine business review in Bangalore. He shuttled between the two cities at least once a month since they were the focal nodes for his business empire. As he sat in his favourite first-row window seat of the Airbus 320 and casually flipped pages of the on-board magazine, he was ready for a repeat of yet another boring hundred and fifty minutes of his life. He did not know that a chance encounter would provide yet another twist to his eventful life.

From seat number 1A, he looked out of the window. The aerobridge was still connected; boarding was not yet complete. He thought of Ritu. He recalled his chance meeting with her—the funny encounter that led to their lifelong partnership.

7

Brigade Road was arguably Bangalore's trendiest hang-out place. It was impossible to walk there without getting pushed once in a while. People loved the stroll up and down Brigade Road, from Mahatma Gandhi Road to Residency Road crossing and back. Some stopped by at Nilgiri's for filter coffee served in stainless steel tumblers or walked into the Sweet Chariot outlet in Curzon Complex to bite into their juicy pastries. Others indulged in window shopping at the scores of bargain outlets on either side of the road. Robin was doing the routine with two colleagues on an insipid Sunday evening.

"Guys, anyone for a pastry? I am, for sure," Robin exclaimed as he walked down the staircase towards the Sweet Chariot outlet while in one of his regular hang-outs with friends during his bachelor days. His friends stopped by the stairs, acted as if they heard nothing and looked away. Although they disapproved of Robin stopping to buy some sweets or ice cream every now and then, they had given up trying to dissuade him from consuming excessive sugar. "You unimaginative bums! What would you know about the romance of biting into a soft, juicy, tender pastry, particularly when the fresh cream gets stuck on your upper lips. What an experience to delicately lick it off with affection! Stay right there as I indulge in some excitement."

His friends continued to act as if they heard nothing, did well to hide their laughter and stayed put. Robin went to the pastry shop and took a visual tour of all the colourful delicacies on display. He had no interest in the young girl who had been doing the same, standing next to him. He shortlisted two: the Black Forest and the

Fresh Cream Mango. There were a few Black Forests left in the showcase, but only one piece of the Fresh Cream Mango remained. Robin thought for a moment and then spoke to the man at the counter.

"Excuse me, that one, please."

The salesman was confused. He heard two voices, one male and one female, at the same time, saying the same thing. He looked at the two customers. Both of them were pointing at the last piece of Fresh Cream Mango! He smiled and looked at both customers in turn, his expressive gesture as though saying, *Now, what on earth am I supposed to do?*

The girl said, after a stare at her challenger for the lone piece of pastry, "This is mine. I came in first to your shop. Come on!"

Robin had a good look at the girl for the first time. The tall girl, probably in her mid-twenties, looked smart in her designer denim and sleeveless turquoise blue top. She wore matching beaded chokers, earrings dangling three inches below her ear lobes and a pair of Prada sunglasses that she did not bother to take off despite being in the basement of a multi-storied building. Amused, curious, and spurred by her fleeting but defiant glance at him, Robin decided to push on. Admittedly, he was not thinking of the pastry at that time.

"I am sorry, but that's not how it works. I asked for it first. It must be mine. Please give it to me," he said firmly, looking at the salesman.

The girl, visibly disturbed, raised her voice with a polite but commanding tone, "Now that he insists, I insist too. That pastry is mine."

The shop supervisor rushed to his colleague's rescue, "Good evening, is there a problem? May I help, sir, madam?" The salesman explained to his supervisor as both the claimants patiently listened. One of them was amused, the other truly upset.

The supervisor said, "I suggest one of you take the Black Forest. They are our specialty. Else, you can also go for one of our most popular varieties, Heavenly Butterscotch Delight. You certainly wouldn't regret it."

The girl replied even before the supervisor ended his last line, "Sure, that sounds cool. Please give him one of those and give me the Fresh Cream Mango. And, please hurry up! I don't have all day."

Robin decided to play on. He hardly cared so much for a specific pastry to get into an argument with anyone, but wanted to know more about the girl. Strangely, he saw in her something that he wished to unravel. He needed to understand why his heart had just missed a beat.

"Not acceptable, just not fair. It is not about the pastry; it is about being right or wrong. Come on! I also don't have the whole day. Let me have it now."

The broad smile on the supervisor's face shrunk to a grin as he said, "Sir and madam, you are both our important customers. I do not have two pastries to give you both. So, either both of you choose another variety, and this precious piece stays on the shelf, or I cut this pastry into two pieces and give you one part each. Please decide."

After quickly exchanging amused smile, they agreed. The pastry was cut into two and served on separate plates. Each of them paid half the price.

They went to the same table with their prized possession and retained their composure till they had their first bites. Then, they burst out laughing together. The girl extended her hand to Robin and said, "This is funny! I am Ritu; Ritu Mehta."

"It sure is. It is the most precious pastry I have eaten in my life! My world would have shrunk to nothing without this half pastry," said Robin, shaking hands with her. "I am Robin. Robin Garg. Very nice to meet you."

They took their time to eat their halves and talked about their respective backgrounds. It was more intimate than a typical chat between two strangers. Robin wanted to propose another round of delicacies. But the guilt of keeping his friends waiting on the footpath prevailed upon his conscience.

"So, Ritu, I got to go now. My friends are waiting for me outside. It was lovely to fight with you over a pastry. But we should follow up on this half a pastry with a coffee sometime soon. What do you say?"

Ritu looked away and pondered. Robin pushed forward. "How about coming Saturday evening, at Indian Coffee House on Church Street, say around six in the evening? Does that work for you?"

She looked at Robin and said, "Okay, six o'clock. this Saturday, at Indian Coffee House on Church Street. Goodbye for now."

They shook hands again and walked up the stairs separately. Two sets of perplexed eyes followed them till they disappeared at the top of the staircase.

As expected, his friends welcomed Robin with a liberal dose of friendly curses for the long wait. They were surprised that the familiar combatant Robin was missing. Instead, he returned their abuses with a smile. They wondered if the pastry had some dope in it!

Back home that evening, Robin replayed the images—the lone pastry in the display case, the girl who would just not give up, sharing bites with a stranger… her voice, her magnetic charm, and the promise of next Saturday. Sensing a world of possibilities in the days ahead, he couldn't divert his mind to anything else. Recalling the set of brown eyes that locked into his while accepting the coffee invite, Robin wondered if there was something more in it. He mulled over it for a while. *It was just a polite acceptance, plain and simple.* Disappointed but unwilling to give up, he retraced her words, moves, and glances for any pleasant clue to a future beyond casual acquaintance. He thought her parting handshake was warmer than the first! It made him happy.

Baffled with his baseless obsession, he switched on the TV for a respite. Next Saturday seemed so far away.

Next Saturday evening, Robin reached Indian Coffee House at twenty minutes to six. After choosing a corner table with a decent amount of privacy, he sat on the chair that offered the best view of the entrance. He would not like Ritu to have to look around for him.

He was amazed with himself. He had met with many female friends, friends of friends, colleagues, business partners. Some of them were incredibly attractive, including a few that any man would desire to be close to, but never had he had such an urge to know more about a woman. Going way back to his late teens and early twenties, he could think of no one like that, with the possible exception of the sweet little darling of a girl who was his neighbour for the first few years of his career. She was exclusive. He used to look forward to meeting her, to see her blush, to hear her nervous greetings, watch her rosy dimpled cheeks and to tease her till she ran for cover. At times, he felt like holding her in his arms, wanting to run his hands tenderly over her hair, her cheeks, and her neck. The next moment, he cursed himself for being stupid! *She is only a kid! Stupid young man, behave and control yourself!* Such restraint usually arrested his flights of fantasy. He put on a big brotherly attitude to cover any traces of interest in her as a woman. Was it infatuation or love, Robin had wondered for years past those delightful days. With time, they lost touch with each other. But he always carried this feeling that she *was* probably his first love. Ten years of age difference—something that seemed colossal in those years but did not look as vast as the years got added to his age. Sometimes, Robin wondered if he had made a blunder. Often, he nursed a craving to seek her out but was not sure where to start.

Ritu had ignited a similar fire in him, something that made one week seem like an eternity. With eyes focused on the entrance, Robin felt his heart pounding faster. All he knew about the young girl was that she was born in Ahmedabad, mostly brought up in Bangalore, lived in Rajaji Nagar, had studied in Bishop Cottons Girls' School, Mount Carmel College and then had done Masters in Sociology from Bangalore University. She worked for an NGO; loved music, food and social work. He desperately wanted to know more.

Seeing Ritu walk into the café a minute before six, Robin jumped out of his seat, nearly ran to the entrance and escorted her to the reserved table. Though he was conscious of a miserable failure in hiding his childlike excitement, there was precious little he could do about it. They chatted, formal cordiality turning to restrained camaraderie and then to a freewheeling discussion on life, society, pollution, the latest blockbusters, the best food joints in town, and the state of the economy. They met again in the subsequent weeks and progressively got more personal in their discussions—talked about people in their lives, discussed their dreams for the future and asked about mutual likes and dislikes. They started dating more frequently, at least thrice a week, and never missed out on their daily late-night telephone chats. It did not take long for them to realise that they were destined for a life together.

They got married after a year at a simple function. Ritu's parents, who had settled in Ahmedabad after retirement, came to Bangalore to attend the wedding. A few of Robin's relatives made it to the ceremony. They could not take time off for an elaborate honeymoon. However, on the Sunday following their marriage, they visited the Sweet Chariot patisserie to share a Fresh Cream Mango. The supervisor gave Robin a meaningful smile. Robin returned the gesture with a wink.

8

The seat next to him, 1C, was not yet occupied. Robin kept his book on the empty seat, stretched his legs, and flipped through the in-flight magazine. Not finding anything of interest, he put the magazine back, stretched out as much as he could in the limited space, and closed his eyes to relax. On second thoughts, he opened his eyes again and looked out the window. Transcending the mundane world of parked aircraft, dollies, chocks, refuelling trucks, and uniformed ground support personnel, he allowed painful images from his past to return in a punishing encore. He went back into the maze of possibilities, slips and misses.

Dynamic, strategic, cunning, visionary, ruthless, pragmatic and generous—these were a few of the many colourful and conflicting adjectives Robin Garg had acquired in Delhi's social circles after moving his base from Bangalore. He did not care either way. He believed he had them all balanced. The anxiety generated by his unrelenting pursuit of wealth was checked by the solace and gratification in his social work. He understood the interdependence of both his passions. He required a thriving business to fund the NGO. Meanwhile, the children's priceless smiles and growing confidence kept him motivated for the long hours needed to run a successful business.

Robin Garg disliked politics; he considered politicians an unavoidable nuisance. He did socialise with a few political figures on occasion to further his business interests. But he found no charm in such events; they were just a call of duty he had to honour.

However, his views on politics would change after he took this eventful flight. By the time the aircraft landed at the Indira Gandhi

International Airport, he was beginning to think politicians were not so bad after all. Maybe the masses were unfair in painting all of them with the same brush.

Boarding was not yet complete. But the initial stream of passengers, struggling through the aisle with bags of various sizes, looking at the business class comfort with envy or with disdain for elite indulgence, slowly reduced to a trickle. Robin was happy that 1C was still empty. It was always a bonus to have the next seat unoccupied. Looking out of the window, he remembered, yet again, the cursed day when his world had come crashing down. He blamed them. He held the entire community responsible for what had happened that day.

However, they were not the only ones. Robin blamed Ritu for insisting on travelling to Ahmedabad for the delivery of their baby. Bangalore had better healthcare facilities. St. John's Hospital was perfect, given his close friendship with senior doctors. Both of them argued about this in the first five months of her pregnancy. Ritu insisted, and he gave in. At the end of the twenty-fifth week, she went home to her welcoming parents, who also believed it was their privilege and responsibility to take care of the birth of their first grandchild.

He blamed himself as well. Events might have taken a different course if he had stayed with Ritu during the last few weeks of her pregnancy. Although his business trip to the USA in those critical weeks was not at all avoidable—he would have lost the nationwide distribution rights for a best-selling skincare product range, causing a loss of millions in revenue year after year—but what good were millions in the face of such a tragedy?

It was the last week of October; the baby was due in two weeks. After consulting the doctor, he decided to travel to Washington DC for a crucial business meeting. He promised his tearful wife to return in four days, well before the delivery date. She was upset but supportive.

After signing up with a large multinational company for the distribution rights of their products in India, Robin had time to spare before his flight back to India. The beautiful state of Virginia was at her best during the famed fall foliage season. He chose to take a drive across the Potomac River along the George Washington Memorial Parkway. Driving leisurely along the thruway without any particular destination in mind, he feasted on the surrounding riot of colours. The maple trees looked gorgeous!

He turned right near the CIA headquarters at Langley and drove up the narrow picturesque road leading to the Bretton Woods Recreation Center. He intended to drive up to the Center, take a detour to the McLean market for some window shopping, and return to his DC hotel in time to leave for the airport. With about a mile left for the Center, Robin's phone rang. It was his father-in-law. He parked the car at the next parking area and picked up the call.

"Robin, there is a complication. We are on our way to Sterling Hospital."

"Oh! What happened? How is she? May I speak to her, papa?"

"She is a little worried and upset. I spoke to the doctor. She fears that her water may have broken and asked us to admit her to the hospital as soon as possible."

"Water may have broken?"

"The amniotic sac where the baby grows has broken. So, the fluid is draining out. Leave those details, Robin, we need to reach the hospital fast. I know you will feel helpless being so far away, but I had to inform you."

"Can I talk to her?"

Ritu's father looked at her.

"Leave it, for now, Robin. I don't think she can talk now."

"Have you reached the hospital? How far are you from it?"

"Not yet; we are still far away. The police have blocked the traffic ahead; cars are not moving at all. I am pleading with everyone here. We can't do anything; the road is full of cars, scooters, autos. Ritu is so scared."

Robin gasped for breath. "Please do something, papa. Did you talk to a cop? Why have they blocked the traffic?"

"There is some religious procession ahead. There is communal tension since the minority community's procession is now passing through a neighbourhood of hardliners. The cops do not want to take any chances. I believe this is likely to take at least an hour to clear."

"Papa, I will call back in minutes. Let me get back to my hotel."

Robin drove back to his hotel, checked out, and sat in a taxi to the airport. He called his father-in-law every few minutes, fuelling frustration at both ends. The Ahmedabad traffic did not move at all. There were rumours that communal fights had already broken out in that area.

Ritu's father saw a senior police officer about a hundred metres away. He ran towards the officer through narrow gaps between stranded cars, buses, auto-rickshaws, and cycles, all along trying to draw the officer's attention. A few yards before reaching the policeman, he hit a truck's bonnet and fell on the road. Undaunted, he got up and limped towards the police officer. Meanwhile, Robin collected his boarding pass and waited in the immigration queue. He knew he could not use the cell phone any further till the immigration process got over.

As Robin walked past the security check, his father-in-law managed to gain some sympathy from the senior officer. He instructed two constables to do the necessary to let their car move ahead. If they could take a right turn a kilometre ahead of the roadblock, they would be able to get away from the traffic as well as any other disruption. The hospital would then be another twenty minutes away.

After completing the immigration and security checks, Robin called his father-in-law again. He was relieved to learn that the police were helping the car to get through the traffic logjam. Nearly an hour later, when their car managed to take the all-important right turn, Robin was in a queue to board the flight. He pleaded with his father-in-law to stay online. As he walked to his aircraft seat with the handset sandwiched between his ear and shoulder, the car picked up speed towards the hospital. Ritu was in distress.

After the air hostess shut the aircraft door, Robin switched the phone off at her repeated directives. The hospital attendants rushed Ritu to the emergency section.

The aircraft took off as Ritu went into an operation theatre. Scared and nervous, she missed Robin by her side. Robin was distraught; he knew that the earliest he could call again was eight hours later from Charles de Gaulle airport in Paris.

The Air France flight took an additional thirty minutes to land in Paris due to airspace congestion. It was nearly nine hours after Robin had last called his father-in-law. Disturbing images of a helpless and terrified Ritu on a stretcher had tortured him. In a desperate attempt to retain some sanity, he had tried everything from sipping whiskey to watching a Tom Cruise movie. Nothing worked.

When he took out his cell phone in Charles de Gaulle airport's transit area, he was confident that Ritu's troubles would have been over hours back. He looked forward to the joyful news that mother and child were doing well. The very thought cheered him up as he dialled the number.

He was wrong. It was only the beginning of a life-long agony; complications from umbilical cord prolapse and the delay in receiving medical attention had already cost two lives. Ritu and the baby had died six hours ago.

All alone in a sea of unknown faces, Robin could not even shed tears. He went through the transit routines like a zombie and boarded his flight to New Delhi. Then, he flew to Ahmedabad with an emptiness beyond words.

He returned home to consoling words and soothing hugs. People comforted him with the age-old adage that time would heal. But his longing for Ritu grew stronger with every passing day. So did his gloom.

9

Minutes before the flight attendant closed the aircraft door, a man walked in to occupy seat number 1C. It seemed that the flight was waiting for him to board. The man picked up Robin's book and kept it on the armrest; the book slipped and fell on the floor with a thud that caught Robin's attention. The two men greeted each other. The gentleman looked distinctly like a senior politician. Robin felt a fleeting sense of familiarity. But, losing interest soon, he looked out of the window again.

He was sure that the amniotic sac was not the real culprit behind the deaths of his wife and the baby. It was one among many possible complications of a pregnancy, well understood in the medical fraternity. All she had needed was timely medical support. He blamed it entirely on the needless procession, holding a specific group of people squarely responsible for his irreparable personal loss. He saw them as the root cause of many problems plaguing the country. The enormity of his personal calamity obfuscated his better judgment. Notwithstanding his secular and tolerant upbringing, he could not steer clear of radical thoughts in his weaker moments. He nurtured a belief that the panacea for all national ills lay in allowing the majority to command.

After the plane was airborne, the man turned to Robin and said, "Namaste! Do you live in Delhi?"

"Hello! Yes, I live in Delhi. And you? I get a feeling I have seen you somewhere!"

"I live in Delhi as well." He extended a hand to Robin and continued, "Manoj Seth. I am the President of the National Patriotic Party."

"Oh! My apologies that I did not recognise you. Very nice to meet you, Mr. Seth. My name is Robin Garg. And congratulations! Your party has achieved unprecedented success since you have taken charge."

"Thank you, Mr. Garg. I appreciate that."

"You are senior to me. Please call me Robin."

"Well, all right, Robin. You can call me Manoj *bhai* as well," said Manoj Seth with a smile. "The success of a political party depends on the support it gets from people. We are lucky to get so much love from people of all walks of life, from every community and religion, across barriers of caste and profession. They relate to us. They see us as their real hope for a safe and prosperous Bharat. Hope you are also a supporter of the National Patriotic Party."

"I am not into politics much. I run a modest business and spend time in social work through my NGO. I dwell on politics only during my cup of morning tea, as I go through the newspaper."

Manoj Seth laughed, "People often tell me this. But one cannot stay truly apolitical in today's world. Politics holds huge sway over our everyday lives, particularly for people like you in business and social service. By the way, what business are you in?"

"I have interests in consumer products distribution, IT, broadcasting, apart from a small venture capital firm to help young entrepreneurs."

"And you call this a modest business! What is the name of the consumer products distribution company? You own that?"

"National Distribution Network Limited. I hold the majority share in the company and manage it as its Chairman and Managing Director."

"Robin, humility is all right, but one does not have to be so humble! You own majority shares in NDNL, manage such diverse businesses, and you call it modest! I believe NDNL is one of the largest in its field, and the company has some of the best products in its portfolio. By that standard, I should call myself the national president of a small regional party!"

The flight attendant offered refreshments. Both of them opted for fresh orange juice.

Manoj Seth asked Robin probing questions about his business, the NGO, his experiences, and his plans ahead. Robin loved the respect he received from the powerful man. He enjoyed chatting with Manoj Seth because of his candid demeanour, his passion for Indian culture, and his vision of a country united in all respects. He respected the senior politician's conviction that bolstering national pride and respect for majoritarian sentiments was vital for the country's future; that blind appeasement of minorities had been a national blunder. Both of them agreed it was high time to undo the wrong.

"A vast majority has silently suffered at the hands of selfish politicians for too long. They have created and nurtured vote banks in the name of religion, caste, language, and regions at the cost of our national interests. Who gives a dime about the sentiments of the majority? When someone from a minority community gets beaten up on the street, the media presents it as an atrocity on the weaker sections of the society; if the same thing happens to someone from a majority community, it is called an unfortunate mishap.

"The majority has to be heard and respected. We are not against any community. We, as the government, must take everyone with us; progress for all, without exception. At the same time, we must not allow anyone to play with majority sentiments. Let's not fool around. If eight out of ten people in a country have one faith, the others must accept this reality and defer to their sentiments."

"I agree. While we accommodate everyone and let one and all live in harmony, the majority sentiments must not be ignored." Robin continued, "On a different subject, I think we should do more for underprivileged children. After years of intense work with my NGO, I know the kind of transformation we can bring to the lives of underprivileged children in our very backyard with suitable intervention at the right stage. A child in the slums may grow up to be a criminal or a professor. It all depends on what *we* do in their early days. I can give you many examples. Our NGO has remarkable successes in this area."

"What is the name of your NGO?"

"Ritu's World."

"I see. Who is Ritu, if I may ask?"

"My wife. Unfortunately, I lost her years back. It was *her* project; it is *still* her project."

"I am sorry, she died at a very young age! What happened?"

"She died at childbirth; both of them died in the operation theatre. However, to me, she was murdered by a wild mob," said Robin in a disturbed voice, looking away from Manoj Seth.

"I don't understand that! Will you please explain? Only if you wish, though; this is a personal and sensitive matter. The last thing I want is to interfere in your private matters."

No one talked for a while; Robin struggled to rediscover his voice while Manoj Seth waited patiently.

"This happened in Ahmedabad a few years back. The minority community provoked the majority by taking out a religious procession in their locality against their wish; the police blocked the traffic instead of banning the procession. Everyone did what they should not have, and I had to pay the price—my wife could not make it to the hospital in time."

Listening attentively, Manoj Seth waited for Robin to finish and then spoke in measured words, "I feel for you, Robin. What you have gone through is something that no one should ever have to go through. It is terrible to lose people close to your heart at any time; it is so much more painful to lose them young, and it must be unbearable to lose them under the circumstances that you have just described."

"You are not the only victim of such unnecessary communal disturbances. As part of my job, I regularly meet people from all over the country, from Gujarat to Assam to Kashmir to Kerala. There are scores of such disturbing stories. It is a shame when the vast majority does not have a voice. Why should a minority religious procession go through a majority-dominated area if the people there do not like it? Pseudo-secularism has destroyed us. This has to end."

Robin looked away. The belligerent words had opened unhealed wounds buried in his subconscious. The long-abandoned urge for revenge sprang up in him. '*The majority must be treated as a majority. They must never feel lost in their own country. Yes, the man is damn right,*' he thought.

Robin said, "What you say makes a great argument, really beyond any challenge. I must compliment you, Manoj *bhai*, on some of the work you are doing, despite stinging criticism from certain quarters. Keep doing the good work."

They continued chatting for the rest of the flight; about politics, Robin's business empire, and his NGO. They discussed the importance of doing everything necessary to make future generations confident, resilient, and patriotic. They agreed that youngsters must become tomorrow's torchbearers of India's rich culture and heritage. Manoj Seth offered his party's support to Ritu's World to improve its reach and scope, which Robin gratefully accepted.

As they bade goodbye, Robin could not believe that he had had such a long discussion with a politician, that too none other than the second most powerful man in the country. With the realisation that they shared a canvas for the country's future, he accepted Manoj Seth's invitation for a drink with him next evening.

The following evening, by the time they had finished their after-dinner coffee, Robin Garg had accepted primary membership of the National Patriotic Party.

10

The unexpected return of a teenage idol took Purnima years back to the most exciting phase of her schooldays. After the brief chat with Robin, she could barely sleep. Vivid images of her happy and dreamy childhood came alive. A shy and sensitive girl, her doting parents rarely raised their voices even to discipline her. They didn't have to. Purnima was an obedient daughter and a bright student. Her parents were concerned about her reserved and extra-sensitive personality. Knowing well that they could do precious little about her basic nature, they did all they could to support and encourage her.

Purnima took time to make friends. But once the ice broke, she stuck to her friendship. Shazia was an exception. Purnima could never get over the sad day of her life when she lost Shazia for reasons she never understood. She could not forget another miserable day of her life when Shiny, her pet dog, passed away. She was in the seventh standard when the milky-white four-year-old Chihuahua suddenly died of an unknown disease. Purnima did not eat anything for two days. She refused to have another pet since then, till a purebred Saluki stole her heart many years later.

Lying on the bed, Purnima clutched her hair to get some relief from a growing pain in the backside of her head. Headaches had been a nuisance in her adolescent days when she had to often struggle with episodes of throbbing pain of varying intensity and duration. Fortunately, its frequency reduced as she went into her twenties and it disappeared in her thirties. Wondering why the pain had returned now, she reckoned it must be a result of the unfamiliar pressure she had been through in the recent weeks. The unwelcome headache brought her some welcome memories. Once in her life, this pain had turned into a delight. She was in the eleventh grade at that time.

"Purni sweetheart, see who's come?" shouted the housemaid.

Purnima didn't respond. Nursing a throbbing head, she was in no mood to talk to anyone.

"Hey, are you sleeping? Get up, lazy girl! Your favourite neighbour is here." Still no response.

Purnima immediately understood who had come. He was the only neighbourhood person she looked forward to welcoming every evening. She wasn't well enough to get up and talk to the man, but at the same time, could not let him go away just like that. While she contemplated how best to handle the situation, the housemaid came into the room.

"Oh, come on, why are you sleeping at this time?"

"I have a headache, *didi*. Can barely get up."

"Robin *da* has come. You wouldn't say hello to him?" The housemaid knew what was in Purnima's mind. Having looked after Purnima since she was a baby, the woman thoroughly understood her. She was aware of Purnima's soft corner for Robin and laughed it off as a classic example of hero-worshipping often indulged in by teenage girls.

"I can't talk to anyone. I do not want to see anyone now," she lied.

The housemaid quickly walked out of the room, saying aloud, "She is in bed with a headache, Robin *da*. Sorry, she would not be able to meet you this evening."

Purnima considered jumping out of the bed. Meanwhile, Robin responded in a loud enough voice to ensure Purnima heard him. "Oh, is that so? The kid is not well this evening? That's not good. Let me see how bad it is. Hey, Purnima! I am coming in." Not waiting for a response, Robin knocked and walked into the room.

"Hello, young lady? What's wrong with you this evening? Never heard of you having a headache! Is it very bad? You must have had a hard day in school."

Purnima hurriedly looked around to ensure she was properly covered with the sheet and said, "Hello, Robin *da*. Great to see you, as always. Yes, I have a severe headache. This happens to me once in a while. Just a coincidence that you have never seen me in this condition."

"Have you taken any medicine?"

"No, I haven't. Usually, I do not take these painkillers unless it becomes unbearable. I will be fine, don't worry. Just that I have to lie down for some time."

"Tell me where is the pain? I mean which part of your head your pain is it centred around? I know a trick or two about managing headaches."

Purnima relished the comforting words from the man she adored. Sheepishly, she said, "Never mind, Robin *da*. I will be fine. This is just a passing thing."

Robin responded caringly, "That's not what I asked, Purnima. I enquired where is the centre of your pain, if at all there is any. Come on!" Purnima understood there was no point in arguing further. She pointed at her right temple. Robin pulled a chair, sat by her bed and asked Purnima to turn over to her left. Then, without saying a word, he massaged her head in firm strokes, his thumb pressing her temple for a few seconds and rolling down to her cheek, repeatedly. Ignoring Purnima's polite protests, Robin continued for some time. Purnima loved every moment. She regretted having to face the wall as the 'best man in the world' relaxed her with his magic touch. It was one of the finest evenings of her life.

"You've got such long and dainty fingers, Purnima! You should be an artist" said Robin once. Indeed, she wanted to be an artist.

A gifted child, her oil paintings and sketches drew everyone's attention. When her own version of Mona Lisa earned her the first prize in a state-level art competition, everyone hailed her as a prodigy. She harboured ambitions of making a career in Fine Arts till, one day, her father called her aside and said, "My girl, I know you love painting and I believe you are contemplating making a living out of it. I am proud of your talent and I have no doubt that you will shine in whatever field you wish to pursue. However, as your father, I want to secure your future. Money isn't everything, but without adequate money, there is nothing in life. You have to monetise your expertise to earn a decent living. It is very difficult to do so as an artist. You are a truly gifted child. You are strong in all the subjects. Take up a profession that gets you money for a good living and also gives you ample opportunity to serve the poor and unprivileged people."

Purnima's parents used to throw lavish parties every year on her birthday. After the tenth birthday party, Purnima asked them to spend that money on poor children in the slums, to give them food, clothes or books. Her personal celebrations were restricted to having pizzas or burgers with a few select friends.

Her father continued, "You have a heart of gold. You have a lot to give back to the society. Take up medicine, and become a good doctor—you can earn a decent living while serving the people who desperately need help. Intelligence, tenacity, empathy, and sensitivity—you have them all to succeed in the true sense of the word in this noble profession."

Her father's persuasive argument had set Purnima on a definitive path leading to the philanthropic medic she became. She was content and happy in her world till the challenges of electoral politics brought wholesale disruption to her life. And then, Robin arrived out of nowhere! She wondered what was in store for her now. *Is he still the incredible charmer he once was? Or has he become an uninteresting businessman always running after money? Will he still treat me like a little schoolgirl? Is he as excited to meet me tomorrow?*

Purnima walked up to the mirror and looked at herself. She hated the streaks of grey hair on the right side. Swiftly hiding them below others, she carefully studied the woman looking back at her.

It's all good! I am ready for tomorrow.

She went back to the bed and quickly fell asleep.

11

A few blocks away from the NPP headquarters, the bigwigs of the UNDP were huddled together on Sunday morning for final deliberations on the candidate for the West Delhi parliamentary by-election. It was not an ordinary contest. The UNDP had to prove that their astonishing victory at the last elections was not an aberration. The win had confounded even their staunchest supporters. It was a moral victory for the party and a significant achievement for their Delhi state unit amid general despair. They had to preserve the gain at any cost.

Further, the stakes were well beyond mere preservation of a strategic electoral gain. NPP exploited their crushing majority in the lower house to pass controversial bills that UNDP believed were against the basic tenets of the nation's constitution. With the general elections years away, it was clear that the ruling party would continue on the same path unless they saw signs of public unease. A win for the ruling party would be an endorsement of their actions considered divisive by many; a loss could press the pause button on their plans.

The party had called for a press conference at fifteen minutes past five in the evening; so a final decision was necessary by afternoon. The UNDP had an all-powerful central high command with supreme control on all critical matters, notwithstanding an elaborate organisational hierarchy right down to the block level. Perhaps as a reward for their stellar performance in the previous elections, the Delhi unit of the party was given a free hand this time to choose the candidate. Harsh Malhotra and top office bearers were unanimous on their choice ever since Purnima Bajaj Bhatt

63

had agreed to be the party candidate. However, it was necessary to review the other contenders as well, as per the party's accepted norms.

The top leaders believed that veteran Durjoy Kumar would be the NPP candidate, and it would be difficult to beat him once again in a routine contest. Like most political leaders, the UNDP hopefuls too had skeletons in their cupboards. An experienced politician like Durjoy Kumar would definitely find ways to exploit them to his full advantage. So, they were determined to surprise him and his party by fielding a new face. They knew that there would be no fodder for political witch hunts in Purnima's past.

The meeting lasted less than an hour, and the leadership rejected all other names with due justification. Harsh Malhotra addressed the meeting after the discussions were over.

"After discussing the merits of each contender for the party ticket, and in deference to our belief that a clean, new face is necessary to defeat Durjoy Kumar, Dr Purnima Bajaj Bhatt is the best candidate for us. Do we all agree? Is there anything else anyone has to say?"

Most attendees nodded vigorously. A few looked less enthusiastic in their agreement, betraying their uncertain minds. Two participants did neither. Harsh Malhotra knew why, ignored them, and spoke again, "So, we pass a resolution that Dr Purnima Bajaj Bhatt gets the UNDP ticket for the West Delhi parliamentary by-election. As per her suggestion—and we have no issues with that—the name shall be released as Dr Purnima Bhatt. A press conference has been called at five fifteen this evening. We shall then announce it to the public."

The meeting was declared closed, and the key executives hurried to another room to prepare for the press meet.

Robin Garg had a busy day. An early morning meeting with the party's regional leadership, a crucial summit with an important

NDNL principal, an address to party workers in the afternoon, a short visit to a Ritu's World event in Badarpur and his party's press conference, before rushing to Connaught Place for his coffee with Purnima Bajaj.

Purnima had been in his mind all through the day despite his gruelling schedule. He was excited, curious, and apprehensive.

Though the distance was not even three kilometre, it was not the best time for a drive in Central Delhi. Given the traffic at the Connaught Place outer circle, it was unlikely that he would make it on time. Robin despised being late for meetings; it was now unbearable to get late for this date. He considered calling Purnima to inform her but opted to pray for the traffic to ease instead. Approaching Shankar Market, Robin sharply cut into the inner lane and then forced his way to Road Number 6. It was already six in the evening. The evening news bulletin broadcast started on FM.

Soon enough, he entered a parking area close to the coffee shop. Certain that he would not get a free parking slot quickly enough, he looked for an attendant to hand over his car keys.

Meanwhile, Purnima had reached United Coffee House five minutes before time. Through the day, she could barely focus her attention on any business. One moment, she thought that a new opportunity had come knocking on her door to bring fresh colour to her life; the next moment, she laughed at her stupidity and reminded herself that she was no more a teenager to indulge in juvenile dreams. Having cancelled all her commitments for the afternoon, she sifted through her wardrobe, selected dresses at random, put them on before the mirror only to reject them and start the process all over again. Finally, she zeroed in on what she thought would be most appropriate. She looked at her watch, begging time to move faster.

There was no way she could skip the press conference. However, she excused herself once the question-and-answer session started.

Keen to be on time and desperate to not face the evening traffic, she decided to leave her car at the party headquarters and take a taxi to Connaught Place.

Waiting at the coffee house, she nervously looked at the time and wondered if she was in for heartbreak.

Looking around for the car park attendant, Robin honked a couple of times. He thought he heard a reference to the UNDP candidate for the by-election on the radio. Robin listened to the headline at the end of the short bulletin. This time he heard it loud and clear. UNDP had fielded someone called Dr Purnima Bhatt for the West Delhi parliamentary by-election. Robin laughed aloud at the coincidence! He was happy to get fresh ammunition to tease Purnima for old times' sake; after all, her namesake would challenge him in the election!

As the attendant took the car key, a relieved Robin walked to the coffee shop at the inner circle. It was already fifteen minutes past their scheduled meeting time. Feeling guilty, he hoped Purnima had not given up on him.

Robin walked into the busy coffee shop looking for a face last seen so long ago. The popular outlet was remarkably congested. It was not easy to locate someone in these busy hours. It was worse when the face was unknown. He stood in one corner and looked at the tables. Single ladies occupied only two tables. He first looked at the table by the left sidewall. The elegantly dressed woman was busy with her laptop. She did not look like someone waiting for a meeting past its scheduled time. The other woman at the last table, a few metres before the cash counter and near the passage leading to the restrooms, appeared nervous. Dressed in a light blue *churidar*, brownish-black hair with shoulder-length sweptback layers, designer eyewear, the woman was looking at her watch, the entrance, and her mobile handset in quick succession. Robin knew exactly where to go.

He walked up to the table and said with a charming smile. "Purnima? Robin."

Purnima jumped out of her seat and held on to Robin's extended hand. Overwhelmed with emotions, she feared she might choke. She prayed for Robin to speak first as she avoided looking directly into his eyes.

Robin came to her rescue. "Shall we sit down? I am so happy to see you again. A million thanks for finding me. How you have pulled this off is something that we shall talk about later. Shall we order something in the meantime?"

Purnima sat down like an obedient child. *Oh, that disarming smile; he hasn't lost even a bit of his charm over the years! And his eyes! They still look straight into one's heart!*

The waiter left with an order for two cappuccinos, a plate each of paneer *pakodas* and fish fingers.

12

Surprised with the NPP's nomination of a political rookie, Harsh Malhotra called for an urgent meeting of the senior party functionaries at half-past six the same evening. His strategy so far had been built around the assumption that Durjoy Kumar would be the NPP candidate. A standby plan with Bhupinder Gupta as the opponent existed on paper but did not get much importance. Now, it was a different game altogether with an unknown candidate without a political background.

The Delhi unit had not had an operational command hierarchy for a long time. A few party functionaries, nominated by the high command, exclusively controlled the decision-making process. The president had to shoulder the responsibilities for all major decisions alone. This gave him an undisputed authority but also deprived him of the benefits of collective intuition.

He addressed the gathering of six trusted lieutenants holding different posts in the state unit. "Gentlemen, we have a different battle at hand now. All our strategies and plans to beat Durjoy Kumar have no relevance anymore. We have to start all over again; that's a lot to do in just a few weeks. Sharma *ji*, do you have any idea why Kumar did not get the ticket? What do your contacts in the party say?"

Sunil Sharma, a general secretary of the party, responded, "I understand they wanted to surprise us with a new face and spoil all our calculations; something that we intend to do with our nomination. The fact is, they have beaten us at our own game."

Harsh Malhotra quipped, "Certainly, they have succeeded in this. How has Kumar taken it? He must be very disappointed."

"Officially, he has come out in full support of the nomination. Many thought that he would revolt and stand as an independent if ignored for the ticket. But it does not look like that. It's very strange but Durjoy Kumar tells his supporters that the party has chosen the candidate in consultation with him, and he fully supports it!"

Looking away, Harsh Malhotra toyed with the paperweight in front of him for a while before speaking again. "There must be something in it. With Manoj Seth at the helm, anything is possible. But that is none of our concern. Do *any* of you know anything at all about this man Robin Garg? I have heard the name before. I may have even met him once or twice at some public functions. All I know is that he is a wealthy businessman, and he runs a well-known NGO that works with poor children to develop their personalities. But I did not know he has an interest in active politics! How do you think he will fare with the electorate?"

Another participant, Jamal Ahmed, responded, "I have done a quick check on him. First of all, he is an affluent, determined, and handsome businessman, well-connected in the corporate world because of his diverse business interests. So, he will have access to enormous campaign funds over and above what he gets from his ultra-rich party. He is likely to attract female voters who constitute about 45% of the electorate. Besides, the head of his popular NGO is a Poorvanchali guy. That is likely to have a significant influence on the large chunk of Poorvanchali voters in this constituency. In short, we would have probably found it easier to fight Durjoy Kumar, whose weaknesses are familiar to us."

Malhotra responded, "It will be good if we can somehow engineer a revolt in that party for giving the ticket to a new face. Even if Bhupinder Gupta contests as an independent, he will take away a chunk of upper caste and Bania votes from NPP. You guys check if there is any such discontent simmering within their party, and if so, do whatever you can to act as a catalyst.

"But this fellow is originally from somewhere in the North-East, am I right?"

"He is from Assam. But that is unlikely to be an election issue. He has lived in Delhi for quite a few years and was earlier in Bangalore, Ahmedabad, etc. I think he left his home state soon after his basic education. He speaks fluent Hindi," answered Ahmed.

"Okay then," said Malhotra, with a tone indicating that the meeting was over. "Let's get to work. Jamal, you closely monitor the events in their party and do your bit when you can to engineer an internal fight. Sunil, let us move at super speed. We must win this contest at any cost. I believe we are all meeting tomorrow. Did you brief Purnima well?"

"Not today. Purnima Bhatt seemed to be in a hurry. You saw that she didn't even sit through the press conference. Somehow, I found her off-colour. I think her mind was somewhere else," responded Sunil Sharma.

"What else do you expect Sharma *ji*?" quipped Malhotra. "She is not a seasoned politician like you! It is not easy to relax on the first day as a candidate for a parliamentary election for someone from a non-political background. She will be all right, give her some time."

Around the same time, the NPP stalwarts were brooding over the challenge thrown at them by their adversary. They had made detailed dossiers on likely opponents. But all the groundwork became null and void with the UNDP's nomination of an unknown candidate. They were amazed at how both the parties had played the same game to deny each other any advantage.

Manoj Seth addressed the senior regional office bearers through a video call. He spoke in his trademark voice. "I bet no one anticipated this googly from UNDP. Suresh *ji*, seasoned batsmen like you should have seen this coming. I always tell you that your team's intelligence gathering is very poor. You had presented various scenarios to me but such a surprise was nowhere on the horizon.

Now throw your information on prospective candidates into the garbage can and get your act together to face the new challenge."

Manoj Seth let a few seconds pass for his message to sink in before continuing. None of the participants in the meeting batted an eyelid. His voice and his stern face staring at them from a large screen sufficed to make them behave like well-trained children in a primary school classroom.

Suresh Ahluwalia was wallowing in self-pity. He believed he deserved to be treated better after decades of unwavering dedication to the party, and its parent organisations before the party's formation. Manoj Seth, younger and a much later entrant to the party, had risen to the top of the party leadership through astute manoeuvring, aided by a few spectacular personal triumphs. He was an efficient administrator, crafty schemer and a ruthless go-getter. Ahluwalia acknowledged that Seth had contributed significantly to the party's remarkable recent rise as the most powerful and well-funded party in the country. But he also believed that Seth ought to show some respect to the senior party leaders; it was simply not right for him to humiliate a state party president before junior party functionaries. Nevertheless, there was precious little he could do about it.

He did not respond. He knew Manoj Seth did not expect him to either.

Seth continued after the pause. "Who the hell is this Purnima Bhatt? I may well have met her in one of the doctors' conclaves though I do not remember any such meeting. Never seen her or heard of her in political circles. Do you have any information on her? Suresh *ji*, anything at all? How serious a threat is she to us?"

"Manoj *bhai*, she is a distinguished general physician. She worked and taught in AIIMS for over ten years; she was like a celebrity in the institute. Quite popular for her professional excellence and her amiable personality. She is also a commoner's darling for her benevolence. Her private clinic has been treating poor patients free of cost for many years. Further, she visits various slums twice a week to offer free consultations. In short, we have a UNDP candidate here who is a political novice but not a new face to the electorate. She is likely to capture a sizeable chunk of the swing votes. I would not be surprised if she manages to slice away some of our traditional votes as well."

Seth retorted, "You sound like someone who has already laid down arms, singing eulogies for a person who is challenging us in this crucial election. Let us think, let's quickly adapt our strategy to this new scenario. There is nothing impossible in politics. You have to be hungry, innovative, and ruthless. Suresh *ji*, rather than discussing her virtues, please think of a winning masterstroke."

Sheepishly, Suresh Ahluwalia responded, "Yes, Manoj *bhai*. We will discuss and come up with a strategy. Just give us some time."

"Let me give you my take on this. *Lohe ko lohe se katiye*! You find another known lady doctor and convince her to stand as an independent. We will bear all her electoral expenses apart from a handsome personal reward for standing in the election. She will, of course, lose but will cut into sizeable votes from the UNDP doctor. Please move quickly. I give you three days, that means we discuss this again on Thursday."

Manoj Seth signed off from the video conference. Most of the attendees admired the party president's perspicacity. However, Suresh Ahluwalia was not very impressed. He believed such murky tricks were unnecessary, and risked hurting their prospects. These negative tactics always ran the risk of being exposed, and could actually turn voters away. Besides, sizeable resources would be wasted on something that was not guaranteed to contribute to the ultimate success. Having no option but to toe the president's line, he asked two trusted aides to scout for a suitable lady doctor for the job.

13

"So here we are, my dear Purnima."

Robin tried to sound cheerful and confident in a poorly disguised effort to hide his nervousness. "You have not changed much, have you? I would have recognised you in a crowd."

Purnima scrutinised Robin. *He still looks the same—well nearly the same—athletic body with a little flab reasonable for a man in his forties, eyes that smiled seductively just as much as they used to, the incredible warmth—he still has them all! His dark hair has aged a bit to let streaks of grey show. But the salt-and-pepper look, with more pepper than salt, added depth to his personality.* Purnima thought Robin Garg looked more attractive than the twenty-something young man she had last seen. However, something was different; it was bothering her that she could not pinpoint exactly what.

'Ah! The moustache!' His thin line of moustache, one which the young man had carefully nurtured, was missing. He was clean-shaven!

"Purnima!" Robin laughed and said, "Will you say something at all? Or are you still the same shy little girl?"

Having himself had a good look at Purnima, Robin searched for the young schoolgirl who had held such sway over him in his twenties. His transfer to Lucknow forced a distance between them; the distance helped reduce his longing to see her every evening. He convinced himself that his fascination with the schoolgirl was nothing but the passing fixation of an attention-loving young man. In times of loneliness, his mind often waltzed back to his Bangalore days and Purnima's face resurfaced to tease his heart. Everything changed after Ritu had stormed into his life. Her company had not left any space for his mind to travel back to his younger days.

Robin noticed that the little girl in a pleated skirt with a matching top had matured into a beautiful lady with an impressive personality. The black ponytail had given way to a brownish-black, tastefully trimmed and layered hairdo that seemed perfect for her face. The dimples added charm to her face, and the teenage blush had seasoned to a mature bloom on her radiant face. The naughty, twinkling eyes were more mellowed but still beautiful. The designer glasses, Cartier, were well-suited to her face. He looked at her long, well-manicured fingers. They looked exquisite with a glittering solitaire on the middle finger of her left hand. A diamond-studded black Rado watch on her right wrist, exposed by her kurta sleeves folding at the elbow as she rested her hand on the table, added to her overall elegance.

With the age difference no more a cause of concern and life with Ritu a distant past, his feelings for Purnima returned with vigour. He was astonished by his desire to hold her in his arms. He wondered what was on her mind that she could not speak a word, just the way Purnima pondered what was in Robin's mind that he would not go further after his initial dig at her.

The waiter came to their rescue. "Sorry sir, the snacks will take a few minutes more. Should I bring the cappuccinos in the meantime?"

Relieved that someone had broken the ice, Robin answered without looking at the waiter, "No, it's okay, we'll wait. Get them all together."

As the waiter nodded and left, Robin seized the opportunity. "So, Purnima. Tell me, what's up with you? What have you been doing all these years? You may recall the last time we wrote to each other. Must have been when Lord Rama was about to invade Lanka with the monkey army! Right?"

Robin's joke eased Purnima's nerves. She finally spoke, "Well, truly, it feels like that. I think I wrote to you once after getting into medical college. I never got a reply to that one. You must have thought enough is enough; no more of this silly girl!"

She giggled like a child and continued, "I was upset that you did not reply. I kept running to the postman for a reply, till I decided to not invite pain. I stopped looking for your reply and never wrote again. Why didn't you reply to my last letter? I don't remember writing anything to upset you!"

Robin cleared his throat and said, "Honestly, it's been a long time. It is very unusual for me not to reply to a letter, Purnima. As far as I remember, I waited for a response from you for a long time, didn't get one, and then got extremely busy with my work in the office. With time, life moved on, just the way it must have been for you too. Let's not worry about what didn't happen. We can't be too harsh on ourselves, can we? There was no social media in those days, unfortunately. But, first of all, let me tell you something. You look gorgeous! Those dimples are tantalising! I curse myself for not looking you up after we lost communication last time!" Robin laughed as he said the last few words.

Purnima thought, *He is still such a charming flirt!* "Robin *da*, come on. Don't pull my leg, please! Let's catch up on what you've been up to all these years. Please, start."

Robin gave her a brief on his career—his transfer to Lucknow, his business interests, his social initiatives, and changing his base to New Delhi. He did not say a word about his family and his new avatar as a politician.

"So, here I am. Now, it's your turn, Purnima."

"Hang on, Robin *da*! What about your family? You did not say a word about that. With so much success behind you, I am sure it was a challenge to pick your partner from many hopefuls. Children?"

Eager to know his past in minute details, Purnima pressed on despite knowing that Robin was a bachelor now.

Robin sighed and looked away. Purnima wondered if she had touched a nerve. She said, "Is this something that bothers you? You don't have to talk about your family if you so prefer. I'm sorry I asked, Robin *da*."

"It's nothing like that, Purnima. I have not had much luck on that front. I will tell you anyway; it is not a secret. Just that this is a part of my life that kills me over and over again!" Robin paused to wet his throat and continued, "I was married to a beautiful woman named Ritu, Ritu Mehta. We had a very happy married life, probably as happy as a couple can get. She has contributed a lot to what I am today, as a businessman, and as a social worker."

Robin stopped again, this time for longer, looked away, and said, "I lost her and our baby during childbirth. I could not give her the required medical care in time."

"I am so sorry, Robin *da*. How did this happen? We don't need to talk about this any further. I don't want to see you sad now. Sorry again."

"No, that's okay. It is not the first time that I have been asked this question. You don't have to feel sorry. However, let's not talk about it right now. I shall tell you the details another time. I am seeing you after an eternity. Let's talk about something else... something pleasant. Well, I am a bachelor now, as it stands! You tell me about yourself."

Purnima spoke about her career, starting from when they had lost touch last, talked about her services in AIIMS, her love for social service and her passion for classical music. She did not talk about her involvement in politics. That aspect of her life was alien and too recent to be mentioned in a routine brief on her career.

She continued, without giving Robin a chance to enquire, "As for my immediate family, it's just me, my Ego, and a housemaid. That's it."

"You're not married?"

"No, I'm single."

"It's interesting the way you mentioned that you stay with your ego. All of us do that. But you do not look to me like someone who needs to highlight it. Someone with a big ego would not have tracked me this way—and thanks again for doing so."

Purnima laughed out. "Ego is my purebred Saluki, truly a fantastic breed! We are just two in the house, me and my lovely dog. And don't get me started on my ego."

"That's a great name for a dog." Robin laughed as well. "I always wanted to have a dog. Ritu was not keen. So, I never got around to getting one… even today."

He continued, in a rather sombre voice, "How come you never married? I know it's a personal question; sorry if I should not be asking it."

Purnima took time to answer. "We shall leave that for another day. I did not say I've never been married. For now, let's just say that I have never met anyone with whom I believe I can spend my entire life. I guess I set the bar very high early in my life."

Robin noticed Purnima's unease as she said the last few words. Knowing that a quick change in subject was necessary to save the evening, he decided not to press on.

"Where are your school friends? I remember you could barely talk those days without mentioning your school friends. Are you still in touch with any of them?" asked Robin, hoping that a mention of her childhood friends would bring back the glow to her face. Disappointed not to see such a change, and with an uneasy feeling that he had added to her gloom, Robin regretted asking another unwelcome question.

Purnima responded reluctantly, "Another unpleasant story that I do not want to revisit this wonderful evening. I have done all I can to avoid any contact even with my best friend ever since the last day of our twelfth-grade final examination. So, honestly, I do not want to talk about any of them."

They discussed music—a common passion—and talked about their wonderful days in Austin Town. Both of them were pleasantly surprised that decades of disconnect had not reduced the intensity of their feelings for each other; they had easily picked up from where they had left off. Their age difference had lost its relevance. Purnima no more perceived Robin as someone well beyond her dreams. Robin felt no guilt in his urge to hold Purnima in his arms. Starved for love, both of them wondered if their coffee date was more than a casual catching up between old friends and if there were promises of brighter days ahead.

Time flew by. Looking at her watch, Purnima said, "Oops, I didn't realise it's eight already! I need to get back home now, Robin *da*, sorry."

"Why, is there something urgent back home? Otherwise, we can order some food here and be done with our dinner. We shall then have more time to talk."

"No, really, I need to get back. For Ego, you know. He waits for me to eat his food. Although my maid gives him his food on time, he takes only a few bites. He returns to his bowl after I get home and cuddle him. After that, he cleans up the bowl! He is just like a child, in fact, more than a human at times!"

"Ah, I understand. In that case, you must go. How did you come? You drove?"

"No, I took a taxi. I didn't want to take a chance with my car and possibly get late for this all-important meeting with my childhood hero!" said Purnima with a chuckle.

"Shall I drop you then? I drove myself, probably breaking a few traffic rules here and there—since I too did not want to be late for this reunion with my little crush—got a few minutes late nevertheless."

Purnima laughed out loud—so loud that the people from the nearby tables looked at them with curiosity—and said, "I like that! 'Little crush'! Is that so? Well, that little one is not so little anymore, however you bet she would have given an arm and a leg to hear you say this in those adolescent days!"

Robin wanted to ask, *And now! What does the grown-up girl think now?* But he chose to ignore the comment and insisted on dropping Purnima.

She replied, "Saket is not at all on your route; you have to go to Dwarka. In today's convenience of on-demand taxi services, it doesn't make sense for such detours. Oh, what's wrong with me! I have to pick up my car on the way! I nearly forgot! You should carry on. I am calling for a taxi now."

Robin settled the bill after an authoritative no to Purnima's offer to pick it up, and both of them walked out of the coffee shop with a promise to talk soon to set up a dinner date. Robin walked with her to the taxi pick-up point before proceeding to the car park. Purnima called from behind, "Robin *da*, what about the exciting development you were expecting last night? Did that happen? You want to tell me about it?"

Robin turned back and said, "Yes, there is an exciting development. I remembered to talk about it right until I entered the coffee shop. Actually, I thought of teasing you with the latest inputs I received on the same topic! Never mind now! It is too significant to be shared this way. Let's reserve this for our phone call, or even better for our dinner date, which I am sure will be very soon. By the way, you were supposed to surprise me with something interesting as well. What was that?"

Purnima walked a step towards him and said, "I shall tell you the same time you tell me. You said it first, so you come out with it first; isn't that fair?" She waved and slowly walked back to the taxi pick-up point. Robin looked at her and thought, *What a lovely woman the kid has grown up to be. Beauty, grace, talent, and wit all rolled into one woman. Terrific!* He regretted that he had forgotten to talk about his candidature for the West Delhi parliamentary by-election and lost a chance to tease Purnima with the funny coincidence that his challenger would be her namesake! There was no fun in teasing her once the names were flashed all over media.

14

Purnima was not the only one to have a sleepless Sunday night. As she tossed around in bed, others also failed to catch the sleep they badly needed.

Suresh Ahluwalia was under enormous pressure. He had a feeling that a loss in the by-election would cost him his job as the president of the Delhi unit of NPP. With his detailed and seemingly fool proof plans rendered useless by a UNDP masterstroke, he had the arduous task of preparing a new strategy to defeat a contender about whom precious little was known. There were many things to do the next day. However, there was something that could not wait till the morning.

He got up from his bed, drank a glass of water, and reached for his cell phone.

The person on the other side did not pick up the first time. Suresh Ahluwalia called again. The receiver picked up the phone just before he was about to cut the call. The man, still half asleep, replied without any effort to hide his irritation. "Hello, who's this?"

"Chowdhury, this is Suresh Ahluwalia. I know this is an odd time to call. But the fact that I am calling at this time should tell you that I could not have waited for a better time."

Ajay Chowdhury jumped out of his bed and cursed himself for not looking at the caller's name. He responded, "Ahluwalia *saab*, *namaskar*! Your call is welcome anytime, day or night, and you know that well. Please, tell me, what can I do for you?"

Ajay Chowdhury was the Chairman of Topaz Investigative Services, arguably the most penetrative detective agency in the country. He privately held the thirty-year-old company. Out of their expansive portfolio of services, background screening, asset search and verification, and due diligence checks for individuals and corporations were in high demand. NPP had an exclusive and confidential agreement with Topaz Investigative Services; they were obliged to take up NPP assignments on priority and were barred from working for any other political party for similar investigative tasks. For this exclusive service, they earned a monthly retainer fee and handsome remunerations for the assigned projects. Chowdhury was more than happy to jump out of his bed for his top client.

Ahluwalia replied, "This is a super classified assignment of supreme importance. I will be brief. Please make your notes, if you wish. UNDP has nominated Dr Purnima Bhatt as their candidate for the West Delhi parliamentary by-election. I want a complete dossier on her. She is not a politician, but I believe she has been in the public domain through her professional contacts and philanthropic initiatives. So, you should be able to make headway soon enough. I want the report with me no later than this Wednesday evening. That is three full working days. And, everything about her. Everything. You want to ask me anything else?"

Chowdhury hesitated a bit and said, "Well, not much at this time, just that I think the time period is too short. We have to start from the very start, you see, without any background on the person. Please, give me three more days. Give me time till Saturday evening, please."

"No. Unfortunately, I do not have such luxury. The election day is just weeks away, and we have so much to do. Like us, they have also revealed their candidate for this constituency at the eleventh hour. I'll give you one more day. Thursday evening, but no later, please. Good night. Hope you get a good night's sleep for the rest of the night."

"Okay, good night, Ahluwalia *saab*. Not sure about sleep now. It is my turn now to wake a few people. Pleasure talking to you, always. Bye."

Chowdhury called his two senior executives and asked them to submit a detailed report by Wednesday. He always kept at least a day for personal review.

Harish Gupta and Raman Srivastava, Suresh Ahluwalia's two trusted aides charged with finding the proxy independent candidate, could not sleep as well. They spent most of the night talking with their close associates and block-level party workers. They needed to have a shortlist by the morning, run a thorough search on each person to finally trim the list down to two prospective options by Tuesday, and then use the rest of the time to convince one of them to file nomination papers as an independent candidate.

Meanwhile, Robin Garg could not sleep either despite an exhausting day. He could not get over the exciting two hours spent with his first crush. *I guess I set the bar very high early in my life … my childhood hero*—Purnima's words, full of promise, would not let him sleep tonight.

Elsewhere in Delhi, Harsh Malhotra gave up his futile struggle for sleep and worked on his strategy. His job was not at stake in this election. But a failure to retain the seat would surely hurt his stature in the party. He hoped Jamal Ahmed and his team could convince Bhupinder Gupta to stand as an independent. But he could not plan to win an election based on one unlikely hope; it was necessary to find more information on the NPP candidate. He called Jamal to stress the importance of their mission to engineer a revolt in NPP. Jamal, well aware of the urgency, did not require the late-night reminder. But he politely heard his president out, knowing well that the call was nothing but a vent for the overstressed man's anxieties.

Malhotra then called Sunil Sharma. "There must be a few chinks in the armour of a successful businessman. We must know them all—any dark spot in his career or his character—corruption, illegitimacy, infidelity, or whatever." Sunil Sharma, himself losing sleep over the enormity of the task in hand, gave his boss a patient hearing, the best that he could do for the moment.

However, the night was the toughest for Purnima. For her, the election and the hectic politicking ahead took a backseat. The aura of a man she had adored as a teenager, the romance of meeting him after ages over coffee in the evening, the things he said, the way he smiled and teased—everything was overwhelming. She smiled, rushed to the mirror, appreciated the dimples that he had admired, and blushed all over again. She saw Robin in the mirror smiling at her from behind, his chin resting on her shoulder, cheek-to-cheek. Excited, she turned to hold him in her arms; he was gone. Embarrassed with her stupidity, she softly slapped her forehead and shook her head in disbelief. She walked to a cupboard near the dressing table, reached for the top drawer, and pulled out a colourful and uncharacteristically large Kashmiri papier-mâché box, and cautiously carried it to her bed. A *Takashi* design with the traditional *Hazara* motif made the box exquisite.

Purnima sat on the bed with her back resting against the headboard slats, stretched her legs out, and carefully placed the box to her left. She stared at it, as if in a dilemma whether to open it or not, before taking the latch off. A dark red velvet cloth inside the box opened up to display her precious collection—a pair of oxidised silver earrings, a Parker fountain pen, and a four-by-six centimetre photograph—all gifts from Robin. She picked up the photo to have a closer look at the young man next to her, the others in the photo hardly mattered. She closed her eyes to capture the image of just herself and the young man.

She hated herself for being a school kid in those days; her life might have followed a different script if their age difference had not been so daunting at the time.

Purnima returned the box to its place. She walked out onto the balcony attached to her bedroom. The Delhi weather was still pleasant. She had a good view of Deer Park from her fourth-story apartment in Safdarjung Enclave. It was too late in the night to see anything. Nevertheless, she could feel the fresh air blowing in from the park. She took a few deep breaths, relaxed her strained neck muscles by slowly turning her head in all directions, and returned to her bed.

The rosy promise of new companionship had reminded her of how lonely she had been. She had not had an intimate relationship ever since her broken marriage. The wound inflicted by the failed conjugal stint had rendered her tough. Never missing a man in her life after that, she focused on her work and took pride in her lonely contentment. The last evening changed it all. She found herself imagining how beautiful life could have been if she had someone to share it with her.

My little crush—was he honest in saying those lovely words? she speculated. At the same time, she was scared of seeing her dreams shatter yet again. She knew she was drifting towards a crossroad—a beautiful future or yet another heartbreak.

15

Dr Shazia Sultana Hameed was driving to Netaji Subhash Chandra Bose Airport to catch a flight to Delhi on Tuesday evening after attending a neonatologist's conference in Kolkata. She was one of the key speakers at that elite forum of paediatricians from around the world. The British delegates had held her up in a discussion on her lecture. She did not worry too much; the airport was a short drive at that time of the day. However, an accident in Rajarhat slowed down the traffic. She had good reason now to worry about catching her flight.

Shazia worked as a senior consultant in the department of neonatology of the Indradhanush Speciality Hospitals in New Delhi for over twelve years. Earlier, she had completed her schooling in Bangalore and then had gone to Kasturba Medical College, Manipal and Jawaharlal Institute of Post Graduate Medical Education and Research, Pondicherry for higher studies. Having spent her younger days in southern India, which included jobs in Mysore and Hyderabad, a move to Delhi had never been a part of her plans. However, when she met her future husband, Dr Mohammed Hameed, in the Indradhanush Speciality Hospital in Hyderabad's Jubilee Hills, her outlook towards life changed in many ways.

Mohammed Hameed was not a flamboyant man, not the kind that a woman would wish to know more at first sight. However, the quiet, well-built, and reclusive radiologist was well-known in his area and for commitment to the profession. He and Shazia worked as a team in a few critical cases in the hospital. Shazia admired him for his work and his unassuming demeanour. She had no idea how and when the admiration turned to love for the man and then to a conviction that they could live a happy life together. Mohammed had never received so much attention and care from a woman before. He immensely enjoyed their time together and had no hesitation in agreeing to marry her the first time they discussed the possibility. They got married a year later.

Mohammed Hameed, the only child of Nasser Suleiman Hameed and Begum Mumtaz Hameed, loved Delhi—the city where he grew up and where his parents and most of his friends lived. So, he always fancied a return to Delhi. With additional pressure from his parents, he took a transfer to Delhi after marriage. The hospital authorities acceded to Shazia's request as well for a transfer due to family considerations. With loving and well-connected in-laws, she did not have to struggle to adjust to the lifestyle and the social circles in Delhi. Nasser Suleiman Hameed had retired as a Supreme Court judge. Due to his reputation as a judge, and thanks to his post-retirement assignments to head strategic commissions, he continued to remain in the public eye along with opportunities to maintain cordial relationships with people who mattered in the political establishment and the bureaucracy. Begum Mumtaz Hameed was the chairperson of an organisation that worked for proper sanitation in poor South and West Delhi neighbourhoods.

Shazia's car raced towards the airport after finally getting past the accident spot. With a real chance of missing her flight, she was tense when the phone rang. By the time she took the handset out of her bag, it had gone silent. She tried to put it back without bothering to check who had called.

It rang again.

"Good evening, Dr Shazia Hameed. I am sorry if I am calling at an inconvenient time. My name is Harish Gupta."

"I am sorry, Mr. Gupta, I don't seem to recall you. Is there something I can do for you? I am just about to catch a flight. We have to be brief."

"Well, I called to seek an urgent appointment with you. I can't explain this on the phone. When are you back in Delhi? Can I have about half an hour with you tomorrow morning, please?"

"It will be helpful if you let me know the subject, Mr. Gupta."

"I am a general secretary in the Delhi unit of the National Party of Patriots. I have something important to discuss with you."

"Okay. This is curious; why would a senior political figure from the ruling party call me of all people? But I have to rush through the check-in process to have any chance of boarding my flight. We can talk in my office tomorrow at ten in the morning. I would have only about half an hour, though; I have to attend to something critical after that."

"That should be fine. See you at your office at ten tomorrow morning then. Have a safe flight, Dr Shazia."

"Thank you. Bye."

Harish Gupta and Raman Srivastava were five minutes ahead of time for the meeting on Wednesday morning. It was a critical mission. They had prepared a list of eight likely candidates by Monday evening. After a careful review of the profiles, they zeroed in on two. Dr Shazia Sultana Hameed was their first choice. They were determined to do their best to convince her so that the second choice would be redundant.

They believed Shazia Hameed had an enviable pedigree for an effective public relations exercise. Given the full support of her in-laws, she could command good traction with the electorate. The West Delhi constituency had a sizeable number of Muslim voters who traditionally supported the UNDP. A large chunk of them were likely to back Shazia. Further, her candidature would split the medical fraternity votes causing significant damage to Purnima's chances of winning.

She was known to be a friendly and easy-going person. However, they discovered that Shazia lived an extravagant lifestyle. She had a penchant for expensive perfumes and branded personal attire. Living beyond her means, she loved opportunities to make additional money and often overcharged her clients by prescribing redundant tests and procedures to earn hefty incentives from the hospital authorities.

Sarita Vihar on Mathura Road was not the ideal destination for a drive during peak morning hours. The NPP officials did well to beat the traffic and reached the hospital on time.

"Good morning. You are welcome, though I must admit I am intrigued by your visit. I tried hard last night to think of a reason but could not, unless someone in your family has any medical issues. Please sit down."

"Good morning to you as well, Dr Shazia, and thanks a lot for your time. This is my colleague, Raman Srivastava. We work closely with the state president of the NPP, Mr. Suresh Ahluwalia." With a warm smile, Harish said, "I know you do not have much time this morning. So, I will go straight to the point."

"I am all ears," said Shazia, fascinated to know what brought two senior politicians to her office early in the morning.

"Dr Shazia, as you must be aware, the crucial West Delhi parliamentary by-election is coming up in weeks. Our party had lost this seat last time to the UNDP, the main opposition party – a result that surprised everyone. Due to the sitting member's untimely demise, this seat is up for election again. Our party must win this time."

"Sounds good, and all the best. I still wonder why you are talking to me about all of this."

"We are well aware of your family's status in this city. You and your husband's professional success, your father-in-law's towering stature, and your mother-in-law's considerable social work together gives your family an enviable standing among the people of South and West Delhi. We have a tough election against a UNDP candidate. We want you to stand as an independent candidate in this election because we believe there is a good chance for a high-profile independent candidate in this fight between two major political parties."

"This is absurd, Mr. Gupta. You want me, a non-political person, to stand in this election to fight against heavyweight candidates who will leave no stones unturned to win this contest, and waste my time and money on a losing cause! Some plan this is!"

"We have approached you after doing extensive research on various scenarios. We believe you have a fair chance to win this race as the dark horse. A regional party may also field their candidate, but we are not concerned about them. People do not vote for them in parliamentary elections. Our party shall bear all your election expenses; all expenses, I repeat. If you win, the party will give you its primary membership. You will be an NPP member of Parliament with chances for a ministerial position at a later date. If you lose, our party shall give you fifty lakh rupees as a token of appreciation for your time. There will be no written agreement to record this, but you shall have them reiterated in person by our state president, possibly by the national president as well. It is a win-win for you either way. However, we need your concurrence very quickly, this evening, if possible, since we do not have much time. I must inform you, with all due respect and in all fairness, that we have another candidate who is keen on this offer. But we believe in you and sincerely hope that you will accept our proposal."

Shazia rested her cheeks against her fist and looked away. She stood up, walked a few steps towards the window, and returned to her seat.

"I thank you for this honour, but with due respect, I decline this offer. I am not into politics; believe me, I am happy this way. No one in my family has any interest in politics. Thanks, gentlemen, for your kind visit. I wish you success."

Shazia got up from her seat again, leaving no doubt that the meeting was over.

Taking the hint, both of them got up. Harish Gupta said, "We understand it is not an easy decision to take. We shall not revert to the other person till tomorrow morning, leaving you with this entire evening, should you wish to reconsider. Here is my card. The UNDP candidate is a lady doctor. We believe that, with your help, we will be able to defeat her."

Walking her guests to the door, Shazia asked casually, "She is a lady doctor, is she? What is her name?"

"Dr Purnima Bhatt. She has worked at AIIMS for many years. Good day, Dr Shazia!"

"Again, please, what did you say her name is?"

Harish Gupta did not miss the sparkle in her eyes.

"Dr Purnima Bhatt. I believe her full name is Dr Purnima Bajaj Bhatt."

"Good day, gentlemen!"

Seeing her guests off, Shazia returned to her seat. She could not believe what she had just heard.

16

Despite a sleepless night, Purnima did not have the luxury of getting up late. She had a packed schedule for Monday that started with a visit to the Akshardham Temple and then a series of meetings at the party headquarters. In the late afternoon, she had an appointment with one of her patients, followed by a meeting with neighbourhood elders to seek their blessings.

She went to the balcony overlooking the park, breathed in some fresh air, and walked towards the round table at the right corner where a large mug of sugarless black tea, a Britannia cake rusk, and a few newspapers waited for her. Her housemaid of many years—more of a companion than a house help—knew what was needed to make her life comfortable and unstressed at home. She was a true blessing for Purnima. She could focus on her work outside without needing to worry about household chores.

Looking at the colourful bougainvillea in the backyard, Purnima dipped the rusk in her tea. With her mind pre-occupied, she held it in for longer than she should have. The sodden piece of rusk dropped into her tea as she moved her hand. She smiled and ate the rest of the rusk dry. She took a gentle sip of the quality Assam tea, stretched her legs, and picked up a newspaper.

The front-page was covered with reports on the sky-rocketing onion prices and the Russian attack in Eastern Ukraine. There was a column regarding the appointment of judges to the Supreme Court. As her eyes scanned the lower half of the front page, she saw a report on the NPP candidate for the parliamentary by-election. She sat up to read.

"Robin Garg! What?!"

She was sure she had read it wrong—it just could not be right—and went through the report again. The ruling party candidate for the forthcoming election was indeed said to be an entrepreneur and social worker by the name of Robin Garg. She picked up the second newspaper to be sure that what she had just read was not a reporting error. It was not! The party had announced it in a press conference on Sunday evening. The details left no doubt that her dear Robin Garg was the NPP candidate. This must have been the important news he wanted to share with her.

She threw the newspapers on the table, stood up and paced back and forth on the balcony. She wanted to confirm the news with Robin but was too nervous to call.

She heard her cell phone ring. Certain that it was one of the overenthusiastic UNDP office bearers wanting to connect with her early in the morning, she dragged her feet to the bedroom to take the call, hoping that the caller would give up. The ringing did indeed stop as she entered the room. She lay flat on her bed, blankly looking at the ceiling. Restless and nursing a heavy head, she got up to splash cold water on her face. The phone rang again.

Robin Garg had got up early that morning. He sat downstairs and talked to the empty chair in silence. He sought Ritu's blessings for the messy politicking ahead. The campaign would have been so much easier and enjoyable with her around!

Time and again, Purnima intruded his thoughts. Robin, confused and mystified, wondered if his life had taken a curious turn.

Taking his eyes off the empty chair, Robin picked up a newspaper to check the headlines. He then realised his blunder: he should have talked to Purnima about the elections last evening. If she got the news first in the media—inevitable with her morning cup of tea—it would not be a pleasant situation for him to handle.

He jumped out of the chair to call Purnima and catch her before she picked up a newspaper. There was no response from her number.

He gave a brief gap and called again. Purnima picked up the call this time.

"Good morning, Purnima. Sorry if I woke you up early. How are you?"

"Hello, Robin *da*, good morning. I was about to call you too. I have just read an interesting report in the newspaper. Is that *really* you? Is this what you were to tell me last evening? I cannot believe you are active in politics, that too as a candidate for the Parliament!"

Robin was not sure whether she was amused or upset.

"You have read the papers already?! I wanted to tell you last evening. But we had such a fascinating journey back to our past that the present did not have a chance. Though you reminded me near the car park, you will agree that this is not something to be told from a distance, that too in a public place. It did not occur to me yesterday that the news would break this morning, if not earlier. I am truly sorry. Yes, I have accepted the NPP ticket for the West Delhi parliamentary by-election. I'm sure I can count on you as my closest and staunchest supporter."

Robin paused. He wondered whether Purnima was still there on the other side. "Purnima, are you still there?"

"Yes, Robin *da*."

"Be ready to support my campaign for the next few weeks. I am not sure which newspaper you have read this morning. If it was *Hindustan Times* or *The Indian Express*, another report on the same page announced my main rival, the UNDP candidate. A doctor named Purnima Bhatt will take me on. Isn't that funny? Your namesake is my main opponent! Now my job for the next few weeks is to go all out to defeat her. At this time, I have no clue who she is. I wish she did not carry your name, though!"

In response, there was only silence.

"Purnima, I still can't believe how I landed up here. I never had any interest in politics, none, honestly. A chance meeting with a very senior NPP official, my frustration with our country's prevalent socio-political challenges, and an enticing offer to be a member of Parliament on a platter, everything conspired to push me towards this." He paused for a moment and continued, "My loneliness often scoffs at my success… it may have played a role too, I guess. You will have to support me, stand by me in these challenging times, motivate me to win and make a difference in the Parliament. You are my old friend."

Robin suspected Purnima was sobbing. It was apparent that she had covered the handset with a tight grip as she breathed heavily.

"Purnima! Hey, have I said anything that bothers you? What's going on? Please say something." Struck by a thought, Robin asked, "Hang on… goodness me… is that possible? Is that why you are so disturbed? Are you the UNDP candidate, Purnima? Is that the news you wanted to share with me?"

After a few seconds, Purnima responded with a choked voice, "Robin *da*, yes, that is correct. UNDP has nominated me to fight the West Delhi Parliamentary by-election. I met with you only last evening after years of waiting! What a way to meet, this—we are the main contestants in a parliamentary poll just a few hours later!"

She broke down in tears.

Letting her take time to recover, Robin said, "What about the name Dr Purnima Bhatt? I know you as Purnima Bajaj."

"I had a failed marriage for a year. That's the legacy."

"I'm sorry about that. You retained the surname?"

"Don't be sorry. It's an unfortunate phase of my life. Yes, I didn't bother to change my name again. I don't exactly know why! Probably, I saw no reason to hide a past that is so much a part of my life!"

"What now?"

"Yes, what now?"

Robin replied, "Let us sleep over it for now. We are already deep into this electoral process; lots of people have pinned their hopes on us. Meanwhile, we met yesterday, after so many years, and enjoyed each other's company, just like the old times."

He continued after a brief pause, "Listen, Purnima, first things first! A whole lot of things are going through my mind since we met last evening. It's probably the same for you. I do *not* take *us* lightly; we could be great friends. We may even have bigger things ahead for our relationship, who knows? So let us stick to our current plans for now and have dinner together next Monday. Monday is the last day for filing nomination papers. Let's complete that process and meet in the evening. We shall then talk details. Till then, we continue as if we do not know each other."

A bit more composed by now, Purnima responded, "Okay, Monday dinner together then. You need to send me the address. It has to be in the strictest confidence. Till then, I agree that we should act as if we do not know each other... Honestly, this is unbelievable, straight out of classic fiction! Probably a horror story, in this case!"

They both laughed and ended the call on a friendly note. But in reality, both were upset and confused, pondering what lay ahead for them.

17

It was not a hard decision for Shazia, to say no to the NPP officials. Having stayed miles away from politics all her life, she was not interested in dabbling in an electoral adventure, that too in an effort that had little chance of success. She knew that a once-in-a-lifetime opportunity for hogging the national limelight had knocked at her door. But she did not want to pay the price with weeks of sleepless nights. The most exciting part of the offer was the fifty lakh rupees. She could do a lot with that much money, but she could not overlook the risks. She had no illusion that the proposed deal was between equals. If the party's promises were not honoured after the election, she would be able to do nothing to receive her dues.

However, when she heard the opposition candidate's name, the situation radically changed. If the NPP officials had looked back, they would have been astonished to see the drastic changes on her face. The stern, uncompromising doctor was distinctly jumpy and muddled.

Shazia knew the candidate very well. Dr Purnima Bhatt alias Dr Purnima Bajaj Bhatt, known to her as just Purnima, had been her closest friend in school. There was hardly anything that the two girls had not shared for six long years—books, clothes, make-up kits, secrets, happiness, and frustration—to the extent that the class teacher had admonished them and urged them to mix with other girls. They had laughed it off.

Purnima had taken admission to the seventh grade in the Central School, Victoria Layout, Bangalore. The compulsion to make friends with a new set of classmates was not novel to

Purnima; she had risen to such challenges before. But the move to Bangalore was hard. Her aptitude for seamlessly making new friends became collateral damage as she grew from a kid to a young girl approaching puberty. Like most grown-up children, her uncompromising likes and dislikes came in the way of acquiring new friends. She spent her first few days in school sitting alone in a corner, eating her tiffin all by herself, and walking the distance from the classroom to the school bus with eyes focused on her steps as if nothing else mattered. She was unhappy, hated going to school, and often cried in bed.

Shazia, born and brought up in the city, had studied in the same school since the first grade. She was intelligent, sincere, and bold. A class monitor that year, she was loved, admired, and feared by her classmates. Purnima, a quiet and well-behaved newcomer, did not draw her attention for the first few days. When the class teacher asked Shazia to help Purnima mingle with the other girls, she took up the challenge in all earnestness. That was the beginning of a friendship that became a topic of discussion among students and teachers alike. Shazia and Purnima were like inseparable twins. There could be no talking to one without hearing the other's name mentioned at frequent intervals. No one was surprised; the girls spent so much time together, after all! Their parents had become good friends, with multiple joint family outings to Nandi Hills, Srirangapatna, Bandipur and other picnic spots around the city. Those were some of the happiest days for Shazia.

She was deeply in love with her classmate Arvind Balakrishnan. Purnima was the only person she had confided in. Naturally her parents would be disturbed to know about their daughter's affair during her early school years. Her conservative parents would also never tolerate a relationship with a boy from another religion. Purnima did not reveal the secret to anyone. She helped them communicate and often arranged for them to spend time together.

Shazia's parents never said no to her request to visit Purnima's house. Purnima's parents, more relaxed about the friend circle their daughter chose to make, allowed boys to come home to hang out with her. Arvind and Shazia often met in Purnima's house and occasionally sneaked out to Brigade Road or Cubbon Park by themselves. Arvind, handsome and intelligent, hailed from a prosperous business family. Where other girls envied Shazia for her intimacy with Arvind, Purnima took pride in it.

Purnima confided in Shazia about her crush on a twenty-something young man, told her about her dreams that the young man would one day hold her in his arms. How she looked forward to seeing him every evening and how miserable she was in the evenings if he did not visit. She never mentioned his name though.

However, everything changed on the last day of their final examinations. Such that one would not even tolerate the other's name from that day on. Their parents did not have a clue about what occurred and neither did their friends.

They never met or spoke to each other since that cursed evening. But Shazia kept track of Purnima's progress and whereabouts, hoping for a chance to settle scores.

Now Shazia was agitated, wondering if this was the chance she had been waiting for all this while. At best, she would become a member of Parliament, and the worst, she would get richer by fifty lakh rupees. Either way, she could make Purnima's life difficult by cutting into her votes.

She picked up Harish Gupta's visiting card to call but changed her mind. *Such critical decisions deserve mulling over for some time. I must assess all the pros and cons. I need to have a word with Mohammed as well.* She left for home early that afternoon. She had only that evening to make the most difficult decision of her life.

Earlier in the morning, Harish Gupta and Raman Srivastava had returned to their car disappointed with the meeting's result and upset with Shazia's asperity. They had not expected an apolitical doctor to agree immediately to jump into an electoral battle, but they did expect at least a fair consideration from her. Looking at Harish Gupta, Raman Srivastava said, "At the very least, I expected this woman to be courteous and be thankful that we thought her to be worthy of this honour. She did not even ask us for a glass of water! Anyway, that doesn't bother me. I am unlikely to see her again in my life. But the fact that we have to do this again with the next prospect is annoying. And if *she* refuses as well, we start with the original list all over again. We do not have much time. Tomorrow is Thursday!"

Harish Gupta fondly patted his back and replied, "I am disappointed as well, but not in despair like you. I have a feeling she has not given up yet, and there may be a slim hope. There is something about the UNDP candidate's name; I don't know exactly what, but the name upset the doctor. There may be some history between these two. I hope there is, and whatever that might be, I hope it inspires her to accept the challenge. We shall wait till tomorrow morning before giving up on this case, though I know that right now, I do sound stupid and over-optimistic."

"Okay then," sighed Raman Srivastava as he took the car out of the car park. "I hope my pessimism is misplaced, and you are right. I would love to be proven wrong."

Back home, Shazia thought through the implications of her decision. In her first brush with politics, she was getting a ticket for the country's parliamentary elections. A win would get her a seat in the country's highest legislative body. A loss would get her fifty lakh rupees. Either way, she would get a golden opportunity to settle scores with her bête noire. And the best thing was that she would have to spend no personal resources. She could not bear the prospect of Purnima becoming a member of Parliament. So far, it had been a fair match, both making good progress in their professional careers. With a stable and happy family life, Shazia took comfort in her conviction that she had been one up on her erstwhile friend. An elevation to the status of a member of Parliament would change the equation forever in Purnima's favour.

She spoke with her husband. Mohammed Hameed said, "You know that I will never say no to something that you sincerely want to do. But politics is a mess. It is not for people like you and me. We run simple lives—focus on our profession and our families, move within a small circle of friends, look for a peaceful retirement, and hope that our next generation does better than us. That is all we do. Politics often involves stepping on others. You do not want to have to throw muck on others to validate yourself. You surely do not want to be forced to wash your dirty linen in public. Are you up for it?"

Shazia replied, "I am not joining politics for the long run. There is no chance for me to win this contest. I know it; they know it too. I just want to have some fun for a few weeks and then get a good reward. That's a good sum of money for us, you will agree."

"And one more thing, Shazia. I am concerned it may affect your health. You know that your heart condition is not great for your age. The stent inside may not appreciate the stress that weeks of campaigning is bound to entail. You may want to consider putting your health above those fifty lakhs."

"My heart is doing great! My doc hubby, a measured amount of excitement is good for the heart. So, don't worry on that front. Come on, don't be a spoilsport; don't talk like a man years ahead of your age. Let's do it."

It was not a surprise that Mohammed Hameed submitted to Shazia's insistence and assured her support. Not taking the risk of waiting till the morning broke, Shazia called Harish Gupta immediately. It was past midnight.

"Mr. Harish Gupta? Pardon me for calling this late. Dr Shazia Hameed this side. I am sorry, but I did not want to wait till morning."

Harish Gupta replied, trying to hide his irritation at being woken up from a deep slumber, "No, that is okay. Thanks for calling. Please, tell me. Have you thought about it further?"

"Yes, Mr. Gupta, I have. I am happy to accept your proposal."

"Oh, that's great news. Thanks. It is a good decision. We shall revert to you soon with further details, most likely tomorrow night. Please keep yourself free on Friday. There is a good possibility that we meet you, along with our senior colleagues, on Friday morning. After that, of course, you shall have a busy few weeks. Please prepare accordingly. Good night, Dr Shazia."

"Good night, Mr. Gupta."

A relieved Harish Gupta shared the good news with his colleague and went back to sleep. Shazia could not sleep at all. A mix of fear, excitement, jealousy, greed, and revenge created mayhem in her mind.

She begged the sun to rise.

18

Dr Satish Bhatt was not expecting any call that Tuesday evening. He sat on a reclining chair with a glass of red wine, looking at the large digital TV on the opposite wall. After a day of complicated surgeries, he looked forward to a relaxed evening by himself. His wife, a banker, had left for Hong Kong for a few days on a business trip. He decided to make the most of it by running through a couple of episodes of his favourite serials on Netflix. He was addicted to the megahit serial *Breaking Bad* and wanted to watch it every night, at least two episodes at one go, to find out how it ended. It was not possible. His wife, a puritan in many ways, did not like the story. She detested the concept of a chemistry professor becoming a drug lord, whatever the compulsions. "Such things should never be telecast in decent society. What example would it set for our youngsters! How would a student look at his chemistry professor now?"

Satish Bhatt had long stopped trying to reason out her didactic views on soap operas conceived merely for mass entertainment. Knowing that nothing he said would make a difference to her world with no shades of grey, he learned to reconcile and saw one episode at a time when he could, dedicating the rest of his TV time to shows that his wife enjoyed. Her absence was the ideal time to watch as many episodes as he could.

He was surprised when his cell phone rang—it was too late for his wife to call from Hong Kong. He picked up the phone. "Hello, Dr Bhatt here. Who is this, please?"

"Dr Bhatt, my name is Pradeep Raina. I am not sure if you remember me. We were together in Burn Hall School. I left after the tenth standard finals. I think you continued till the twelfth."

Satish Bhatt could not recall anything. However, the caller was right about his alma mater, one of the oldest schools in the Kashmir valley. "Hello Pradeep, forgive me, but I'll be lying if I said I remember you exactly. It has been a long time. Never mind; what do you do now, and what can I do for you?"

Pradeep Raina briefed him on his journey from Burn Hall School to the corridors of Delhi High Court, where he practiced as an advocate. He did not allude to his private investigative assignments to earn the cash his weak practice failed to bring home. The claim that they had studied in the same school was correct. But he could not be truthful about why he reached out to his long-lost schoolmate all of a sudden after so many years.

Satish Bhatt, a brilliant student, had earned admission into AIIMS, New Delhi, with high ranks in the qualifying examination. Since his parents were in Srinagar, he kept close contact with the gorgeous Kashmir valley till his family had to flee their ancestral home in the early nineties. After that, the beautiful childhood memories and a bitter sense of betrayal were his only connection with the valley. He wished they could go back to settle in Srinagar once again one day but did not brood over it. Life moved on. With a successful academic life and an acclaimed practice as a general surgeon, Satish Bhatt had no reason to hunt for peace in his past.

He had one regret—an unfortunate decision in his life with lasting consequences. He had fallen in love with a beautiful post-graduate student in Internal Medicine, who was a few years junior to him. He and Dr Purnima Bajaj had shared interests in books, music, contemporary art, and food. It was his first serious relationship. One evening, he dramatically proposed to her in the Hyatt Regency coffee shop, a few kilometres away from their institute. To his delight, Purnima accepted the ring immediately. Their marriage followed soon.

However, it did not take him long to regret the wedlock. The first two months of nuptial euphoria were eclipsed by increasingly bitter fights over the next few months. It ultimately led to the inevitable—a divorce. The painful memories of the recent past were unbearable. Looking for a change, he quit the institute and joined Shanti Hospitals, on the outskirts of Delhi, as a Senior Surgeon.

After their divorce, Purnima and Satish never met again. They occasionally saw each other from a distance in medical community gatherings but made no effort to interact. He was surprised to read reports on her nomination for the West Delhi by-election. Though convinced that Purnima was unsuitable for the rough world of politics, he believed it was none of his business and treated the news as just another mundane headline.

Their bitter separation left deep scars unlikely to heal in a lifetime. However, Satish Bhatt harboured in his subconscious a sense of antipathy towards Purnima. He believed she had taken undue advantage of his simplicity.

He was now happily married to a lovely woman from Chandigarh, employed with a multinational bank. Their son studied Computer Science in the United States of America. With a small and contented family, his life centred around his workplace and his large South City One condominium.

Satish Bhatt patiently listened to his schoolmate. He traced the caller back to a blurred image of one quiet classmate in Srinagar and replied, "Very well, it is always so nice to hear from school friends. I appreciate you reaching out to me. Please tell me if there is anything I can do for you?"

Pradeep Raina replied, "Thanks. Let me come to that. I am working on a project to put together profiles of some successful alumni from our school. You are certainly one of them. I am not sure whether this project will work out but I want to give my best shot in any case. Please, can I request you for an hour tomorrow morning?"

"That sounds good. It must be a challenging project. But does it have to be tomorrow? Can it wait till the weekend?"

"I am afraid no. I am doing this in between various other commitments. If not tomorrow, I may have to keep this on the back burner for a few weeks. Please, any time of the day, if you can give me just an hour. I promise I shall not take more of your time."

Satish Bhatt laughed and replied, "Okay. In that case, the only possibility is early in the morning. You may have to get up a bit early for that. We can meet at my house at seven thirty in the morning. That will leave me with enough time to be in the hospital for my first commitment."

"That works for me. Don't worry, I am an early riser. See you at seven thirty tomorrow morning."

Pradeep Raina noted down the address and patted himself on the back as he hung up. Though apprehensive about how the call might play out, he ultimately managed to get the appointment. An assignment from Topaz Investigative Services warranted his best efforts. Thanks to his excellent rapport, its chairman entrusted him with the most challenging projects when he wanted nothing but the absolute best.

While Pradeep Raina got the impression that he had a unique assignment, Ajay Chowdhury asked his senior executives to meticulously profile the target on their own—from AIIMS back to her years in Bangalore. He believed that the report to his clients had to be comprehensive, authentic, and vetted by multiple sources. For that, he could never depend on just one source of information.

Meanwhile, Jamal Ahmed asked a friend, a wealthy businessman with close relations to both leading political parties, to contact Durjoy Kumar to find out what was on his mind.

The man met Durjoy Kumar for tea on Monday afternoon.

"I must say I was shocked with your party's nomination. Where the hell has this one come from? You—an ex-parliamentarian from this constituency, a seasoned and revered politician, someone who has served the party for so long—on one side, and on the other a novice who has no experience in electoral politics. Why electoral, any political activity for that matter! And they nominate him! NPP is going to lose this seat again; mark my words. It is also an insult to you, Kumar *saab*! If they had nominated Bhupinder Gupta, I still would not think of it as a good idea; but at least I would not have considered it crazy. But this man!"

Surprised with lack of a response from the seasoned politician, he stopped for a moment and hoped that the man would reveal his cards.

The clever politician showed no emotion. He answered, "What you say is not quite how it has been, my friend. We have discussed this matter in the party at the highest level and then decided on the nomination."

The businessman persisted, "That is your big heart talking, Kumar *saab*, one of the many things that I love about you. Truly magnanimous! For a non-political person like me, this looks like a straightforward case of insulting one of the tallest leaders in the party. NPP may win this or lose, but one thing is sure, there is some vested interest in this nomination, either to snub you or to sabotage the party's prospects. There could even be some other financial considerations behind the scene.

"In your position, I would have never taken this lightly. I would have taught the party a lesson by filing my nomination as an independent. With your enviable support base and with friends like us to fully back you, you would have gone to the Parliament, and then the same party leaders would beg you to rejoin the party."

After a minute of silence, Durjoy Kumar replied, this time in an authoritative tone with a shade of irritation. "Look, I respect your good feelings and your kind words for me. I really do. But let's not discuss this issue further. The fact is, we have decided in the best interest of the party. Now it is our responsibility to ensure a resounding victory for our candidate. Please, let's work towards that. Thanks for seeing me, and thanks again for the kind words about me."

The message was loud and clear. The businessman did not believe for a moment that Durjoy Kumar unequivocally supported his own humiliation. A ticket for a parliamentary seat was central to every politician's dreams. There could be no place for generosity in that matter, certainly not in one's backyard. Durjoy Kumar had already started his campaign in anticipation of the ticket and had asked him for a sizeable contribution towards his election funds. The businessman understood that there was some deep political intrigue behind Durjoy Kumar's volte-face. Whatever the case, one thing was clear to him—the veteran would stay with the party, and anything said to the contrary might be counterproductive.

They discussed family issues, the economy, and weather for the rest of the thirty minutes together.

Around the same time, Jamal Ahmed's brother-in-law had a friendly telephone call with his close associate Bhupinder Gupta. The veteran politician sounded like someone who had personally given the ticket to Robin Garg. When he declined a face-to-face meeting blaming it on his busy schedule, it was clear that there was no hope for a rebellion from him. Jamal Ahmed knew he had no good news to report to his boss. Their only hope was to find chinks in Robin Garg's armour. He further strengthened the team assigned to prepare a dossier on the NPP candidate with some of the best people he had at his disposal.

Later that evening, Durjoy Kumar had a closed-door meeting with his core supporters at a resort in Surajkund. The resort was chosen as it was far away from the busy city, so as to keep the attendees out of public eye. His friend owned Vivanta Surajkund. So, security and secrecy were not a concern. Eight loyalists with strong grassroots connections—people who owed Durjoy Kumar everything they had and whatever they were—reached the resort separately, within a span of thirty minutes, covering the distance from various parts of South and West Delhi by different routes. No one except the participants knew about the meeting. Even the security men at the entrance had no reason to suspect a political gathering in the hotel.

They met at the hotel's Bliss Suite where the furniture had been rearranged to host nine people in a relaxed ambience. Durjoy Kumar entered the suite once all the others were seated. All of them rose from their seats and queued up to touch his feet. He gestured at them to take their seats quickly. Then, he got straight to business.

"So, how do you guys feel?"

The oldest among them, the only one greeted by Durjoy Kumar with a hug, responded, "We are all upset and angry with this. You are our leader; we are in the party only because of you. We cannot tolerate this snub and such an injustice to our leader. We are only waiting for your instructions on how to react. We have not told anyone anything so far. We have avoided our block-level workers ever since the decision was made public. Now, please, tell us what to do. We are totally demotivated. This way, none of us want to work for this election."

He looked at the other men and asked, "Do I speak for all of you? If not, this is the time to speak."

Everyone nodded. One of the participants spoke out, "You are unquestionably speaking our mind. We work for Kumar *saab*. That's all we know."

Durjoy Kumar looked at each of them in turn and then looked at the man who had first spoken. "Good, so what do you wish for me to do under the circumstances?"

The senior man replied, "*Saab*, we wish you fight these elections as an independent candidate. We understand from reliable sources that the Social Justice Party (SJP)—you know they have a significant hold on Delhi voters—is not fielding any candidate for this election. That makes their core supporters, who do not like to vote for either NPP or UNDP, available to back a third candidate. We understand that a significant section of the UNDP leadership is also unhappy with a rank outsider for the ticket. You have a solid support base in traditional NPP voters, and many UNDP leaders have good relations with you. With support from the SJP high command and the disgruntled UNDP factions, we can win this election. I think SJP is not fielding a candidate because they wish to save their resources for the state elections. But they would do anything to see that NPP loses this prestigious contest again. As for the UNDP rebels, you, as an independent, will be the obvious choice given their dislike for NPP. Kumar *saab*, we need only your blessings. We will do the rest for you."

Durjoy Kumar thought for a while and said, "You have proposed a good plan. I like it. I also must thank you for this loyalty and love."

Everyone looked up and smiled as he continued, "But you have to appreciate that I have given my entire political life for this party. I am as upset and angry as you are. But it is hard for me to rebel against a party that I have built myself. I cannot file nomination papers to contest my party. That choice is out."

The smiles disappeared on everyone's face. The senior was about to say something when Durjoy Kumar intervened, "Wait, I haven't finished yet... so, where was I? Yes, I said I will not contest as an independent candidate. But, and this is a *big* but, I would like to do everything possible to ensure that the party high command pays for their mistake. They must not get away with this insult to me. It is my constituency, my backyard, my own turf, and they dare bring a good-for-nothing boy from somewhere to take my place? Damn! If they gave the ticket to that joker Bhupinder, I would have still sulked but not felt as sick as I do now."

Durjoy Kumar continued his tirade, getting angrier and more agitated with every word, "I want to prove to them who is the boss here. I want to fight this battle without taking out my sword. I want to demolish the party's electoral chances, so badly that next time, the so-called 'high command' comes crawling to me for help. A bunch of idiots, that's what they are! That stupid usurper of a party president, he knows nothing about the ground realities. He knows nothing about state politics. Riding a handful of lucky breaks in a few elections, he thinks he is all-powerful, ignoring and often insulting the state-level politicians. It is a path to disaster for the party.

"So, I want you to do the best that you can to ensure our party candidate *loses* this election. As always, you will have a lot of electioneering to do in the coming days. You must act like you are working very hard for the party's win. But in reality, you should work against the party's interest. You all are hardened politicians; you have been through many conflicting situations before. Let's do it again. This time do it for me. We have a clear decision here.

"We shall meet only once like this again, a few days before voting day, to take stock of the situation. I shall communicate suitably, where, when, etc. Till then, no group meeting like this. Any doubts, anyone?"

They dispersed as they had come. The participants received their leader's message loud and clear. The work ahead was complicated, but they had to deliver at any cost for his sake.

Pradeep Raina met Satish Bhatt as scheduled on Wednesday morning. They spent an hour discussing Satish Bhatt's journey from Burn Hall School to Shanti Hospitals. Pradeep asked the doctor many questions during the interview. Most of them were on his personal life since, as he said, the humane aspects were more relevant for the project. Satish Bhatt did not want to delve into the finer details of his past, particularly ones that hurt him deeply. But the interviewer had a gift for making people open their hearts out. He created a relaxed and friendly environment and asked cleverly-worded yet persistent questions. Once the interview was over, the doctor realised that the talk had centred more around his failed first marriage and not his successful second one. In hindsight, he wondered if this had anything to do with the elections but brushed such thoughts aside as he hurried to get ready for the hospital.

Pradeep Raina left a happy man. He had gathered potent ammunition that would please his employer.

19

Robin and Purnima were not finding life easy. It was easy to agree to let business be as usual till next Monday evening, but it was tough to spend seven long days with uncertainty. They stuck to their agendas but found it very difficult to stay on top of their conflicting emotions. Both wondered, as greenhorns in the world of politics, if they should have bothered with politics at all. Deprived of love for a good part of their lives, they had found hope and promise through their reunion. Now working on a campaign that had the potential to destroy such prospects, their efforts seemed futile and self-defeating. Their busy schedules kept them occupied late into the evenings. But distressing thoughts invariably returned within the four walls of their bedrooms.

By Wednesday night, Purnima could not handle the pressure anymore. In between repeated rehearsals for her debut public speech the following evening, she sat in front of the mirror and asked herself what on earth she was doing with her life. She was preparing to contest against the man she grew up admiring—that too soon after she had met him after so many years, when her dreams had just found new wings, when she saw a ray of renewed hope that could bring colours to her monotonous personal life. It was bizarre. One instant, she decided to quit—to refuse to sign the nomination papers on Monday morning; the next moment, she cursed herself for being utterly irresponsible and selfish—that she could never let down so many people who put their trust in her. Going crazy, she desperately needed to speak to someone.

Past midnight, she dialled the only person she could think of, Radha Saluja. They had spoken to each other a couple of times since the nomination was made public. However, Purnima had not mentioned that she knew Robin to keep their relationship strictly under wraps. In the late hours of an exceptionally twitchy night, she decided to break the vow to retain her sanity.

It took a few rings for Radha to wake up. As one would expect after calling someone late at night, Purnima heard a groggy hello from the other side.

"Darling, I am so sorry. Hit me next time we meet as a punishment for waking you up like this," said Purnima apologetically.

"You bet I will. Damn, is this any time to call, my dear future member of Parliament?"

"You know, Radha, I was prepared for a tough time. But it seems this is going well beyond my imagination. Caste equations, nasty intra-party politics, God only knows what else. It is too complicated. But there is another challenge for me now, a *big* one!"

Radha replied like a schoolteacher admonishing her student. "Stop talking like that now. You have taken a conscious decision to enter electoral politics—and very well knew that it would never have been clean. Now focus and win this election. Win you must! So do whatever you need to do; play what needs to be played; win at all costs. The winner takes all, remember?

"Anyways, I wanted to share with you something interesting before you talk about your new challenge. Do you remember I had asked you to meet a handsome, bachelor business tycoon? I am sure you would have deleted the snap from your phone by now. He is the NPP candidate in this election. I am so surprised. Another lost opportunity for my dear friend. He is your challenger now!"

Purnima intervened, "Listen, I—"

Radha would not stop. "No, really, in hindsight, it is good I did not get to connect you two. You would have found it so funny to have to now fight each other like cats and dogs. Damn you! If you were not the UNDP candidate, I would have quietly joined his camp to be his ambassador to the media. Poor me, now I have to work against him."

Purnima replied, "Have you finished? Once you start, you never stop, do you? *This* is the big challenge I mentioned. But I cannot discuss it on the phone. We need to talk in person, like right this moment. I will not ask you to come home at this time, but—"

"You can ask, but no way will I be stupid to run to you at this time just to hear yet another of your boring stories."

"Listen, please. This one will not bore you; I promise. You are likely to hit the roof once I tell you. You don't have to come right now but tomorrow morning please have breakfast with me, here, at half-past seven sharp. I must get out of the house latest by nine. So, you cannot be late. You are allowed to come in early."

"Do I have the chance to suggest another option?"

"No, you don't.'

"Okay, see you tomorrow morning then. Bye and good night," sighed Radha.

"Good night, Radha."

Radha quickly went back to sleep. Purnima struggled.

Around twenty kilometres away, another man was wrestling with solitude. It was not new for Robin to be alone in his private hours ever since Ritu was gone. But he never experienced such intense turmoil where confiding in someone became the only recourse. Robin did not have a circle of intimate friends. There were many friends, but none that he could pour his heart out to without any inhibition. Essentially a loner in his private life, he had not missed such support till now.

Sunday evening's happiness disappeared faster than he would have liked. After three days of campaign work, Robin thought about what he would like to discuss with Purnima on Monday evening. They cannot retreat without serious consequences; their nominations were already made public. But was it sensible to sacrifice personal happiness at the altar of electoral politics?? He was delighted to meet the charming teenage schoolgirl he was infatuated with as a young man. The cute little girl grew up to be an impressive and attractive lady who took the initiative to reconnect with him after so many years. She definitely looked excited to meet him. What if there was more to it than just a chance meeting? Should he turn a blind eye to an opportunity knocking at his door to end his biting loneliness? It was a tough call. If he dropped out of the contest, oblivious of any repercussions, there was no certainty that their relationship would blossom. On the other hand, if he ignored the relationship, there was no assurance that he would win the election, and even if he won, it would still be no guarantee for his happiness.

To make things more complicated, could he handle losing an election to Purnima? Would it not hurt his self-esteem?

Must he choose one, or was there a way to ride both horses simultaneously?

He struggled to fight his sleeplessness. The harder he pressed his eyelids the stronger his worries returned. At some point, he convinced himself that lack of sleep for a night would not kill him. He got up from his bed and picked up a copy of NPP's manifesto for the last general elections. Tiring of it quickly, he fetched an old album from the topmost drawer of his wall cabinet.

It was not the album that Robin turned to when he felt lonely. That hosted a collection of carefully selected photos of Ritu in different poses, alone and with Robin, in various moods and occasions, including one taken inside the famed patisserie.

He picked up an older album instead. It contained photos from his bachelor days, not arranged in any specific order. Robin browsed through them in a hurry until he reached one page. The right-hand top corner had a photo of a cute schoolgirl posing for the camera with her back to Ulsoor Lake. He had clicked the picture during one of the outings he had in Bangalore with the Bajaj family. A shy Purnima had agreed to pose after her mother reprimanded her for being impolite. He looked at the mysterious smile and wondered where it came from—was she nervous or playful, upset or excited, adoring or scornful? Still unable to decrypt it, Robin smiled. He had fallen in love with this picture so much that he had never shared it with anyone, not even Purnima. The larger photo at the centre had the entire family; Purnima had a copy as well. In this, Robin had wrapped his arms around her shoulder. Staring at the picture, Robin in his mind was back to his carefree days. When he went back to bed this time, he slept.

Radha reached Purnima's apartment fifteen minutes early, knowing well that Purnima could not afford to get late for her appointment and that she was unlikely to be concise in telling her story.

She walked into the dining room, where a sumptuous breakfast awaited. With everything ready on the table, only the *parathas* were to be served straight from the pan. Purnima had instructed her maid to prepare a breakfast according to Radha's choice—fresh fruits, plain *parathas*, scrambled eggs, yoghurt, hot pickles, orange marmalade, and a large mug of weak black tea without sugar.

Seeing Purnima join her at the table, Radha wasted no time. "So dear, shoot. I am all ears."

Purnima took a deep breath and spoke, "This is a truly filmy story. You will see that the problem is much bigger and messier than you can imagine. It has become a nightmare for me. You know I haven't been able to sleep well for the last few days."

"Oh, will you cut the crappy intro and get straight to the point, Purnima?"

"Okay, here it goes. I met Robin Garg last Sunday evening. It turns out that he was my first crush … actually, my only true crush forever!"

Radha was about to bite a piece of *paratha* dipped in orange marmalade. Unable to believe what she heard, she dropped the *paratha* piece and looked at Purnima with disbelief. "You're kidding? Say that you're joking!"

Purnima explained.

"This is truly a very difficult situation. My goodness! What will you do now?"

"I need your advice, Radha. Tell me: what choices do I have?"

They discussed and agreed that the only choice was to wait till Monday evening and hear what Robin Garg had to say. Not filing the nomination papers was not an option.

20

SkyDeck by Sherlock's was not busy on Monday evening.

Aditi Kasbekar took a table with Maria D'Souza at the open-air bar's right-side corner to celebrate her thirtieth birthday. The view was good from the table. On one side, they saw the busy junction where Brigade Road branched out to the iconic Mahatma Gandhi Road. On the other, Kamraj Road led the traffic to Cubbon Road. The Manekshaw Parade Ground was not clearly visible at that time of the day.

Their friendship dated back to their primary school. Both grew up in Indira Nagar, went to Bishop Cotton's School, and then to Mount Carmel College; they even worked in the same place. They had joined National Distribution Network Limited together as trainees and had a great time in one of the fastest-growing companies of that time. Maria had continued to work for the company till a few months ago, but Aditi left it years back. Her exit from the company had been bitter and contentious.

Aditi had invited her friends for a birthday bash in her house the coming Saturday since no one would enjoy a midweek party. However, she had to do something to celebrate on the actual date of her birth. There was nothing like some quality time with her best friend, whom she had not seen much of late due to their busy schedules.

The circumstances that had forced Aditi to leave her first job made her angry even now. Happy with her job and the ambience, she would have never resigned had she not been forced to. An urge for revenge lingered in her even though her unpleasant relationship with her boss was left in the distant past.

This evening, Maria gifted her an elegantly-wrapped box. She opened it in a childlike hurry, screamed with joy, and jumped up to give Maria a tight hug. It was a beautiful set of pearl earrings.

The waiter greeted them and asked for their order. He returned quickly with two pints of Kingfisher Draught and a plate of nachos. Sipping their drink, they talked about different things: current boyfriends to parental pressure for marriage, the latest fashion to recent politics.

Maria said, "Talking of politics, I wanted to tell you something ever since I read the newspaper this morning. Have you heard the news?"

"It depends on the news. If you are referring to a mob lynching or a similarly gory incident, I am not interested."

"No, it's about our ex-big boss! I mean our first boss. No one has told you yet?"

"Tell me what? In any case, why should anyone tell me about him, and why should I bother?"

"He is in politics now. Robin Garg is the NPP candidate for the by-election to the West Delhi parliamentary seat. So, given NPPs hold over the electorate these days, your dear ex-boss shall be a member of Parliament very soon."

"Oh, shut up, Maria! My *dear* ex-boss! Seriously, is that freak trying to be an MP?"

"Yes, it is all over the news. Check out one of the national TV channels when you get back home. I bet you will see it being flashed as Breaking News on all the news channels."

"Oh Maria, I do not want to remember those awful days and not that man for sure. I have forgotten my stint in NDNL and nearly forgiven him for all his excesses. But I can't imagine him as a member of the highest legislative body of the country. Anyway, good luck to him. It means nothing to me whether he becomes a rickshaw puller or the president of India. Let's talk about something else. Did you watch the latest Ben Affleck movie? He is *so* good! I have *really* fallen for him!"

Soon after they drew the last drop of their second pint of draught beer, they left for their homes since the next day was a working day.

Aditi switched on the television as soon as she reached home. Robin Garg's smiling face, flashing repeatedly as breaking news on a national platform, opened her old wounds. Although she had no reason to be concerned about a man with whom she had severed relations years back, she believed that the man should not be allowed to grab a public position, not without a fight, at least.

In this dilemma, Aditi fell asleep. Later, she woke up with her mind made up.

Thousands of kilometres away, Dr Anil Hazarika also had an uneasy evening at his Guwahati residence. The celebrated surgeon worked for his alma mater Guwahati Medical College. Given a stable professional career and a happy family life, he did not dwell on his whirlwind campus romance with his batch mate from Bangalore. Their tumultuous love affair lasted barely a year. The parting was abrupt, though neither acrimonious nor friendly.

Purnima Bajaj averred that their obsessive relationship had seriously hurt their studies. Despite his ceaseless efforts to convince her otherwise, Purnima insisted. They separated to bring their by-now famous romance to a sudden end. True to her strong character, she embraced her new life on the campus with remarkable ease. Anil sulked and went into a shell for some time.

In the end, both of them did well in their chosen specialisation. Purnima moved on with her life well. Anil was not in her mind anymore. However, Anil could not forget her so easily. He kept track of her developments. He knew about her jobs, marriage, and divorce. With time, her memories, and her betrayal of his true love, stopped troubling him in recent years.

Monday's news about Purnima's candidature for the by-election intrigued him. His first concern was whether she was good enough to stand the inescapable public scrutiny. He was also curious how she got involved in active politics and claimed the powerful national party's nomination for a parliamentary by-election. Spurred by streaks of jealousy, he dredged up memories of her wanton betrayal and pondered how many more men she had destroyed to get to this level. He considered his options—from doing nothing, to helping her win, to creating hurdles in her path to victory. He wanted to play a part in the election process but didn't know exactly how. He was determined to share the story of Purnima's ruthless betrayal with the electorate.

Another person in Bangalore, a few kilometres away from Aditi Kasbekar, took special note of the breaking news. Arvind Balakrishnan had spent his entire life in the same city. There was no reason for him to look elsewhere; after all, he was the scion of a prosperous family with diversified business interests flourishing through three generations. His father—a man of high integrity and exemplary modesty—wanted him to imbibe a commoner's ethos, tenacity, and humility along with the confidence and finesse of the privileged. He sent Arvind to Central School instead of other elite options while keeping him in touch with his business circles and his affluent lifestyle. Arvind grew up to be a respected, kind, and influential businessman. The family business expanded multi-fold due to his business acumen and dogged perseverance. He made his father's dream come true.

Arvind remembered his first love with mixed feelings. It was at once glorious and childish. He laughed at the thought that he had considered spending his life with her. The memories seemed inane—the relationship and the break-up—and he was grateful that the love affair did not survive their high school years. Those were the simple days of falling for pretty girls. Tall, handsome, and rich, Arvind did not have to struggle to befriend them. He could choose whoever he wanted. But Shazia was different. Her initial arrogance and repeated snubs surprised him, but his grit and diligence paid off. They became close friends and, by the end of the tenth standard, they fell in love.

However, in the last few months of school, Arvind developed reservations about Shazia. He discovered a new person—insecure, moody, jealous, bitter, and vengeful—hidden behind the girl he had known. The get-together to celebrate the end of their high school days confirmed his suspicions; there was no future for him with Shazia. They broke off that evening itself and never met each other since.

Arvind was fond of his classmate Purnima as well. Purnima was a sweet and friendly girl. Besides, she went out of her way to help him meet with his girlfriend. She was a true friend. There was no way he could blame her for that evening's fiasco. She should not be the scapegoat for his girlfriend's jealousy and insecurity. Realizing this, he remained in touch with Purnima but lost touch with her after she got married.

When Arvind learned that Dr Purnima Bhatt was the UNDP candidate for a parliamentary by-election, he wondered if she was his old friend but did not bother to investigate further. An electoral contest in distant Delhi did not interest him, even if it involved someone he had known.

His perspective on this election was to change in a week!

21

Jamal Ahmed and Sunil Sharma spent the entire evening on Wednesday deliberating how else to find exploitable leads in Robin Garg's past. They wanted juicy material, things that would excite and antagonise the electorate even if the stories were dubious. They needed allegations of corrupt practices, clandestine love affairs, or controversial statements on issues of national import. They wanted stories to catch Robin Garg off-guard, to send NPP strategists scurrying for covers. The UNDP had detailed plans built around their candidate's clean image to appeal to the voters for support. However, negative propaganda against rival candidates had become an essential part of contemporary electoral battles. Many voters fell for such smear campaigns. There were other benefits as well; such propaganda upset the opposing candidates' campaign plans. They often landed up spending valuable resources defending against such attacks.

Though each political party pursued such tactics to different extents, NPP was exceptionally effective in recent elections. Their use of electronic media to spread unsubstantiated but well-articulated rumours on opposition candidates was unprecedented. The UNDP leadership knew that NPP would conduct nasty assaults on Purnima Bhatt's character and her past. They would have by now prepared plenty of ammunition against her to release in bits and pieces at convenient times during the campaign. But UNDP could so far find no significant chinks in Robin Garg's armour. He seemed perfect—a self-made entrepreneur with a big heart and clean track record—both in business and personal life. But it seemed implausible that a nouveau riche and socially-active man had no dark spots in his past. The state president would be upset with the team's failure to unearth any usable information on the candidate.

Harsh Malhotra called Jamal Ahmed for interim feedback on their progress and, as expected, pulled him up for an incompetent job. Reminding him that Thursday evening was the deadline for the first draft, he insisted that they could achieve a lot in the remaining twenty-four hours if they got their act together. Meanwhile, he rested his hopes on an impending report from the party's Ahmedabad unit. Robin had spent two years in this city as a student. Besides, his in-laws were based there. His hopes were not baseless.

He would have found some comfort if he had known that there was another team— weathered, zealous, and ruthless—busy searching for dark shadows in Robin Garg's past.

Suresh Ahluwalia had formed a dedicated team headed by Harish Gupta to oversee Shazia Hameed's campaign. The instructions were clear; no one else should have even an inkling of NPP's link with the independent candidate. Their efforts should be to cut into UNDP candidate's votes. So, there must be no campaign for her in the NPP-dominated assembly segments. Her campaigns should focus extensively on UNDP strongholds and give special attention to the minority-dominated areas.

He eagerly awaited the report from Topaz Investigative Services. Going by their earlier record, Suresh Ahluwalia was confident that he would not be disappointed. He was ill-prepared for his meeting with Manoj Seth scheduled for Thursday night. It was never easy to please the man. With nothing substantial in hand and with only one more day to go, he knew he was heading for a dreadful meeting with a boss who loved sneering at others. His only achievement so far was the discovery of Shazia Hameed. He hoped the president would approve the candidate and, for once at least, applaud the seemingly impossible work done by his team to find a dummy candidate.

Both the camps had reasons to be happy on Thursday evening. Suresh Ahluwalia received Ajay Chowdhury's report well within the deadline. He read the executive summary as soon as it got delivered to him. He was pleased; one particular paragraph delighted him.

Dr Purnima Bhatt is a ruthless, uncompromising woman. She does not give an inch when it comes to protecting her turf. A detailed chat with her ex-husband revealed the dark side of this seemingly amiable and compassionate person. Their marriage failed in less than a year due to the mental torture her simple and easy-going doctor husband had to go through. She was abusive and even violent at times.

Suresh Ahluwalia loved it. He ran through the fifty-four-page report stopping at parts that were very critical of Purnima. He saw great scope for a juicy anti-campaign. It was evident that Satish Bhat and his short-lived marriage with Purnima Bhatt was great for their campaign arsenal.

A section of the report focused on Purnima's views on social issues and current topics. The professional investigators had hacked into her social media accounts, sifted through her posts, and run a check on friends with whom she often interacted. Some of her comments on topics like minority rights to caste-based reservation policies were highlighted. Suresh Ahluwalia could not hide his glee; the explosive comments were perfect ammo for counter-attacks if she indulged in making populist statements on her campaign trails. He congratulated Ajay Chowdhury on a job well done.

Later in the evening, he waited for Manoj Seth to arrive for the meeting. Though he was well aware of his boss's uncanny flair to hit where it hurt, his nerves relaxed a little.

Manoj Seth was happy. He approved Shazia Hameed as their proxy candidate and asked for a meeting with her at Harish Gupta's residence at eleven o'clock the next day morning. Any public place, or his own house, was not safe for the undercover summit.

Four persons attended the meeting—Shazia Hameed, Harish Gupta, Suresh Ahluwalia and Manoj Seth. The party president spoke the most in the brief interaction.

"Dr Shazia, we appreciate your accepting our proposal. This one is an important strategy for us. You have nothing to lose and much to gain."

He continued, with the tactical pauses he so effectively used in his speeches. "First of all, I have full knowledge of whatever Harish has told you, every detail. You have the word of the NPP president that all the commitments shall be honoured.

"Now, your campaign is our responsibility. You shall play your role in executing whatever we chalk out for you. If you succeed in impressing the electorate, if your words and promises resonate with them, if you can make them rally around you, you may even become the dark horse to win this seat.

"One critical thing to expressly understand here. I'm sure my colleagues have already explained this to you. I must repeat it since there is no scope at all for any slip-up. It is a very confidential agreement between our party and you. No one, I repeat, absolutely no one else should know about this. I will make an exception for your husband since it would be unfair to expect you to hide it from him. If we get to know—and we *will* know if that ever happens— that you have breached secrecy, we shall stop all support for your campaign at that very instant, and our deal shall be dead. We shall then publicly deny all rumours and claim that talks of such a deal are nothing but a stunt from the publicity-hungry, independent candidate who is set to lose even her deposit. The press and the people will believe us. We shall not rest easy with leaving you stranded amidst the campaign. I will use the *entire* party machinery to make life difficult for you. *Please*, do not get me wrong. I do not mean to sound discourteous to you. But I am known to be blunt and forthright. All the cards are in front of you; there is no scope for misunderstanding later. What I just said remains true, from now and till forever, notwithstanding the results.

"Having talked about the most unlikely situation, I congratulate you on this courageous decision."

He continued after a pause. "Now I want to ask you something. My colleagues believe there was a noticeable change in you after you heard the name of the UNDP candidate. We are pleased that you carefully considered our proposal and changed your mind late evening, overriding your firm rejection earlier in the morning. We have a hunch that the UNDP candidate's name has something to do with it. It may be just conjecture. Nonetheless, if we need to know anything about the UNDP candidate, or about a past relationship between the two of you, you should let Harish know. It may be of help in planning your campaign."

Manoj Seth paused again and stared at Shazia. "From now on, you shall not contact any NPP functionaries, including Harish Gupta. Harish will introduce you to Srikant Tiwari and his team, who shall take care of your campaign all the way. He will report to Harish, but Harish shall not be seen with you in public from now on. He is a senior party functionary. We do not want any mix-ups. Harish will also give you a new number to call whenever you need to contact him for any emergency. Please delete his present number from your records soon after this meeting. You do not know any of us. You have never had anything to do with NPP. You have joined the fray only to serve the people. You are determined to defeat the mainstream party candidates, who you believe serve only personal interests and not the country's. And, of course, it goes without saying, this meeting has never taken place.

"Is this all clear, Dr Shazia Hameed?"

"Yes, Mr. Seth, all clear."

"Thanks. Very nice to meet you. All the best, and my regards to your husband. Bye."

In sharp contrast, the evening did not start on a good note in the UNDP office. Harsh Malhotra was livid with his colleagues for failing to make any inroads into the NPP candidate's past. A veteran of many electoral battles, he refused to believe for a moment that a candidate could have a clean past.

Upset and worried, he prayed for divine intervention.

Right on cue, a mysterious envelope addressed to the UNDP state president was delivered to him. Preoccupied with multiple challenges, he casually picked it up and, observing that the envelope did not carry the sender's details, tossed it to his right. On second thoughts, he stared at the envelope for a while and chose to open it. It contained two pages of typed text without any sign-off. The title of the text read, 'Robin Garg—the Darker Side'. He minutely scanned the document for any indication of the despatcher. There was none. He excused himself, and sitting on a corner sofa in the privacy of his own office, read the document with keen interest.

The report presented a new perspective of Robin Garg as a ruthless man who could do anything for his business. It reported how he had left his heavily pregnant wife alone and flew to Washington DC on a business trip only to multiply his wealth.

It read: *His wife Ritu Garg was in an advanced stage of pregnancy when she fell seriously ill. Robin Garg left her with his in-laws and flew to the United States of America on a routine business trip. When her condition deteriorated, his father-in-law pleaded with him to come right back. Robin Garg insisted that he could not return before the multi-million-dollar business deal, for which he travelled all the way, was finalised. His wife pleaded and had heated arguments during their last telephone call. She was very depressed after he refused to advance his return. A day later, she died in the operation theatre. Robin Garg still did not return. He hung on further to sign a landmark distribution deal with a multinational company. By the time he got back home, the last rites for his wife and his still-born baby were long over.*

The report quoted a few more instances to expose Robin Garg as a cruel mercenary who put business interests above everything else in life, as one not trustworthy enough for a responsible public position. Further, the report contended that his NGO was nothing more than a convenient contrivance for money laundering and expansion of his business interests.

He showed the papers to Jamal, who read them with great interest.

"Have you received a report from our Ahmedabad team yet?"

Jamal Ahmed replied hesitatingly, "Yes, we have received it a few minutes back. Their report is of no use to us. They report that there was nothing noticeable about the candidate's character and conduct during his IIM days. Though he married a girl from Ahmedabad, the couple did not live in the city for any length of time. Hence, there were hardly any details available on him from there. There is a mention of his wife's death, but the perspective is quite different. Let me read it out for you."

He opened the file he carried to the room and read it out: *After their marriage, Robin Garg and his wife rarely visited the city except when she was to deliver their first child. Unfortunately, her amniotic sac ruptured a week before the baby was due. She and the baby died in the operation theatre. He was away in the USA on a four-day business trip when this tragedy occurred.*

Harsh Malhotra thought for a while and said, "Our Ahmedabad guys have not gone deep into the matter. I do not know from where this report has come. But someone wants us to know the darker side of this man. Use this report."

Both of them returned to the meeting room. Harsh Malhotra then continued from where he had left and urged his colleagues to look for leads, however small or insignificant, that could help them mount attacks on the opposition candidate.

Leaving the room, he could not help wishing for more mysterious envelopes to land at his desk in the next few days!

Back home, Shazia recounted the day's extraordinary developments. She had never before met an active politician face-to-face. An eventful meeting with the national president of the country's most powerful party was overwhelming. It was intimidating as well. However, she now had a chance on a platter to take revenge on her childhood friend who she believed had betrayed her trust.

Those were the days of a heartbreak that Shazia never fully recovered from.

Her best friend Purnima's young man had moved out of Bangalore a few months before their school finals. She was distressed. Shazia comforted her, encouraged her to stay in touch with him and see where the relationship was headed, or to remember him as just a teenage infatuation. Shazia advised her to focus on her days ahead when she would make many new friends, meet with fine men of her age group, and fall in real love when the time was right.

As days passed, Purnima's gloom faded. She seemed to have reconciled with the reality and regained her chirpy best. A surprised Shazia was happy to notice the swift change in her best friend's moods. Initially, she thought that her endless discourses had worked, and Purnima had decided to move on. But intrigued by Purnima's ever-increasing exuberance, Shazia speculated if there was something more. She got sceptical. Closer scrutiny led to suspicion. She was convinced that there was something sinister behind Purnima's newfound cheerfulness.

Around the same time, Shazia saw distinct changes in Arvind's attitude. During the months leading to their final exams, the three friends met in Purnima's house more frequently thanks to the convenient alibi of group study. She minutely observed the chemistry between Arvind and Purnima. Blinded by jealousy, she believed they were getting cosier with each other, thought they laughed together more often—sometimes at things that were not funny at all.

She felt Arvind sat closer to Purnima than he used to do before. He hugged her more often. While in school, they often turned to each other to silently communicate with their eyes. Shazia was sure that Purnima also did not talk to her as much as she did in the past. She thought Purnima called her less than before, and even when she did, there was an air of detachment and restraint.

She felt Arvind was going to ditch her for Purnima. She also believed that Purnima was looking for an excuse to break their friendship. It had to happen one day.

The events of that awful evening, when the friends got together to celebrate the end of their board examinations, remained fresh in her mind. She lost two friends in one go; Arvind walked out of her life, and her relations with Purnima broke beyond repair. Shazia blamed Purnima and had craved revenge ever since.

She believed it was her time now to settle scores.

22

Once the deadline for filing the nomination papers was over, the battle lines were clearly drawn. No one expected any party other than the NPP, the UNDP and the SJP to field candidates for this contest since they had hardly any presence in the state's politics. But it surprised many that SJP did not field anyone despite their pre-eminence in the state. The grapevine said that they had struck a secret deal with UNDP to defeat the NPP candidate.

So, everyone was astonished to find that an independent candidate—not known to be active in public life in any manner—filed papers to take on the two leading contenders. It did not make any sense for Shazia Hameed to challenge the two big national parties. Only a handful of people knew her in the city as a good neonatologist. The public, in general, searched for her name on the internet to find information on her. Everyone agreed that the doctor had made a big mistake and she would lose her security deposit.

Purnima Bhatt was shocked and dismayed. It was beyond her wildest imagination that her erstwhile best friend had chosen to drag their teenage fracas to the national arena. Purnima had followed Shazia's career progression out of general curiosity; she did not harbour any desire for retaliation. There was also no longing to revive their friendship. But Purnima was happy to see her erstwhile friend do well in life and settle down with a happy family. She had long excused Shazia for her bigoted insinuations in the shameful brawl at the farmhouse and dismissed them as a crazy outburst from an insecure adolescent in love.

Purnima's friend working at Indradhanush had once told her at a wedding reception a few years ago. "I had a bad day today. One of our colleagues complained of severe chest pain early this morning. The doctors had to operate on her immediately. Three stents; she seemed so healthy! She is barely in her thirties! Things are so unpredictable these days!"

Purnima replied. "Oh, that's unfortunate. Thank God she got the necessary treatment at the right time. What's her name?"

"She is a neonatologist, Shazia Hameed."

Barely managing to hide her deep concern, Purnima responded. "Hope she recovers fully soon enough." She truly wished her erstwhile friend was out of any danger.

However, the unwarranted political challenge opened old wounds. Purnima knew Shazia could not be serious about winning the contest. It was difficult for an independent contestant to defeat the party candidates, given their formidable resources and organisational prowess. Her only intention seemed to be to pre-empt Purnima's win.

Purnima had been in a strategy meeting in the party office when she first heard about a surprise independent candidate in the fray. Already in a tight spot having to contest the man she loved, the new twist sent her head reeling. She looked forward to a candid discussion with Robin to get some clarity for the days ahead. The new challenge from her childhood friend and anxiety about her evening rendezvous with Robin were too much for her. Citing a severe headache, she excused herself for the day and returned home early in the afternoon.

She stood under the shower with the waterjet hitting her face in full strength. She stayed still for a while to soothe her nerves. It worked. Minutes later, she went to her favourite corner table on the balcony with a cup of strong black coffee. Fortunately, there was enough time left for her to hopefully return to emotional stability before the all-important tête-à-tête with Robin.

With her eyes trained on distant nothings, her mind raced back to her teenage years—Austin Town, Central School, Brigade Road, Robin, Shazia, Arvind *et al*. She smiled. She recalled her joy in bringing the lovebirds together in her house and occasionally in isolated corners of Brigade Road where no one could notice them. She believed Arvind and Shazia were a perfect match. She remembered Robin's transfer out of Bangalore, her emptiness, her subsequent recovery thanks to the amazing friends around her, the final school exams, and then the appalling farmhouse evening.

The smile disappeared from her face the moment she thought of that.

She wished they had not gone there to celebrate the end of their schooling days. The three-bedroom farmhouse on Kanakapura Road was a perfect getaway for the group of eight friends—Arvind, his two friends, Shazia, Purnima, and three other girls from their class. Arvind's father allowed them to spend the night there and instructed the farmhouse attendants to ensure that the children were taken good care of and served sumptuous food.

The Bangalore traffic was notoriously unpredictable. To ensure they did not have to waste their time honking at cars in front of them, they left the city early and reached the farmhouse by four in the evening. The girls were jubilant. The final exams' worries were behind them, and their parents had allowed them to spend a night with friends for the very first time. Their parents had called Arvind's mother to ensure that the get-together had her blessings and the children would be under supervision.

The driveway to the farmhouse had tall trees on either side with colourful bougainvillea plants in-between them. On the left side, partly concealed by the trees, there was a playground big enough for a round of family cricket. There were seesaws, swings, and a badminton court. On the right, various vegetables were being grown, cabbage, cauliflower, tomato, beans, chili, etc. There were cowsheds, chicken coops, duck pens, and rows of mango trees at a distance to the right. Purnima had never been to such a large farmhouse before. She loved it.

The house was L-shaped. The large wing had two bedrooms with a shared bath, a kitchen, and a living room. The smaller wing had a large bedroom with an attached bath. There was a swimming pool on an elevated concrete base by the side of the veranda. It had been re-filled with clean water in case the young guests fancied a dip.

Arvind and his friends checked in to the large bedroom, leaving the rest for the girls. Greeted with sumptuous snacks— bread *pakoda*, grilled paneer, *mysore pak* and masala tea—on arrival, their party could not have started better. Everything was perfect for a group of children celebrating the end of an epoch.

There was only one thing in the house that Arvind's father did not arrange. He also did not envisage that it would be sneaked in by the young visitors. They quickly looked around the property and gathered in the living room to open a crate of beer, well out of the caretakers' sight. In the next two hours, they drank, watched a short film, indulged in gossip, sang karaoke, and played a few rounds of *antakshari* before going out to have an elaborate dinner laid by the poolside.

Post dinner, they went back to the living room and drank more beer. Although drinking alcohol was nothing new for the boys, they managed to consume excessive amounts in a short time. Purnima and the three other girls had casually tasted beer before but were not comfortable with drinking. So, each toyed with a can for the whole evening. Shazia had never even been close to spirits. She frowned and twisted her lips with disgust after the first few sips.

The bitter lager invariably surprised first-timers. But, for reasons best known to her, she persisted. She drank one beer after another as if she had been at it for years.

About an hour later, Arvind got up, subtly gestured at Purnima to follow him, and casually walked out of the room. As the rest of the friends watched a Shammi Kapoor hit, his unique dance sequences often replayed in fast forward mode, and laughed their guts out, Purnima followed Arvind to the large bedroom.

Arvind burst out, "Tell me, Purnima, what the hell is wrong with your friend these days? She is not the girl I knew till a few months back. That bubbly, loving, jovial girl I loved has disappeared. What I have for a girlfriend now is a cribber who is grumbling non-stop. A girl who gets angry for no reason, someone who wants to own me and tells me when to breathe and when not to. What the hell has happened to her?"

Choking with emotion, he panted, took out a handkerchief, and covered his eyes.

"Arvind, listen, please don't get so upset!"

"Wait, I have not finished yet. Look at the way she is drinking! She has gone nuts! I thought I have a girlfriend with whom I can spend my whole life. I was ready to take on society, my family—goddamned anyone—to make her my wife. I knew bloody well that even the whisper of such a marriage would create an upheaval in my community. Why is she doing this to me? If she wishes to break up, damn it, just let her tell me that. I will then go away from her life. You know, I screwed up my exams as well. I am not sure I want to continue this relationship anymore."

"Okay, relax and listen to me. Both of you are my dearest friends. I will do everything I can to resolve whatever issues you have between the two of you. The thing is, I also don't know what's going on. I have not noticed anything so drastic. Maybe I love you guys so much that I am blind to aberrations."

Arvind, inebriated and highly emotional, quoted multiple instances of Shazia's strange behaviour. Purnima defended each instance with genuine attempts to give positive twists to Arvind's perception. At one stage, Arvind started crying like a child. Unhappy to see a friend in distress, Purnima moved to sit very close to him and patted him like a young child.

Shazia noticed that Arvind and Purnima were the only ones missing from the living room. Highly intoxicated, she tiptoed out of the room and followed Purnima's voice to the large bedroom. The door was wide open. Stretching her neck from the right side of the door to see them without being seen, she was furious and disgusted. Her worst fears came true as she saw Purnima wrap her arms around Arvind's shoulder, hold his hand in hers, and engage in an intimate conversation.

She heard Purnima say, "Please, don't worry at all. I am there for you. You can trust me. You know that, don't you? Stop getting so worried. You are wonderful, Arvind. I will take care of everything. Now relax."

Shazia stormed into the room with shaky legs and stopped a few inches short of Purnima. With a set of livid eyes, she shouted, "I knew this was going on the whole time, you bitch! You are a bloody venomous snake! You stabbed your so-called best friend in the back. Have you no shame?"

Purnima looked at her with pleading eyes. Arvind tried to get up, but Purnima pulled him down, afraid that things might get out of hand with two drunk persons close to each other. As he sat back, Arvind told Shazia, "Keep quiet. Let me tell you something. If there is *any snake* or *bitch* in this room, that is *you.*"

Shazia shook Purnima with both her hands and shouted, "This one is the culprit. She has been planning this for a long time. You always had an eye on my boyfriend, didn't you? You were jealous of me all the time. Do you think I am *stupid* that I didn't see all your cosy conversations in the last few months? You think I am *blind* that I don't notice that you go out of the way to sit close to Arvind every time we meet, ensure that your arms and thighs touch his, laugh at anything he says even when there is nothing funny, run away together from our group given half a chance. Damn it, how could you do this to me?"

Purnima was dumbstruck. She was stunned by this vicious attack from a girl she had always thought to be her dearest friend. Arvind again said, "I know what's wrong with you, Shazia. *You* are a jealous, insecure woman. *You* are messing up things, no one else. I can't believe that I planned to spend my life with you; life with someone so green, so virulent, so possessive, and so stupid!"

Shazia continued her tirade, "Yes, of course, now that this witch has charmed you, I am all bad. This woman knew that you and I have huge social hurdles to cross to live our life together. So she laid this trap for you. Till that damned old guy was around for her to fancy, she was all right. After he left, her true colours showed."

Purnima was shocked by Shazia's unwarranted personal attack. She retorted, "Don't bring *him* into this. Where the hell did that come from? We are here. Talk about us."

Shazia got wilder. She yelled at the top of her voice, "*You* don't tell me what to say and what not to! I will teach you a lesson right now." She pushed Purnima down to the ground and pulled her hair hard. Arvind struggled to get to his feet but finally managed to stand straight. Unable to disengage them, he grabbed Shazia by her shoulder, shook her up, and shouted, "This is the end of my relationship with you. And Purnima, I am sorry that I dragged you into this. Forgive me."

Shazia was speechless. She wept inconsolably. Moments later, she recovered enough to hurl insults at Purnima—words that hurt Purnima even today.

It was the worst night. Purnima never saw Shazia after they returned to Bangalore the next day.

She met Arvind twice, once at a wedding and then again before leaving Bangalore for her medical studies. They, too, lost touch over time.

Back in the present, Purnima closed her eyes to take a catnap before getting ready for dinner with Robin.

Meanwhile, Shazia waited in her Sarita Vihar residence for her husband to return from work. She wanted to share her overwhelming experience of filing the nomination papers, describe the new campaign headquarters in Rajouri Garden, and recount the briefings received from her mentors. In her mind, the mission was to destroy whatever chances Purnima had for a win and to enjoy the fruits of her weeks of labour with the bounty. As soon as Mohammed arrived, she started with her story. Too excited to take notice of his indifference, she talked non-stop as Mohammed went through his daily routine: wash up, change of clothes, and enjoying a mug of black coffee.

In the end, he said calmly, "Listen, Shazia, this is a game you opted to play. You know very well that I was not keen from day one due to multiple reasons. This thing will consume too much of your time. There are risks as well if anything goes wrong. Father also has concerns, but he has agreed to go along with you; you know how fond of you he is. He will never say no to you! Take help from him and Ma. That may help you to retain your deposit and save your face. As for me, you know I am not a socially hyper person. So, don't expect much from me. I will, of course, come to your help whenever you ask for it. But please, let us not discuss this election at home. Let us keep our home private and peaceful as it has always been. I don't want the next few weeks of politics to take that away. Sorry for being so brutally frank. But you know me well. I would rather be clear from the beginning."

Shazia did well to hide her disappointment and replied with a smile, "Of course, my dear. It is clear. Let us not bring politics home. I will expect you to join me on a couple of campaign trails, though!" Her winking left Mohammed confused about whether she actually meant it or just wanted to pull his leg. He certainly had no such plans.

Nevertheless, Mohammed replied, "Of course! All the very best, Dr Shazia Hameed, for the forthcoming elections!"

"Thank you, Dr Mohammed Hameed." They shared a good laugh.

23

The two national parties' headquarters were only a few blocks apart in the exclusive Central Delhi neighbourhood. Though they looked similar from the outside, there was hardly any actual resemblance. The imposing gate at the entrance to the UNDP headquarters was a mute witness to the country's eventful history—scores of national leaders had walked tall through the gate over the years. The long driveway led to a porch large enough for two big cars. A Range Rover parked close to the steps indicated that the party president was in the office.

The hall inside had a reception counter with rows of cushioned chairs for visitors. Large portraits of the Father of the Nation, the first prime minister, and the first president hung on the wall on the right side. The wall on the left showcased an imaginatively crafted collage that reflected significant national achievements since independence. It depicted a village with paddy fields, a nuclear power plant, a geostationary satellite, an aircraft carrier, armoured tanks, various handicrafts, etc. A picture of the national president, flanked on either side by two senior general secretaries, was prominently displayed behind the reception,

The E-shape building had three distinct wings. The left wing, open to senior party functionaries only, had an automatic door with biometric access. There was no security guard on duty at the door leading to this part of the building. The guard in the middle wing let people in after checking their identity badges or security passes. This wing housed the permanent workers and people with specific long-term assignments at the head office. The right wing was open to all. It was usually full of party workers, sundry contractors,

142

caterers and the like. The cafeteria, at the end of this wing, was open to everyone.

People with access to the middle wing could visit the right side at any time. The people with access to the left wing could access any part of the head office without restrictions.

The left wing had five well-appointed offices; the largest one had a small meeting room attached. It also had two conference rooms, a data centre, a luxurious dining room, and an extended veranda opening out to the backyard garden. The extension, adorned with cane furniture and flower vases, was reserved for casual senior-level discussions. The greenery outside was visible through the glass facade but one could not see in from the outside.

The mid-wing had a few open offices, two meeting rooms, a library, an audio-visual studio, office equipment, and other utilities.

Harsh Malhotra was the first to enter the left wing on Tuesday morning. His national president was to join him to discuss various matters—a status report on the West Delhi by-election topped the agenda. Six senior-most officials from their Central and Delhi party units were to attend. He wanted to review his presentation a couple of times. Since it was not easy to get an appointment with his boss, he had to be at his best.

He was unhappy to hear the intercom ring. That was not the time he wanted to indulge in mundane discussions. He grudgingly answered the phone.

"Sorry to disturb you, sir. There is someone on line from Bangalore, who wants to talk only to you," said the operator.

"I am busy. Forward the call to Jamal. He should be here by now."

"I suggested that, sir. But the lady wants to talk only to you."

"A lady, is it? Tell her I am unable to take any call at this time. If she wishes to talk to us, she needs to speak to Jamal Ahmed." He put the receiver down without waiting for a response.

A few minutes later, a visibly angry Harsh Malhotra picked up the intercom again.

"Jamal, it had better be something important. You know I have something urgent this morning."

"I do Malhotra *saab*. I am sorry, but the woman from Bangalore insists on talking only to you."

"And I insist on not taking any random call now."

"She says she wants to talk to you about Robin Garg. And that our party will miss critical information if you do not take her call. She gave her number and said she would wait for half an hour for your call. After that, she will not be available at all."

"Hell! I would normally not respond to such threats, but given the condition we are in now about this man… fine, connect me to her. This better be good."

"Okay, *saab*. I'll do it right away. Do you want me to join you in the call?"

"No."

Two minutes later, Harsh Malhotra was in a call with Aditi Kasbekar. He started with a curt statement, "I believe you wanted to talk only with me. Here I am, I just have a few minutes for you. Please talk."

They spoke for nearly fifteen minutes. By the time the call was over, Harsh Malhotra was friendly and respectful. "Thanks for your call, Aditi. I will then expect you in our office by eleven in the morning. You can take any return flight after five. And don't worry, you shall have a return ticket in your mailbox in an hour. Give me your email address." He noted down the details.

The next day, Aditi Kasbekar walked into the UNDP office like a celebrity. A party worker guided her from the gate to a meeting room in the left wing. Though she was a first-time visitor, she did not have to report to the reception. Minutes later, she was ushered into the state president's office. Harsh Malhotra welcomed her and directed her to the sofa at the far end of his office. For the next one hour, Aditi gave a vivid account of her tenure in National Distribution Network Limited, her relationship with Robin Garg, his autocratic management style, and his ruthless defence of his own interests.

Jamal Ahmed took extensive notes throughout the meeting without saying a word. Later, he took her for lunch in Khan Market before seeing her off at the airport.

Harsh Malhotra was delighted like a child. He had received an invaluable lead for besmirching Robin's seemingly spotless profile. It was not necessary to cross-verify Aditi's story. A seasoned hand in politics, he knew that it was unlikely that the story was entirely true. It must have been spiced up to suit one's argument by a person who clearly felt victimised and longed for revenge. However, the truth behind the serious allegations did not matter. The rival candidate, when caught by such allegations, would be busy defending himself. That's all that mattered in an election.

He read Jamal's notes at random.

I would not like to be physically involved in this—campaign trail, press conference, statements, etc.—these are not for me. You can quote my name, though, I don't care. If the press people find me, I'll manage. I shall not deny anything.

Robin Garg is a narcissist. He thinks he is God's gift to this world. This sense of superiority drives him to treat his subordinates as lesser human beings. As new recruits, we felt worthless, non-entities! Though there was a hierarchy in the organisation—we did not report to him—he often took our appraisals himself. He was so nasty that we often cried after those appraisals.

… after a couple of drinks, he was high. He slurred, stared at me to the point that I became very uncomfortable. He moved closer, held my hand, and got emotional. He wrapped his arms around me. I tried to excuse myself and join my friends at the party. He insisted I sit with him

in the corner. I was scared to go away against his wish; after all, he was the big boss! He talked, mostly a monologue, and touched me now and then despite my obvious discomfort all through the evening.

Another day, he asked me out for dinner. I accepted, and I must admit it started nicely. He selected a very posh restaurant—beautiful location, lovely ambience, and great food. He was a graceful host too. But after a few glasses of wine, he became very emotional. We knew that he had lost his wife a couple of months ago. He lamented over his lonely life and described his craving for intimacy. Despite my unease, I gave him a patient hearing out of respect, as expected from a young trainee. While driving me home, he asked if I would like to join him for a coffee in his house. I politely said no. He persisted. When his pleading started to sound more like a command, I said no firmly. He reprimanded me as being ungrateful and impolite. I curtly asked him to stop the car immediately and drop me off right there on the road. He sobered down and saw me home.

Later, he asked me out thrice. I found excuses to say no each time. He looked very annoyed at the last instance. He never approached me after that.

However, my life at work became hell after that. My immediate supervisor shouted at me all the time. Robin Garg rebuked me in public for my so-called poor performance. Everyone thought that something was wrong with the quality of my work; even the security guys looked at me funnily. My manager gave me inhumane amounts of work—enough for three trainees—and shouted at me before everyone for not meeting the deadlines!

...pushed to a corner by a resentful boss and subservient managers, I had to resign. They did not even settle my dues.

I have nothing to gain from sharing these details with you. I have long forgotten about this awful man. But I want the voters to know who he really is before casting their votes. After all, these are the lawmakers who decide the future of our country.

Beaming with happiness, Harsh Malhotra asked his social media head to report to him immediately.

Around the same time, Arvind Balakrishnan searched for information on candidates who had filed their nomination papers. For a man with hardly any interest even in Karnataka state politics, it was very unusual. When he asked for his secretary's help, she was intrigued.

Arvind suspected that the independent candidate was none other than his ex-girlfriend. Her looks had not changed much over the years. The UNDP candidate also looked familiar. Though he believed Purnima was not the kind to go in for active politics, he could not overlook the glaring similarities. He wondered if the juvenile battle had survived time only to launch into a finale in the national capital. He scouted the internet for information and corroborated his findings with the secretary's reports. He knew now, beyond any doubt, that his schoolmates—close friends at that time—were now locked in an electoral battle in the national capital. It seemed like the stuff of movies.

Arvind tried to analyse the various possibilities. Purnima represented one of the two leading national political parties who typically engaged in all-out fights in national politics at every opportunity. Her nomination had to be a well-considered decision taken by a group of senior politicians. But Shazia's candidature as an independent did not seem to make much sense. He checked with his well-placed contacts in Delhi if she engaged in public service in any capacity. The feedback from all sources was the same—she was known only in a limited circle, that within the medical community and among her patients. He correctly deduced that her move was intended to reduce Purnima's chances of winning. That meant Shazia was willing to endure personal humiliation only to hurt Purnima. This implacable pursuit of teenage bitterness left him astounded.

He tried to divert his mind by focusing on the business at hand. There was no reason to be unduly concerned; after all, his friendship with them was now a part of his childhood history.

However, he was disturbed. He realised he could not remain a mute spectator to Purnima's punishment yet again for a crime she had not committed. Ultimately, he made up his mind to help Purnima out to take on the unfair challenge.

He pulled a few strings to get Harsh Malhotra's mobile number for a brief chat on Wednesday afternoon.

"Dr Malhotra, this call shall be brief. I am Arvind Balakrishnan, and I have a family business here in Bangalore. I know your candidate Dr Purnima Bhatt very well. She was my classmate in school. I may be of great help to your campaign since we were close friends. After I hang up, I will message my contact details to you. Please retain them. You may need it. Goodbye."

Getting Purnima's number was not difficult. She was happy to hear from Arvind after years. She was also relieved to share her frustration with the only person who knew the details about her rivalry with Shazia. His pledge for active support cheered her up. She felt herself relax a bit.

Far away in Guwahati, Anil Hazarika did not bother much about the UNDP nomination after the initial agonising. It would have been a forgotten piece of news if he was not drinking with his Guwahati Medical College batch mates when the 'breaking news' on filing of nomination papers for the West Delhi parliamentary seat flashed on television. One of them clapped his hands to divert everyone's attention from a heated discussion on Virat Kohli's merits as captain of the Indian cricket team and spoke at the top of his voice.

"Hey, guys, look at that. Look who is contesting a parliamentary election. Dr Purnima Bhatt, alias the great Purnima Bajaj. Do you guys remember the most romantic couple of our times—the couple that took the campus by storm, although for a short time?"

They all looked at the TV and quietly sat through the report. When the anchor moved to another piece of news, they looked at Anil together. Anil knew they were taking a dig at him, knowing about his relationship.

One friend, befuddled by a couple of drinks, rubbed salt into the wound. "This girl has always been extra ambitious. She took our dear friend Anil—the most honest and unpretentious boy in our batch—for a joy ride for a few months. Then she dumped him when she was done with him, talking about career—as if she did not know in those wild mooning months that she was here for a career—so let's not talk about her. She *has been*, and will *always* be a cunning chess player, making calculated moves with scant love or regard for anyone else."

Anil protested, "Come on guys, why go back to the days that we have left so far behind. She…"

Someone else cut him short with an alcohol-inspired emotional outburst. "Please, Anil, you don't have to play a Yudhishthira; call a spade a spade. She *dumped* you after manipulating you for months. She wanted to work hard for a *great* career—good for her. But to become a lawmaker of our country, that's another matter. It is your time now. Play your part in this. The voters must know her profile—the *full* profile—not just what her party portrays. Take my suggestion: contact the NPP—a great party doing great things for this country, not done since independence—and tell them what you know about their opponent. They will do the rest."

Another doctor added, "Doing *great* things for this country… my foot! They are actually…! Oh, leave that aside, no point. Let's focus on the key issue. This guy is spot on! Buddy, do it for yourself, for us, and the country. We need members of Parliament who do not take far-reaching decisions only with their vested interests in mind. It *may* sound childish to dig into campus life to define a candidate. But it is *not*. One's carefree student life reflects one's true traits."

Comments and advice poured in aplenty till Anil forced a change in topic. However, once his friends left, their words returned in full force. He saw merit in their arguments. Impelled by painful memories of their separation, he wondered if it was indeed a time for payback. The notion of social obligation was a convenient excuse.

Anil mulled over his options for a day. Once absolutely certain, he called Suresh Ahluwalia on his mobile phone. It was not difficult to get the number; one of the NPP state president's doctors in AIIMS was Anil's close friend. It was Wednesday evening.

Happy to get invaluable support from unexpected quarters, Suresh Ahluwalia thanked Anil profusely. Dark stories from candidates' younger days invariably resonated with the electorate. He smiled at the prospect of demolishing Purnima Bhatt's image of a clean, compassionate social worker. He asked his social media head to report to him at nine o'clock the next morning.

24

Radha Saluja had never been so nervous. Forthright and carefree by nature, she never liked doing things in secrecy. She was uncomfortable with performing a confidential act with significant political implications. But she had to do it for Purnima.

They had been close friends since their first meeting at a dreary party seven years ago in Green Park Extension. The owner of a pharmaceutical company had hosted a grand dinner to celebrate the silver anniversary of his company. The city's elite, particularly the crème-de-la-crème of the medical community, were invited. Radha received the invite as a journalist covering the healthcare industry. Lost in a crowd of unfamiliar faces and tired of formulaic pleasantries, she nursed her drink in a quiet corner when Purnima joined her for a chat. They struck an instant bond. Their friendship grew with time. Radha's husband, a friendly gentleman, spent a significant part of the year in business travel for his multinational employer. Their young daughter in the ninth standard was very fond of Purnima. They often met for family get-togethers.

Once the nomination was official, the candidates were under relentless public scrutiny. Robin recognised that inviting Purnima to his house for the dinner appointment would be risky. They could not meet in a public place as well. If the press spotted them together, it would be difficult to explain. It had to be a neutral and private venue. He and Purnima discussed options and agreed that Radha's apartment in Saket was their best choice. Robin drew confidence from Purnima's assurance that if there was one person in the world to be trusted, it had to be Radha Saluja. Purnima requested Radha to allow them to meet at her house in the A Block of Delhi Development Authority's Saket Self Financing Scheme housing complex.

Radha agreed to it, setting her apprehensions aside. There were high risks of getting involved in a political spectacle. But friendship reigned supreme and she felt honoured by the confidence reposed in her. It was a blessing that her husband had gone to Europe for the week, and her daughter happily agreed for a night out in her friend's house. So, there would be absolute secrecy.

Well aware that Radha and Robin did not know her history with Shazia, Purnima preferred to keep it that way. With challenges on various fronts, she chose to take them one at a time, starting with the most complex one, Robin Garg.

Though a drive from Safdarjung Enclave to Saket in peak hours took no more than forty minutes, she got into a taxi an hour and a half before the scheduled time to take a detour; she knew she could be under surveillance. She wanted to leave even earlier but got delayed while dressing up. Purnima took quite some time to decide what to wear, to try different sets of ornaments, and then review her overall appearance from various angles in front of the mirror. She wanted to look her best for the evening.

The shortest route was to take the Shaheed Jeet Singh Marg and get on to Sri Aurobindo Marg to avoid traffic congestion on the Outer Ring Road. Purnima booked the taxi instead for Sarojini Nagar Market. She got off at one end of the market, joined a horde of shoppers to cross to the opposite side, and called for another taxi to Saket. The waiting time for the cab was ten minutes. She walked around the busy alleys along with the swelling crowd, stopped at odd places, and then quickly moved on. After getting into the taxi, she asked the driver to drive through the Inner Ring Road to join Sri Aurobindo Marg at the AIIMS junction. She chose the worst approach to Saket to ensure that tracking her car was nearly impossible. Half an hour later, she looked at the traffic jam and wondered if it had been a good decision. But when the taxi turned to Shivalik Road, she was relieved; she would not be late.

Robin Garg had planned his late afternoon engagements with the all-important dinner appointment in mind since driving from Dwarka to Saket on a weekday evening would have been difficult. He was equally discreet. His driver dropped him at Ansal Plaza on Khel Gaon Marg for a meeting with a colleague working for Ritu's World. After their discussions, Robin requested him to drive him to Saket DLF Mall, from where he took a taxi to the flat.

Purnima was with Radha by the time Robin pressed the bell.

Radha opened the door and greeted Robin like a long-lost friend. "Hi there! A hearty welcome to you. It *is* my privilege to see you again soon. Our first meeting was so impressive that I have been looking forward to the next. Come on in."

Robin laughed and responded as he walked into the apartment, "Oh, that's so kind of you. You have a beautiful place. Hello Purnima! How are you doing?"

"I'm good." Pointing to a sofa set at the far end, she continued, "Please have a seat."

Radha said with a sense of urgency, "Listen, guys, I have decided to watch a movie. Kevin Costner and Woody Harrelson—I love both these guys—it will keep me busy for a little over two hours, after which I shall warm the food. Let me warn you; it's not a fancy spread, just some basics. But there are plenty of nibbles on the table—peanuts, cashews, kebabs, and samosas—and alcohol in that cabinet. Please feel at home and relax."

Once Radha had disappeared through a door on the right, Purnima asked, "Do you care for a drink?"

"Yes, I'll have a whiskey if there's some."

"Sure. Radha has a good collection though neither she nor her husband is much of a drinker. Any preference?"

"I will have a single malt if it's available. Should I come help?"

"No, you relax, Robin *da*. I'll do it." Purnima checked the cabinet and said, "Okay, fifteen years Glenlivet for you, does that work? How do you take your drink?"

"That sounds perfect. Just four cubes of ice please, thanks. What about you?"

"I see a Grey Goose here. I'll have that with a dash of tonic water."

As Purnima prepared the drinks, Robin had a good look at her. She looked stunning in her cream-coloured, fitted trousers and a bright-red top. Her chic beige leather sandals displayed her beautiful feet. He observed her dainty fingers holding the whiskey bottle carefully as she poured a drink, the solitaire, the Cartier—they were all so gorgeous!

After serving the drink, Purnima moved the snacks over to the coffee table at the centre of the sofa set and took a seat facing Robin. They sipped their drinks and sat quietly like strangers for a few minutes. After a while, Robin looked at his watch and realised they were losing precious time.

"So, here we are, Purnima. Our story must be unique in this world. We meet in a strange twist of destiny, only to fight each other in a public spectacle."

"Well said, Robin *da*. Destiny has been cruel, at least to me for sure. With a happily married life, you found love and bliss for a few years at least. I have no such salvation. Searching for true happiness, I need to return to my distant childhood, the love I got from my adorable parents, my happy-go-lucky school days, and you, Robin *da*. With time, those days are getting hazier."

Robin did not interrupt her. He wanted her to speak her heart out before they discussed politics. He walked over and sat next to Purnima.

Purnima continued, "I have had a successful career as a doctor. I can't complain. Blessed with an opportunity to work for a premier institute, I command respect within the medical fraternity. I am loved by many for my practice and social work; I am grateful for all their affection. But I have been a failure in my personal life. Looking back at my teenage years, I now believe I was deeply in love with a young man ten years older and did not even know! I was not seasoned enough to understand the difference between a crush and true love. I was too young to realise that ten years of age difference was not a huge barrier to a lifelong relationship.

"The young man went away and slowly disappeared from my life. I shrugged it off as teenage madness and tried to move on. I fell in love with a batchmate in my first year in medical college. It happened so quickly—I was surprised with myself. Maybe because he had many qualities similar to the young man—his features, accent, warmth, intelligence, humour, and mischief; perhaps I saw someone else in him. After about seven months of a passionate relationship, I sensed a void, found something amiss in the intimacy. The smokescreen collapsed in the face of closer scrutiny. I realised that my poor academic performance had a lot to do with our wild romance. I insisted on breaking-up. After that, I never considered getting into another relationship till I fell in love with a colleague in AIIMS, years later. I rushed into a marriage—probably conscious that I was not getting younger—it failed miserably. God knows I tried my best. After that debacle, I convinced myself to stay away from intimate relationships. I devoted myself to my profession and spent a significant amount of time in social service. It worked very well. The emptiness in my personal life was filled by the love and respect I received from the poor and the unprivileged. I learned to live with the illusion that I am never lonely with so many people to love me."

Purnima's voice cracked. She bit her lips to rein in her emotions. Robin took her hand in his, held it tight, and caressed it with the other hand.

"I have surrendered to reality and been content with what I have. Then, you arrive from nowhere like a comet to make a mess, to make me feel sad again about what could have been, to feed me to my wild dreams and I started seeing possibilities. The next day, you present yourself in a new avatar—my rival in an election! What am I supposed to do, Robin *da*?"

Purnima could not hold back her tears anymore. Robin put his arms around her, held her closer, and stroked her hair gently.

"I thought of quitting many times in the last one week. But that would be highly irresponsible. Too many people are involved in this now. Besides, though my feelings for you are real, an enduring relationship with you is still nothing but a figment of my imagination. So, I am *more* confused now than I have *ever* been in my life." She spoke now with more clarity and confidence. "Let's discuss this, Robin *da*. Honestly, I have come with an open mind. I do not have any solutions to suggest. *You* tell me."

Robin gently released Purnima from his arms, held her face like it was a fragile treasure, and looked at her for a few moments. He let his fingertips caress her cheeks, the thumbs parting ways to feel the corners of her quivering lips. The feather touch sent a shiver down her spine. Robin was pleasantly surprised; he had unwittingly done something that he had fantasised about ages back. Suddenly nervous and apprehensive, he adjusted his shirt collar and looked as far away as he could.

Taking time to regain his composure, he shifted to his original seat facing her and said, "I am happy that you have spoken your heart out, Purnima. I was in my early twenties when I saw you for the first time. You were such a cute girl—naughty eyes that always wanted to say something, cheeks that turned red when I teased, the tantalising dimples, your giggles! I loved it when you ran for cover when I teased you. But I cursed myself for being romantic about a schoolgirl so many years younger than me. I did everything I could to steer my thoughts away. The next evening, it played out all over again. On top of it, I got so much love and warmth from your family! I was sad when I could not visit you for a couple of evenings.

"Then I got a transfer. After I reached Lucknow, I missed you a lot, I'm not sure in what way. I was confused. You thought I was too old for you, I thought you were ridiculously young for me. However, you did not let me be in peace in the new city for many weeks."

Robin stopped talking. It was apparent that he was trying to suppress his emotions from bursting out. This time, Purnima walked across and sat next to him.

Robin continued, "I waited for your response to my letter. It never came. My confused mind found an easy explanation. I understood—the lack of any response from you was proof that your enthusiasm when we met was nothing but natural warmth from a well brought up, kind-hearted kid—I was nice to you, so you returned the favour. It dawned on me that whatever I had read in your eyes were only delusions to suit my fancy. I felt stupid that I had misconstrued my infatuation for a girl ten years younger. I worked hard to get away from it; I succeeded. In less than a year, your face faded into a beautiful past.

"If I knew that you were also waiting for my letter, our future may have unfolded differently! In a few more years, the age difference between us would not have looked as daunting."

He again stopped talking and looked away to hide his moist eyes. Purnima gathered the courage to take his hand into hers. Her dainty fingers caressed his hand with a touch of restrained intimacy.

He spoke again, "It seems we both erred. I have since met many women and made friends with a few wonderful women. But I could never develop a close relationship. I can't blame it on you, but that's how it was, till I met my Ritu. Can you believe it? We got to know each other because we fought over the last piece of pastry in a patisserie! The shopkeeper had to cut the pastry into half to serve us both!"

They laughed together. It was a good break. The environment had been getting too emotional. They discussed the past, their profession, and plans for the future; talked about the state of the economy, social challenges, and exchanged views on Delhi's latest popular eateries. Robin looked at his watch; it was time they got down to business.

"I think before Kevin Costner finds Clyde and Bonnie, let us get down to our main challenge in hand—the elections. What shall we do? How do we compete? I believe these elections require a killer instinct to win. How do I develop that against you, or you against me?"

"Yes, indeed, Robin *da*." Purnima moved back to her earlier seat and continued, "We are in a mess here. I'm sure campaigns get quite nasty, very personal."

"Yes, I believe so. Let me ask you something, Purnima. How did you land up in an electoral contest? What do you want finally?"

Purnima did not respond for a while. Shuffling in her seat, she was noticeably uncomfortable. With her elbow resting on the armrest, and the chin nestled in between the thumb and the index finger, she asked in a heavy voice, "What do I want finally? Robin *da*, I want to ask you something."

"Sure, of course. And, please, can you call me just Robin?"

Purnima giggled, reminding Robin of the teenage sweetheart he had once known. "Give me some time, Robin *da*! It is not that easy to switch, you know!"

Robin chuckled and said, "Okay, I take that. Now, your question, please."

"Do you see a future in *us*?"

25

The Third Eye, a low-budget, web-based publication, survived on donations from readers and independent organisations. The paper was widely popular among people interested in reports and analyses from journalists with no links to certain families, political parties, corporates, or lobbying groups. They published their stories based on merits and facts free from any pressure groups, unlike other news outlets. With increasing polarisation of the media, only a handful of such publications held the fort for free press. *The Third Eye* was somewhere at the top. Though they covered various topics—social, political, cultural, religious, sports, entertainment—politics usually got the most space. They regularly published scathing critiques on the leading national parties. They were generally considered authentic.

Tim Jacob, the lead partner and the chief editor of *The Third Eye*, was briefing his senior journalists on Thursday morning. "This West Delhi by-election for the Parliament is a crucial one. I am so confused by the independent nomination. In a prestige battle between the two most powerful parties in the country, when even the SJP did not field a candidate, why has an unknown candidate filed her papers as an independent? A doctor from an apolitical family is unlikely to believe she has a fair chance to win. She cannot be so stupid to contest merely to hog a few weeks' limelight. I suspect some political chicanery behind this. Find out exactly what is going on here. Dive deep into the candidates' profiles, their backgrounds, their campaign trails; find out everything and let the people know. Guide them to an informed decision."

The journalists listened to the chief editor like a set of disciplined students. It was a familiar message ahead of an assignment of national import. There was no response; the chief editor did not expect any.

Tim Jacob had an enviable network of contacts cultivated over years of intensive work in the profession. He had worked for leading international news agencies at various stages of his career. His final assignment had ended in bitter dispute. When, as the chief executive officer of a prime national television channel, he refused to toe the line on national issues, he was dismissed with a day's notice. He decided that he had had enough. He started his own publication in collaboration with like-minded journalists. As expected, they had many critics. Many considered them a bunch of radical intellectuals. However, no one had ever charged them with bias towards any particular organisation or ideology. Their issue-based reports carried critical analyses from a neutral perspective. All the major national parties got their fair share of rebuke at some point or the other.

He was keen to personally investigate the curious case of the third, independent candidate to complement his team's report.

Around the same time, Suresh Ahluwalia was having a closed-door meeting with his party's key media relation executives. The chief of the IT cell, the head of the social media section, and the chief spokesperson were present with a few others.

"Each one of you now has a folder with valuable information on the UNDP candidate. First of all, check out her failed marriage. This report is from a top-class investigative agency. They even had an interview with her ex-husband. Some of the information is priceless. I believe the candidate has cultivated a public image of an honest and compassionate person. Her party will try to capitalise on this. They will project her as a selfless person who forsook family life to serve the poor. But the agency's report shows that she is a self-centred woman. Also, carefully read the Guwahati doctor's feedback, the man with whom she had her first fling. His frustration as a used-and-dumped classmate is all too obvious. It reconfirms the agency report.

"Your job is to take advantage of this invaluable information and destroy her image. Mount a coordinated attack on her profile—WhatsApp, Facebook, Twitter, Instagram, and what have you—use every possible tool; start early. This one is a must-win battle for us. Is this clear to everyone? We must win at any cost."

The social media head responded, "Agreed, we will run an aggressive campaign. But we need to be ready to manage a counter-offensive from the opposition. We must know whether this data is verified. We should also know if there are any gaps."

The state president gave him a sharp look.

Getting the message, he said, "No, please, I do not doubt the reports. Just that we should have as many details as possible to react at lightning speed to any opposition rejoinders. We caught them by surprise a couple of years back when we launched our social media offensive. But now, I must say, they have done significant catching up. Their digital media management is now pretty sharp."

"There is solid ammunition in your hand. When the opposition reacts, you do what is necessary to give back to them in equal measure. I am sure you do not expect me to do your job," roared Suresh Ahluwalia. "Each adult in West Delhi and beyond must believe that Purnima Bhatt is a ruthless, self-absorbed person who has ditched many people, including her boyfriend and ex-husband—to create an image for herself; she is an unreliable person for a public position."

The meeting was dismissed. Suresh Ahluwalia requested one of the executives to stay back and asked if the Poorvanchali head of Robin Garg's NGO had already been inducted into the campaign team. He was aware of Robin's qualms about drafting his NGO officers for a political campaign. However, Suresh Ahluwalia insisted, keeping in mind the proven role of ethnic influencers in garnering mass votes. He was happy to find that the man had agreed to join the team in a few days.

Later that evening, he called Manoj Seth to give an update. At the end of the call, the president said, "It all sounds good, Suresh *bhai*. But the proof of the pudding is in the eating, as they say. By the way, is Durjoy Kumar actively involved in the campaign? I hope he is taking responsibility for mobilising voters in his areas. And, his committed grassroots supporters, what about them? I believe they are so committed to him that they will walk into wildfire if Kumar asks them to!"

"Yes, Manoj *bhai*, I have no idea how you managed this—a miracle of sorts—he is very supportive. In fact, he is giving useful suggestions. He has asked me not to worry at all about his pockets of influence. We all know that he has significant influence over this constituency."

"That's good. But if I were you, I would watch Kumar very closely. I would not trust him to be a part of my top decision-making body for this particular election. A veteran of many political battles, he is shrewd and also miffed. This is a lethal combination in politics. Be very careful."

The last few prophetic words struck Suresh Ahluwalia. Encouraged by the enthusiastic support, he had so far engaged the old hand in all high-level meetings. At no point in time had the wily politician allowed him to doubt his commitment and loyalty. But Suresh Ahluwalia saw immense logic in what the party president said.

Durjoy Kumar would have weighed the various options at hand. If he revolted, the party would undoubtedly expel him, leading to a slow but sure demise of his political career. If he showed sincerity in helping the party win the contest, his stature as a loyal soldier would soar. A win for the party might even bring him handsome rewards. But rewards would not placate a snubbed politician. Indeed, there was nothing for him to gain from a Robin Garg win. However, if the party lost the election despite his wholehearted support, Durjoy Kumar would be the undisputed claimant for the ticket in the next parliamentary election. Suresh Ahluwalia reluctantly admired the sharp foresight of his boss. The best bet for the smarting veteran was to exhibit absolute loyalty to the party and quietly work towards its defeat.

Suresh Ahluwalia decided to beat Durjoy Kumar in his own game. He planned to continue inviting the senior politician for all crucial meetings but take every strategic decision in his absence. It was not a route free of hazards. There was a fair chance that the crafty man would sense this game. Nonetheless, Suresh Ahluwalia opted to choose the option that seemed less risky at the time.

The same afternoon, Harsh Malhotra had called a meeting of his social media team and an external public relations consultant the party had recently contracted to help them with an image makeover. Losing two consecutive national elections had been hard on the party. Their high command decided to seek professional help from a reputed firm. Since then, senior executives from the consultancy were part of all strategy meetings, often to the disquiet of its senior leaders.

Not wasting any time in pleasantries, Harsh Malhotra got to business right away. "You all know what we are up against in this election. NPP's overwhelming grip over social media for the last decade has cornered us time and again. Now, they own most mainstream media. You have to do what it takes to beat them at their own game. We have made extensive plans involving most of our assets, but a lot will depend on your work.

"We have collected critical data for you. The files you have now contain confidential information that debunks certain myths about the opposition candidate. He is a hard-hearted businessman who lets his wife die rather than lose a business contract. NPP would like people to believe their candidate has not married again due to undying love for his departed wife and that he has dedicated his life to strengthening her dream NGO. But the reality shows something else. You have a direct report from one of his trainees who had to leave her job due to his harassment just a few months after his wife's death. It is a formidable challenge to the public portrayal of his character—enough fodder for your stories. Any questions?"

The public relations consultant asked, "What about the independent candidate?"

Harsh Malhotra replied, "That one is a real surprise. No one thinks she has any real chance of winning this election. That is good *and* bad news. It is good to be able to write off an opponent. So then why has the lady filed her nomination papers at all? Is there a game plan that we don't see? We should have no doubt that this candidate will cut into our votes. She is a reputed doctor and she belongs to a well-known family. Further, our constituency has significant number of minority votes. I suspect a sinister design behind this surprise nomination. We are looking into it. Meanwhile, you focus, for now, on the NPP challenge."

Meanwhile, Srikant Tiwari and his team met Shazia in a nondescript Rajouri Garden house. They showed some of the campaign material to Shazia and discussed an action plan for the next few days. Shazia, as expected, did not have any comments. She was, however, intimidated by her tight schedule. The campaign plan consisted of various rallies, public engagements, door-to-door canvassing and press meets. She received three different drafts for her public speeches. She would be asked to deliver one of them depending on the specific audience. Srikant Tiwari asked, "I believe the NPP President had asked if you and Purnima Bhatt have history together. They still think you do. Do you want to talk about it? It may help us in the campaign."

Shazia had no intention of talking about her enmity with Purnima. She was sure that a reference to those days would bring the spotlight back on herself—her love for a boy from another community, clash with closest friends, the drunken brawl—and things would get out of control. The farmhouse incident would unfairly paint her as a jealous and selfish individual. The muck would stick to her otherwise clean image long after the elections were gone. She believed Purnima would also not risk going public with their teenage fracas. Considering Purnima's impending defeat as a fitting punishment, Shazia felt there was no need for personal slander.

"No. I said this before as well. There is nothing as such. You made me an offer, I took some time to think about it, and later I accepted. That's it."

Srikant Tiwari sighed. "Well, then, we take your word for it. We hope we do not get any surprises later. I must tell you that this is going to be wild. No good can come from getting major surprises during the election campaign."

Shazia left their first formal strategy meeting on a happy note. Though the schedule was frightening, she was pleased that the campaign was on a reasonable scale. With nearly no chances for a win, she preferred low-key electioneering.

Late Thursday night, three senior politicians had a covert meeting in a two-bedroom apartment of a middle-income group housing society in Vikaspuri. Durjoy Kumar met two of his close confidantes to review and thrash out their action plan for the next few days.

Kumar addressed his colleagues. "The good news is that I have been a part of the highest decision-making committee for the election. Ahluwalia discusses all major issues with me, and he values my inputs. So, we shall be on top of whatever the party is planning at any point in time and will adjust our plans accordingly. For now, they have advised the social media team to unleash a major offensive to malign the UNDP candidate personally. We are trying to find data on both the candidates, not counting that silly independent candidate. Once we have useful information—either *for* the opposition or *against* ours—we shall feed them to the right people in the parties. Have you briefed our block-level workers properly? They shall be decisive factors in this election, like always. What do you have so far?"

His confidante reported on the block-level activities in detail. Durjoy Kumar was happy that an elaborate campaign against the party candidate had already commenced in parts of the constituency where he held significant clout. He was confident that the usurper would find it very difficult to make inroads in those areas.

The senior politician said, "Don't worry. They are all as upset as we are. They will take up the party's electoral assignments as loyal soldiers but ensure poor execution. In fact, they are asking for my permission for some anti-campaigning. They want revenge on the party leadership for the injustice done to you. I am holding them back with great difficulty."

Durjoy Kumar replied, "That's good. Our focus should be on block-level work. Whatever investigative work we do on the candidates' profiles, given our limited resources, our reports are unlikely to better theirs. Besides, feeding negative information on our candidate to the opposition is fraught with high risks; it can potentially take us all down. But the ward-level activities and the door-to-door initiatives are entirely in our hands. It is difficult for the party to monitor such acts in a campaign and impossible to retrace after the election results are declared. Stay active, do not campaign for the party, and furtively encourage and facilitate UNDP canvassing activities. Talk to the opinion leaders, highlight how the ghost of internal politics is devouring the party—how injustice has been done to a devoted senior party veteran and an outsider imposed—but do not ever explicitly ask them to vote for the opposition. No one should be able to quote any of our supporters. You must understand this well since you have to further explain this clearly to our grassroots workers.

"We may meet again in a week. I will call you from the new number that I gave you if anything important comes up. Do not save that number with my name."

They moved out of the apartment keeping some gap between their exits.

Back home, Shazia reviewed her speeches before going to bed. She was surprised that the drafts had contradictory things to say on various issues. A stranger to politics, it did not make any sense to her. A skilled politician would understand the obligation to say different things at different times based on what motivated the audience and what would lead them to believe that the person giving the speech would save them from their daily struggle for survival.

26

"Do you see a future in *us*?"

The blunt question had disconcerted Robin. He had been searching for an answer to this question ever since their United Coffee House meeting. Afraid that the surreal reunion was nothing more than a chance get-together with a long-lost friend, he had wanted to ask her the same question but could not gather enough courage to do so.

He got up, walked to the far end of the hall, and looked at a vitrine containing beautiful showpieces. One of the shelves displayed high-quality crystals. He picked up a Swarovski lotus and brought it closer to his eyes. The diffused light from a nearby lamp bounced off the sparkling petals creating an exquisite display.

Purnima was afraid she had been aggressive in asking the question. In order to relax the tension, she said teasingly, "Careful, that crystal is delicate. If it breaks, her heart will break as well—she had personally picked that up from the Swarovski Crystal World store in Innsbruck!"

Walking up to Robin, she stood very close and continued, "Robin *da*, this is a problem with me. If I feel close to anyone, I don't hesitate to open up my mind—with zero concern for diplomacy and restraint. I have lived my life with the burden of not asking you. Now, I wanted to make amends by asking a direct question. If I have crossed my limits, sorry. Please assume that I did not ask this."

Robin turned to face Purnima, walked inches closer, and held her arms with both hands. Looking deep into her eyes, he said, "Yes, the answer is *yes*."

Purnima was trembling. "What did you say, Robin *da*?"

"Yes, I said *yes*, I *do* see a future in us. Do *you*?"

"I do, Robin, I do."

Purnima broke down again. This was the first time she addressed Robin only by his name. Robin loved it. He quipped, "Great! Finally, you did it! That's how I want you to call me, Purnima!"

Robin held a weeping Purnima in his arms. He led her to the sofa and helped her settle back on her seat. A few strands of hair that had parted way from her neat hair-do fell into her eyes and dropped down to her chin. Robin held them by his fingertips and guided them to where they belonged.

"Robin sounds so good! Stay with it, please. Another drink?"

Without waiting for an answer, he walked back to the cabinet and brought her some more vodka. After making another drink for himself, he joined Purnima on the sofa.

Unsure of what to say next, both hoped that the other would say something. Robin picked up his glass, had a good look at the intense golden Speyside beauty, relished its fresh fruit and flower on the nose, and took a large sip. He held the drink in his mouth for a while to feel its rich notes of almond, sweet spice and fruit. He savoured the lingering spicy finish. The experience helped him organise his thought process.

"Purnima, we definitely have something going on here. Given how we feel for each other; we shall do ourselves grave injustice if we do not grab this second chance. Now, the challenge is: how do we handle the next few weeks? Our respective parties oblige us to go all out to win this election. How do we handle this campaign, the result, and the aftermath, and at the same time build further on our relationship?"

Purnima recovered enough to speak, "I am at a loss, Robin. I am ready to renounce my political ambitions for a happy personal life. I was not excited about running for Parliament in any case. I only agreed because there are a few people to whom I am unable to say no. Now, it is not possible to quit at this stage—I know there are a few days left to withdraw the nomination—as I will humiliate the party that has reposed so much faith in me. More than that, I will lose the goodwill of some people I hold in high esteem.

"However, I can happily lose and let you become a member of Parliament. I reject your party's ideologies and detest many of their political actions. I hate a few things your government has done and lament many things that they have intentionally not done but should have. But why should I bother? You win, and after the elections, I quit politics."

Robin took another sip of his drink and said, "I could repeat what you have just said. I am also not desperate to become a member of Parliament. However, I joined the party sometime back of my own accord. I like some of their agenda. I also thought being a member of the ruling political party would help me improve and further expand my NGO, something close to my heart. I, *too*, do not care who wins this election. And, I cannot withdraw now for the same reasons as you. Apart from our obligations, it is not a good idea to upset political bigwigs. If we leave them high and dry after they have trusted us with their ticket, they are not going to be kind to us for a very long time. They are merciless when it comes to defending their own interests."

"Okay, a few things are clarified," said Purnima. "While we further build on our relationship, none of us withdraws the nomination. We do not care which of us wins this election; we shall celebrate the result either way. All of this sounds perfect. But how do we manage ourselves in the next few weeks? Fierce competitors in public and close friends in private!"

Robin thought for a moment and asked, "What about the independent candidate, Dr Shazia Hameed? Any idea about her? Everyone is surprised by her candidature. Since she is also a doctor, do you know her by any chance? Shouldn't we be concerned about her?"

Purnima was not sure of how best to answer. She was quite certain that Shazia had filed the nomination papers only to reduce her chances of a win. However, there could be other political explanations as well. In any case, she did not see any sense in discussing a friendship that had ended so bitterly long back. Acknowledging the long-buried relationship would invariably involve detailing everything that had happened, including their nasty fight at the farmhouse. She considered it prudent to deny any links with the independent candidate.

"All of us are surprised by this nomination out of nowhere. I would not give an independent contestant a chance in this election. I believe we should be concerned about ourselves."

A worried-looking Robin—the chin resting on folded hands and the eyebrows touching each other over a shrinking glabella—shuffled uncomfortably on his seat and said, "This, I am afraid, does not have a simple solution. Going by what we have seen in recent elections, the bitterness, unrestrained character assassination, childish one-upmanship, and at times violent canvassing by the two parties has often been out-of-control. These guys will even exhume the dead to sully the opponent's image. I am sure people on either side are working overtime to discover, and if necessary, fabricate the missteps in our past. They have a powerful machinery and ample resources to do so. They employ consultants and investigative agencies. The damned social media has been a great gift since they can take their message and stories directly to those they wish to brainwash.

"It will be naïve for us to sit here and agree to have a clean and respectable contest. What *we* say or do in public shall only be a small part of our overall communication with the electorate. So, be ready for a few surprises. They are coming your way very soon."

"You scare me, Robin! How I wish I could just run away from all this!"

"You can't. So, let's do the best we can. Let's go through this campaign with a clear understanding between us. Our relationship—even that we know each other—must remain a closely-guarded secret between us; well, actually the three of us now. We shall avoid meeting each other till the election results are declared. If we must meet for any reason, we must ensure that no one can track us. We shall not personally attack each other in our campaign rallies. Though we shall not be able to control the propaganda unleashed by our parties, we must resist personal vilification in our direct interactions with the electorate. Otherwise, our relationship, in the long run, may get hurt beyond repair. Do you think this makes sense?"

"Makes a lot of sense, Robin. I will brief Radha as well; you do not have to worry about her. As a journalist, she may have to cover the election, but she would not do anything to hurt me. As I told you earlier, she is the most reliable person I know.

"Our association in Bangalore was so exceptionally private that I haven't talked to anyone about it. Even my best friends have never heard your name. A few knew of my crush on a man much older than me, and that is it. You surely haven't referred my name to anyone; you never had strong feelings for me anyway." Robin did not miss her mischievous smile as she said this.

"Only we know about our love that has always been platonic. No one can think of us as *together* unless, of course, they trace us now. So, all agreed."

She paused, as if struck by a thought. "Does it mean we shall not even hear from each other till the results are out? That's harsh!"

Robin smiled and said, "I have a solution for that. Keep this SIM card, a prepaid connection loaded with some credit. Please activate this card tonight in a spare handset. Even if the handset you are using has an empty slot for a second SIM, please use a different handset. Tomorrow morning, I will call you at this number from a new mobile number. Now onwards, you will call me only at that new number using your new SIM. Please do not call my regular number under any circumstances till all this is over. I suggest you delete my present number from your handset's phone book if you have it there."

Purnima responded, "Thanks for this. It did not occur to me that our phones may be tapped. You bought two new prepaid connections in your name today?"

"Not in my name. One in the name of my houseboy, other in name of my driver. I'm trying to be as discreet as possible."

"This is great planning! That means you have come prepared with the new SIMs—you knew what was to happen in our discussion this evening—that we shall reach this kind of an agreement?"

"No, I did not. However, if we had no agreement, I lose the cost of two prepaid SIM with some credit, that's it!"

"Impressive, Mr. Robin Garg!"

"Thank you Dr Purnima Bajaj Bhatt."

"Come, let's end this with a warm hug," said Purnima with open arms. Robin walked into her arms for an embrace, tight and passionate on this occasion. They froze for a while.

Behaving like a child after a forbidden act, Purnima moved away abruptly and said, "I think it's time to call Radha, shall I?"

Robin, trying to regain his poise, smiled and said, "Must we?"

Radha responded to Purnima's knock, "Coming guys! Give me a minute, please."

She came out as chirpy as ever and addressed both of them. "Hey, are you guys done with your consultations? The movie's climax is not over yet. Clyde and Bonnie are alive and kicking! Is everything all right here?" Without waiting for an answer, she continued, "Oh, the poor kebabs! You have been very unfair to them. And you did not even touch the samosas! I am going to give them the respect they deserve." She picked up a samosa and took a large bite.

"Haha, we have cleaned up your bar, though," jested Purnima.

"I am glad you did that! I love people who do justice to my well-stocked bar! Shall I serve dinner? Well, not a proper dinner, though. It's going to be the very basics."

"Sure, thanks," Robin answered gratefully.

"Yes, time for dinner. And please do not be so formal to talk about the spread. Come, let me give you a hand," said Purnima as she followed Radha to the kitchen.

"May I offer some help?" asked Robin. Radha shouted back, "Yes, sure, you can help by having a great appetite."

Robin felt much relieved as he left the apartment after dinner. On his way home, he crooned his all-time favourite song, *Lady in Red*:

I've never seen you looking so lovely as you did tonight,
I've never seen you shine so bright.

It was no coincidence that Purnima had been wearing red silk.

Tucked inside his lonesome bed, he reflected on the beautiful evening. Never having been as happy since Ritu had left, he turned left and stared at the empty pillow. He imagined Purnima resting her head on it, clothes unchanged, hair still the way it was styled earlier in the evening. He lovingly touched her hair, making sure the hairdo was intact. He then felt her cheeks and let the fingers roll down to her chin, her neck, and then to the cleavage that teased him all evening from the shelter of a low neckline top. A pleasing twinge moved down his chest.

The late-night call from the party office brutally brought him back to reality; the meeting next morning was advanced by an hour.

He got up earlier than usual, went to the extended sit-out downstairs with his cup of tea, and sat on the left chair. Moments later, he abruptly got up and sat on the other chair. It was a rare sight. The houseboy, passing through the hall after dusting the entrance, was shocked to see his boss sitting on the verboten chair. Robin noticed his dazed look and asked, "What happened? Anything?"

The houseboy answered awkwardly, "Nothing sir, nothing at all," and moved on. Sipping his tea, Robin resolved to let hope win over his past agony. He had to move on. For that, such symbols had to go.

Spending some more time in the apartment, Purnima briefed Radha on her discussions with Robin Garg. Radha promised her absolute confidence. She reassured that, even if she covered the election in any manner, her reports would not personally attack Robin. She further assured Purnima that her house was open to them anytime they wished to get together again. Purnima slept well that night. When she woke up, the busy schedule ahead did not bother her; she had to somehow bear with the electioneering nuisance and get ready for a happy time ahead with the man she always loved.

27

Tim Jacob was happy about the latest lead he had received from one of his associates in Bangalore. He took a flight to Bangalore early Monday morning. His first scheduled stop was the Central School in Victoria Layout.

The information collected from the meetings with the principal and two senior teachers set to retire in a few weeks was so encouraging that he cancelled two unrelated appointments to devote the remaining time in the city to interview Arvind Balakrishnan. The school records did not have his telephone number, but they gave him the office address registered with the school long back. Taking his chances, Tim Jacob assumed that the address location was likely to remain the same for a family business running for generations. He was correct in his assessment. However, the receptionist informed him that Arvind was in his farmhouse, far away from the city, with official guests from abroad. On his insistence, she reluctantly connected Tim to her boss. Though uninterested in taking a call with his guests around, he knew it would be reckless to refuse the chief editor of an influential publication.

"Good afternoon, Mr. Jacob. I believe you have been trying to get in touch with me. What can I do for you?"

"Well, first of all, I know you have guests, and I appreciate you taking the call nevertheless. I wanted to talk to you about something that is not easy to do on the phone. Is there a way I can meet you? I promise that I will not take more than half an hour."

"It is always a pleasure to meet respected journalists like you. But I am not sure how it will work. I cannot leave this place till my guests depart for the airport. How long are you in Bangalore?"

"I am afraid my flight is this evening."

"Oh! Then it is difficult."

"How about this—I change my booking to a late-night flight, and I come over to your farmhouse if you can spare that much time. I will then drive to the airport from your place."

Arvind thought for a moment and replied, "Well, you can do that. But it will not be a pleasant drive at this time of the day. By the way, may I know what this is about?"

"Sure, although it may not be of much interest to you, personally. It is about the West Delhi Parliamentary by-election."

Trying to hide his unease, Arvind said, "Politics and me! We stay very far from each other, Mr. Jacob. How come you want to take so much trouble to meet me on such a topic!"

Tim Jacob laughed and replied, "Don't worry, sir. As I said, it is nothing that involves you personally. More when we meet. I shall take the location from your office and leave for your farmhouse right now."

"Oh, don't bother to take locations. Be my guest; I will ask one of our company cars to bring you here."

"No, let it be. My taxi will take me to the airport after our meeting."

"My company car will do the same, sir. Please, let your cab go. As it is, you will not find it easy to locate this house. So, kindly have a cup of our special filter coffee. Meanwhile, our car will be ready to bring you here. I will instruct my secretary right now. See you then, Mr. Jacob."

"See you. Thanks a lot, Mr. Balakrishnan."

When Tim Jacob reached the farmhouse, Arvind received him in a separate room away from his foreign guests.

"Welcome, Mr. Jacob. My sincere apologies that you had to travel so much to ask me a few questions. I am aware that you have a flight to catch. So let's start. I have already asked the boys to serve us some coffee with a few special snacks of this state."

"I thank you for taking time off your busy schedule to see me. Much appreciated. Now, coming to the point, I understand you had two very close friends, Shazia and Purnima, in your school—the Central School in Victoria Layout. You may be aware that both of them are standing in a parliamentary by-election in Delhi. We are doing a story on this important event. Since the candidates grew up in this city, I am meeting some of their old friends to know more about their childhood. We came to know that you had very close relationships with both of them, particularly Shazia. Please, would you be kind enough to tell me something about them—their relationship and your relations with each of them."

Arvind was surprised by the precise information the journalist already had. He wondered if the man knew everything and was just looking for validation. With two choices in hand—either refute any relations with both candidates and risk being confronted with irrefutable facts or accept what he had said and risk an awkward situation of narrating childhood melodrama—he opted to stay with the truth. With no stakes or interest in a Delhi election, he had nothing to lose by sharing facts. On the other hand, hiding the truth could irreversibly hurt his personal integrity if subsequently exposed.

After their meeting, Tim Jacob hurried to the airport. He could barely wait to work on the report that would hit the internet no later than Wednesday morning. It would be a sensational newsbreak with substantial bearing on the election.

Arvind took some time to get over the crafty interview. Such were Tim Jacob's interrogation skills that he had ended up revealing substantial details, much more than he had initially intended to.

The same morning, Durjoy Kumar sent one of his men to Lucknow to investigate a sketchy lead he received on Robin Garg about his little-known bachelor years in the city. The man returned the next day with sensational information. Fed up with the noisy, crowded parties every weekend, the neighbours had complained to Robin Garg's landlord in the posh Gomti Nagar neighbourhood. When Robin did not heed two warnings, the landlord reported him to the police. The cops caught him and his friends red-handed with recreational drugs during a late-night raid. A day after he had spent a night in the police station, the landlord threw him out of the apartment. He had to put up at a colleague's place for a few days before finding a newly leased property in Hazratganj. Durjoy Kumar was over the moon—rave parties, drugs, and reckless youth were ageless fodder for juicy anti-campaigns.

On Tuesday night, someone left an unmarked envelope for Harsh Malhotra with a brief note inside. It read: *This piece of information may be of great interest to you. The NPP candidate Robin Garg was, and probably still is, a drug addict. Going by his reckless youth, he is a man of questionable character. He had to be evicted from his apartment in Lucknow's Gomti Nagar after a drug squad arrested him and his friends with call girls, all high on alcohol and drugs. It happened during a late-night raid after the police had received intelligence of repeated drug abuse. They found drugs in his possession, and he spent the night in a lock-up. The neighbours had reported that such parties were a weekly affair that led to considerable nuisance. The grapevine has it that he made a name for himself in the city's youth circles for doing drugs and womanising during his short stint there. Multiple sources in Lucknow corroborate this account. If you wish to run your independent checks, you are welcome. In that case, the following references shall be useful.* The note then listed details of the locality, police station, and names of the neighbours.

Harsh Malhotra carefully looked at the document. There was no clue as to its source. Whoever it was must badly want the NPP candidate to lose. It could certainly not be from his party cadres, otherwise they would have come out into the open to claim credits. It could also be from a well-meaning citizen who did not want to get drawn into a political crossfire.

There was a third possibility. There could be a significant revolt within the NPP ranks. So much so that the disgruntled group wanted their official candidate to lose the election and they dug into their own candidate's past in search of dark spots to feed the opposition. It was an exciting possibility for UNDP. Infighting within the opposition ranks was a dream for any political party. Internal discord often snowballed into revolts with far-reaching implications for the ultimate results. Harsh Malhotra had a feeling that the latest incendiary feed on the NPP candidate might not be the last.

After a hectic day of campaigning that included a series of meetings with party workers in his house, Robin retired to his bedroom. The head of his NGO had joined the campaign for the first time. The man was least interested in politics. As a committed social worker, he would have never joined an election campaign if he had a choice. But he could not ignore a request from his boss. His job was well cut out—to accompany Robin to rallies with sizeable Poorvanchali participation in the audience. He was a talented singer who loved to croon to the tunes of popular Bhojpuri numbers. The mandate was to be the cheerleader—to regale the audience with his songs before the political speeches began.

The party workers were delighted since they knew the peppy songs would set the right tone for successful public rallies. However, after everyone left his house, Robin allowed his apprehensions to return. He was nervous about the likely adverse effects on his NGO's performance in the long run and regretted that he had not been able to convince the party leadership to not drag his NGO executive into electioneering. Robin believed the expected nominal upswing in votes was not worth the risks, given his clear priority of Ritu's World over his politics.

Suresh Ahluwalia reviewed the stories created by his social media team. He did not like most of them because they lacked teeth. He told the team, "Social media posts must instantly hit hard. In case the reactions from the target audience turned out to be mixed, or if the opposition aggressively cries foul, or the Election Commission objects, all you have to do is withdraw the posts from the media. But by then, we would have achieved the desired impacts on the electorate."

He gave them another day to come up with a more vigorous campaign. He reminded them that the polling date was less than two weeks away, and the social media battle must peak without any further delay.

Durjoy Kumar toured some of his strongholds, ostensibly to gather support for his party candidate. He was happy that not many posters for the NPP candidate were put up in his areas. In fact, most of the preferred locations were occupied by the opposition. When the party officials accompanied him to the meetings, he pulled up the workers for not doing enough and gave fiery speeches to enthuse them. His senior party colleagues were happy and grateful to Durjoy Kumar for his selfless loyalty to the party. Feedback on his dedicated and generous efforts promptly made its way back to the party higher-ups.

Shazia Hameed was happy so far. She had adjusted well to the canvassing pace. Unused leaves in her account and enthusiastic support from hospital seniors allowed her to concentrate fully on the election without worrying about her medical duties. Nevertheless, not used to running around so much regularly, she was exhausted after the first few days. Throbbing chest pain on Tuesday night made her uncomfortable for a few minutes, but she fully recovered in less than an hour. The sermon from her husband, who believed the campaigning stress was taking a toll on his wife's health, bothered her more than the chest pain. Mohammed asked if there was still time to stop the madness. Shazia promised to go through a medical examination before moving on with the campaign the next day.

She consulted a cardiologist in her hospital, did a blood test, ECG and echocardiogram, and got a confirmation that there were no new health issues. Delighted, she shared the good news with her husband and left for a meeting with Srikant in Rajouri Garden on schedule.

Shazia enjoyed the attention received on her campaign trail. She was thrilled to see her portraits on scores of posters displayed in prominent parts of the constituency. Her speeches improved with every delivery, and the press meets packed more punches as the campaign progressed. Srikant had to put up an act to praise Shazia in her first few public interactions as a kind effort to encourage a newcomer in politics. But with time, his compliments became more natural since she demonstrated remarkable spontaneity. As she basked in the glory of unprecedented publicity and her confidence grew in leaps and bounds, Shazia wished she had a genuine chance of winning the contest.

She had no idea of what was to come her way.

28

Media reports rarely drove so many people to a collective frenzy the way the recent *The Third Eye* scoop did. Usually, reactions to a sensational exposé were typical and predictable: one part of the political community ran for cover while others gleefully watched the fun and added as much spice to it as they could. *The Third Eye's* Wednesday afternoon post was unique in many ways. It surprised everyone on either side of the fault line. Some of them were angry, some confused, and a few disappointed. But everyone was shocked.

Shazia received a call from Srikant Tiwari during her lunch break. "What is this we are reading in this darned e-magazine? I asked you repeatedly, and you denied it repeatedly. This is not the way one works in a team, Dr Shazia. I have been working my guts out for your campaign, and now this blow! It is so disappointing!"

"What are you talking about, Tiwari *ji*?"

"Please read the cover story on *The Third Eye* today. If what they write is true, I can only say that you have been very unfair to us. If you believe they are planting a story, then you need to vehemently deny it and sue them for messing around with you. First, please read the report and revert to me quickly, please."

"Okay, I will. Thanks."

Manoj Seth was raging in his call to Suresh Ahluwalia. "Suresh *ji*, it is pathetic! Your team must be one of the poorest I have among all the states. You selected a candidate for a covert, critical operation, and you have not done even basic research on her. How does such a thing happen? Don't you and your team feel terrible reading this report? Please make a decent counter plan right away. Otherwise, this scoop will end up helping the opposition and our strategy will boomerang to take *us* down. I give you tonight to come up with an effective counter-strategy."

On the other side of the fence, Harsh Malhotra was upset with his candidate. Even if Purnima Bhatt had no prior indication that her friend would contest the election, it was inconceivable that she did not recognise Shazia after the nominations were made public. He read the explosive revelation in *The Third Eye* again and slumped on his office sofa in sheer disgust. If the report was correct, there could be sweeping repercussions. It was hard for anyone to ignore reports released by the prestigious publication. He was too shocked and disappointed to call up Purnima to enquire.

Radha was hurt as well. She sounded upset when she called Purnima, "Darling, you disappoint me! I am surprised that you have not told me about your friend. Even if you did *not* know about her intentions beforehand, you could not have missed her name after she had filed her nomination papers. Do you know the implications now? I know how the voters as well the political parties react to such bombshells. Each party shall create and plant sub-stories based on this one designed to suit their game plan. And the electorate? Unless they get a plausible explanation, the swing voters will desert both you and the independent candidate. But all of these are secondary issues. More important, I cannot believe that you did not share this with me though you have been upfront with me about a relationship with much bigger political consequences."

"My dearest, are you talking about *The Third Eye* post?"

Yes, of course! What else?"

"Well, then, it was not my intention to hide this from you. Even Robin *da* does not know about it. He must be angry with me as well. The fact is, I have not talked to Shazia ever since we left school. Do you get that? We are talking about decades, not years. Yes, she was my school friend for six years, but our friendship did not end on a happy note. Life has moved on. I did not think that an antique, forgotten story of childhood friendship needed to be rehashed for this election. I used to know a girl called Shazia. This independent candidate is Dr Shazia Hameed, whom I do not know at all, Radha. Please understand."

Radha thought for a while before responding. "Well, you see it that way. Unfortunately, the murky world of politics will not take it so easily. Anyway, it does not bother me much except that I felt a bit let down. But I'll let it pass. But you should get ready for fireworks from all sides. I have to go. Bye for now."

Purnima was on a coffee break during a meeting with her campaign managers. She repeatedly looked at her phone in anticipation of another call, expected sooner rather than later. Robin would likely be furious; she had no clue how to respond to him. But her phone did not ring.

After the meeting, she walked into Harsh Malhotra's room as per his request.

"Please, come in, Purnima. I understand the campaign is on schedule."

"Yes, thanks, Malhotra *ji*. All credit to you and your great team."

"Now, can you please explain to me *The Third Eye* report? It is incomprehensible that you did not consider it proper to brief me on your friendship with the independent candidate. It may now lead to a lot of complications."

Purnima took a minute to sort out her thoughts and said, "First of all, she is *not* my friend. I have not met her or had a word with her in a quarter of a century. Yes, she was in my class in school, and we were good friends. That way, I have many friends and countless stories to talk about from my youth. I didn't see the relevance of a timeworn, buried relationship to this election. We had not parted on a happy note. I guess that's why we have not been in touch ever since. It is as simple as that, Malhotra *saab*. Now that this article has dressed up a regular teenage friendship as a political conspiracy, what can I say? It is blown so out of proportion that I find it amusing. If you wish me to do anything about it—give a fitting riposte, say nothing, or whatever—please advise. You can't be surprised that I have no great skills in political manoeuvring!"

"So, you have never met or talked to her after leaving school. Is that right—an unquestionable fact?"

"Yes."

"Do you think there are any reasons for her to nurse a grudge against you, something that she wishes to settle by reducing your chances of winning this election?"

"I do not think so. What you have read in the article is correct. We had a bitter end to our friendship due to a big misunderstanding. But to assume that Shazia has carried that teenage grudge to a mid-life political battle on the national stage— that would be stretching the imagination beyond limits."

"Okay, thanks for your frank clarification. Leave this issue with me. You focus on your campaign activities. If anyone questions you in the election meetings or press briefings, you handle it the way you have just done. Good luck!"

"Thank you, Malhotra *saab*."

She read the article once again, later in the evening at home. It was largely factual, apart from its dramatic analyses and inferences. Despite her by now well-rehearsed plan to effectively respond to an angry call from Robin Garg, her heart missed a beat every time the phone rang. There were five calls that evening—three from her campaign team, one from a patient, and the other from a close relative. Robin Garg did not call. It was most unlikely that he had not seen the report till then. She assumed that Robin was too upset with her to call. The thought of losing him yet again shattered her.

Earlier, Shazia retired to a quiet corner with her laptop and read the report:

A hidden agenda in the West Delhi parliamentary by-election?
It is straight out of fiction, suitable for a potboiler!

Since the news of a surprise independent candidate was made public after the nomination papers for the West-Delhi by-election were filed, political corridors have been abuzz with whispers. Earlier, there were debates in social media and the mainstream press about whether the SJP would field a candidate or leave this battle to the two main national political parties. It was clear to all concerned that the NPP and the UNDP will deploy all their resources to ensure a big win in this prestigious constituency. As far as national politics is concerned, a win or loss in this contest will not make much difference to the overall political equation in the house. However, for the political strategists in either party, this election goes well beyond the additional seat on the bench. UNDP needs to retain this seat to show that their win last time was not a fluke. Besides, they need this win to boost the morale of their party workers after the hammering they received in the previous national elections. For NPP, it is a must-win to avenge the last embarrassment in this constituency besides the urgency to retain their momentum for the forthcoming elections in key states.

SJP thought it smart not to spend their limited resources for a losing cause. But a 'brave' independent candidate, unknown and unprepared, considered it wise to file nomination papers and spend a personal fortune for electioneering, knowing well that she might even lose her deposit. This one has been a riddle for everyone. We wondered if this is a wealthy doctor's foolish adventure for a few weeks of sunshine. Or if there was something more than what meets the eyes? We checked up. The candidate has a well-paying job. She belongs to a respectable and resourceful family but is not rich enough to throw personal money into a national election just for a few weeks of publicity.

Our unrelenting search for some rationale behind this mystery took us to her days in Bangalore, where she had spent her youth. Lo and behold, what we found goes well beyond our expectations!

The unearthed information further strengthens our suspicion—not suspicion really, let's call it uneasiness—about the real motive behind this nomination.

The story continued with a stagy narration of her intimate friendship with Purnima—how inseparable they were in the high school years—and went on to talk about Arvind Balakrishnan and the troika that broke up in a rancorous country house fight. The account was reasonably accurate except for the intended dramatisation meant to excite readers. It was evident that the journalist had done extensive investigative work, including detailed discussions with Arvind Balakrishnan. There were some facts in the report that only Arvind knew apart from Shazia and Purnima.

The report ended in a way that raised more questions than it set out to answer:

We would have passed this off as a mundane story of teenage friendship, intimacy, jealousy, parties, alcohol-induced madness, bitterness and break-up. Under the present circumstances, we cannot do that. The question is whether this election has become a platform for an extended teenage rivalry? Is it possible that the sole intention of the independent candidate is to cut into the UNDP candidate's votes? Let us not forget that the independent candidate is from the same profession. That makes it so much easier to achieve this goal since they have shared links to the electorate.

But going by the way the independent candidate has campaigned so far, this interpretation does not stand up to scrutiny. If her entry is indeed a solo enterprise to settle old scores, her campaign should have attacked the UNDP representative directly and viciously. Unless there is a direct denigration of her bête noire, how will revenge be exacted? We do not see this happening. The doctor could have also chosen to canvass hard for the NPP and helped them with information to beat the UNDP candidate instead of jumping into the fray. She instead took the big step of personally contesting the elections. Is Shazia Hameed ready to spend so much of her personal wealth merely to reduce Purnima Bhatt's share of votes? It somehow doesn't add up.

Consider this—a possibility that comes to our mind, but we have no proof at this time—is there some ingenious political brinkmanship behind this move? Is one of the main contesting parties backing this candidate for a specific purpose? Or, even more interesting and tricky, is this a result of some undercover in-fighting within the rank and files of one of the national political parties? Either way, she would just be a political pawn deployed by a party at their cost. Then, why would a respectable doctor agree to play the role of a political poker chip unless there are some attractive personal gains? Has there been a secretive financial deal behind fielding a third candidate? We suspect, not a claim but a suspicion, there is an attractive bait behind convincing an unassuming doctor to jump into an unwinnable electoral contest.

One thing is beyond doubt—there are questions that cry for answers in this saga of the dark horse. The jury is still out. We shall continue our efforts to get to the bottom of this story. Please stay tuned.

Shazia was scared stiff. She had not anticipated such controversy while accepting the deal. The description of the events did not bother her; they were true but also very old. If and when confronted, she would brush the events aside as nothing but routine teenage excesses. But the clever insinuations were disturbing. It seemed as if the reporter knew about her deal with the party. If the party was exposed for their electoral deception, that would be their headache. However, if the journalist dug deep and somehow associated her nomination to the cash reward, she would lose face beyond any hope of recovery.

When Srikant picked up Shazia's call, he understood that she was agitated. "Tiwari *ji*, this is a terrible report. I am so sorry. I did not have a reason to hide it from you. It's just that I did not believe a teenage friendship dead more than two decades back was important enough to be discussed in a national election. The story is a docudrama, but its fundamentals are true. I have not met or talked to Purnima Bhatt—Purnima Bajaj as I had then known her—ever since we left school. That is the explanation for my not talking to you about it. I don't think anyone would wish to talk about their drunken teenage brawls. I thought if I referred to our childhood friendship, it would invariably lead to details of our break-up. I did not want to go there. Now, please help me. Please tell me, in case I have to do or say anything. I will lose face very badly among my friends and relatives if they come to know about our monetary deal. I am very disturbed now."

Srikant Tiwari replied, "Shazia *ji*, I understand. Don't worry about it. I still insist that you should have told me about it. We would have probably done something to pre-empt such a report. We know how to handle these things if we get to know about them early enough. But what has happened cannot be undone. Let's see how to manage it from now on. Don't worry about the reward. That is something only a handful of people know in our party. None of them will ever leak that to the press. As far as the party's strategy is concerned, we are working on it. We have handled worse challenges from the media. In any case, this is not a challenge thrown directly at us. These people attribute possible motives behind your nomination, hoping that someone will blink and go on the defensive. It is a blind shot. We shall do nothing of that sort. Let them do their research and throw their bait. We shall not bite, and they will never find out. I suggest you stay with the same explanation that you have just given me. Own up to the facts, laugh them off as a typical teenage mess, and stress that the two of you have not even been acquaintances for a quarter of a century, and hence, this is not a relevant issue for this election. Then, quickly divert them to the conventional election buzzwords. You will be all right."

The next day, the UNDP issued a press release accepting that Dr Purnima Bhatt and Dr Shazia Hameed had been classmates and good friends in high school. It further said that they fell out at the end of their schooling years and have never met since then. The press reporters persistently asked Shazia about her relations with Purnima. She responded as advised.

The NPP also issued a strongly worded press release: *We congratulate The Third Eye for their brilliant work and welcome such efforts from any quarter to get to the bottom of all political deception. We must have a clean election where the electorate can choose their representative in an environment free of all manipulations. It is a matter that demands urgent attention. We call upon UNDP leadership and the independent candidate to immediately explain their position on this momentous exposé. Our party shall focus on our campaign undeterred by our opponents' negative tactics. However, the question remains pertinent till a convincing explanation is made available. We note that neither of the concerned parties has refuted the report and hence believe that UNDP has fielded a friendly independent candidate to cut into NPP votes. We also know that the public shares our logical assessment. Such sinister designs will not be able to distract our wise voters. The people are solidly behind us. With their overwhelming support, our candidate shall win this election with a thumping majority.*

Purnima waited the entire Thursday in vain for a call from Robin Garg. Unable to wait any longer, she called him before going to bed. There was no response.

29

Wednesday was an awful day for Robin Garg. Till then, the canvassing had been running very smoothly. Buoyed by the promise of a happy future with Purnima, he ran an inspired campaign. He delivered energetic public speeches, held knowledgeable interactions with belligerent press reporters, deftly presented an adorable man-next-door image in door-to-door campaigns and provided valuable inputs in internal review meetings. It was all playing to a script. However, the canvassing changed gears after *The Third Eye* report. It was till now focused on the party's manifesto with minor variations to suit local aspirations. After the report was published, the campaign managers believed it was time to attack the opposition candidate personally in all their publicity. The party was getting ready to flood the internet with a barrage of Twitter, WhatsApp and Instagram posts to tarnish Purnima's public image. They wanted to project her as someone untrustworthy, selfish and of doubtful integrity.

Robin believed the sea change in approach was due to the report. A political rookie, he was unaware that personal attacks were an integral part of the present-day campaign strategies; they were always a part of the overall plan of his party. It usually intensified as the polling day got closer.

The news about Purnima's association with Shazia frustrated him. He believed it was too trivial for Purnima to hide from him, particularly in the backdrop of their budding relationship. However, he sympathised with her too. He appreciated that she might have her reasons to avoid talking about regrettable teenage interactions, more so with a man she had met after so many years, with whom she hoped to have a serious relationship. He considered calling Purnima to soothe her nerves immediately after reading the report. That's when Suresh Ahluwalia called him for an urgent meeting.

Robin walked into a room where, apart from the state president, three others waited for him. Suresh Ahluwalia spoke first. "Hello Robin! First of all, you are doing a great job so far. I must confess that we did not expect such professional work from a man in electoral battle for the first time. Keep it up, and we will soon see you taking the oath in the lower house of the Parliament."

"Now, the campaign has to shift to the next gear. A few things in this phase, running up to the polling day, may surprise you; you may feel like resisting them. But I want you to know that these are an integral part of the election process, and we shall not be the only ones in the game. The opposition, the press, corporates with vested interests, and many other unknown forces will definitely up the ante in the coming days. You need to focus on winning, even if it means stomping on someone else's feet once in a while. I understand you objected to a part of the speech prepared for your meeting this evening at Uttam Nagar. Please tell me, what is the issue?"

Robin replied in a low voice, "Thanks a lot for your kind words. I shall, of course, continue to do my best. Well, we have been doing good so far in all the meetings, drawing good crowds, thunderous applause, etc. We have always stuck to positive stuff—detailing our poll promises, promoting our party's track records, and things like that. Now, I am required to target the UNDP candidate personally. Where is the need for that? I mean, making statements doubting the integrity of a respectable woman! It is not required to win an election. It should not be so. I have serious issues with such an approach."

Suresh Ahluwalia smiled and said, "Robin, listen, I have seen many elections. This is how it goes. It is not enough to highlight your positives; you need to show the voters that the other options they have are dreadful. Besides sealing your own supporters' votes, such strategies help the fence-sitters decide. UNDP will do just the same, you wait. Whoever carries out a more effective campaign will ultimately win. Can I have a look at the objectionable part in the speech?"

Robin took out a paper and read a paragraph from it. "Quote, 'I want to ask you, do you think a woman who couldn't hold on to her marriage to a fine gentleman for even one year, that too when she had accepted the proposal after months of maintaining a romantic relationship, can hold on to you and our interests for five years without losing focus? Will she be able to stay with you during your good and bad days, look after your needs at all times without losing her patience? Our family is where it all begins. If she can't take care of her own family, she can't take care of others. Look at me. Many years have passed, but I still miss my wife, taken away from me by cruel destiny. I wish she were here by my side', unquote. What is the need for this in my speech?"

"Robin, you want to win this election as much as we want to. Have faith in us. We shall do what it takes—nothing more and certainly nothing less. So, please cooperate. It is only the beginning; more aggressive speeches are to come in the days ahead. I have asked these gentlemen to show you a few social media releases scheduled for the next few days. We are sharing these with you only to drive home the intensity of our efforts. They will be broadcast from unofficial accounts and will not involve you directly in any way. Be clear that we do not own, disown, comment, support or criticise any social media releases, except what is released by our official handle. We shall stay away from any comments on these posts and let them do their intended job on the electorate.

"I've got to leave for another meeting. You have some time before your next public engagement. Please spend a few minutes to check out some of their work. These are not up for discussion; they are for your information only."

After Suresh Ahluwalia left the room, Robin looked at some of the social media campaign templates. Feeling sick and helpless, he left the room in a hurry.

Left with no choice, Robin made only oblique references to Purnima in his evening speech. However, he took extra care to skip the derisive words proposed by the speechwriter. Robin felt ashamed to imagine what Purnima would think of him once she knew the details of his speech. Over and above his belief that maligning an opponent in a public meeting was wrong, he was conscious of his agreement with Purnima. He could claim ignorance of the party's social media excesses but he could in no way disown his own public statements.

He, by now, knew that the opposition would not be far behind in playing similar tricks; very soon, Purnima would also be obliged to talk personally against him. Her party would fiercely attack his personality on social media to prove him unfit for public office. Hence, he considered it sensible to wait for some time to talk to Purnima, with the hope that she would understand his helplessness after herself being instrumental in his vilification.

Purnima headed for her campaign headquarters early Thursday morning for an urgent meeting to discuss the next phase of canvassing activities. Harsh Malhotra presided.

"I believe we are making good progress so far. First of all, let me record our party's appreciation for the excellent work done by Purnima. I feel as if she had contested many elections earlier. But now, we get into a more complex phase in this contest. NPP will not hold back any punches from now onwards. We can expect wild personal attacks on our candidate—I believe he has already started it last evening in his speech in Uttam Nagar. Soon there shall be large-scale social media mischief. As we have seen before, there is no point in crying foul, and there is no use in going to the Election Commission with complaints. We have to counter them and hit them harder. We have managed and contained any adverse effects due to *The Third Eye* report reasonably well so far. There are some merits in their subtle insinuations—I also wonder if this is an NPP ploy to cut into our votes. However, that's a risky angle for us to exploit because the independent contestant was *our* candidate's good friend at one time, not *theirs*. Hence, we do not press this further and stay with our present stand. If they come up with new findings, we shall then take a call.

"I guess you're all ready to change the tempo of Purnima's election speeches? Pack some fire and aggression; make those guys run for a cover!"

After the meeting got over, Purnima received a new set of guidelines for her speeches. Parts of the text read:

Tell me, if a man chooses a business deal over his pregnant wife's life, should you trust him with your votes?

Fights and altercations between husband and wife are not new. Though unpleasant, such quarrels are natural when two persons live together. They blame me for my divorce. Mutually agreed separation of incompatible spouses are also not new in our society. No one likes or encourages divorce, but they happen when differences are irreconcilable. That is what had happened to me. There is no shame in it. Let me tell you where shame is. Think of a man who pretends to have a blissful married life but chooses a business deal over attending to his dying pregnant wife. That is shameful! But he has the cheek to take a dig at my divorce? Yes, I have had a divorce within the first year of my marriage. I do not blame my ex-husband—may God bless him! But doesn't a woman have a right to be happy? Will you trust people who throw muck at others without looking into themselves? You teach him a lesson on polling day so that no one dares to target a woman unfairly in the future.

Purnima shuddered in disgust. She had not agreed to such mudslinging. Throwing muck on others had never been a part of her persona. Besides, the draft was totally against the baseline she and Robin had set. She needed to talk to her party boss immediately.

"Malhotra *saab*, thanks for taking my call, and I am sorry to have to call you back so soon. But this matter is urgent." She continued without waiting for any response. "I have read some of the new guidelines for my election speeches. They are sick. With due regard, I wish to remind you that I am not a regular politician, and by nature, I cannot slander anyone this way. So, I cannot be a part of such a campaign even if that means losing the election."

"Purnima, while I understand your concern, let me make one thing clear to you. This election is not only for *you* to win or lose. The entire party machinery right up to the top is invested in retaining this seat. So, *please* do *not* consider this a personal contest. You should not speak as if you are the one to decide whether to win or lose. Having made that clear, let me now tell you that it does not help if only one party swears to play by the book. You may not know it but the NPP candidate has already started throwing muck at you from last evening. He has painted you as a self-centred, impossible woman who failed to hold a marriage together for even a year. He insisted that you are not good enough to be trusted with a public office."

"Robin Garg said that?"

"Yes, you need more? I'm not sure if you've seen a WhatsApp message that is doing the rounds since this morning. I guess you haven't. I am just sending that to you; see it and then call me back."

Purnima watched the short video in horror. Angry and disappointed, she played the clip again. After walking around the room to try and relax, she looked for the privacy of a restroom.

Inside the room, she stared at herself in the mirror. She had grown much older in recent weeks; she noticed a few wrinkles near her eyes that she had never seen before. The skin on her neck was not taut anymore. She wondered if the woman in the mirror was confused about her dreams for the rest of her life. Standing at the crossroads of politics and family, she doubted whether a mid-life crisis was driving her to tread hopelessly divergent paths. In riding two horses—political rivalry and personal bliss—at the same time, was she chasing a mirage? Looking at the mirror, she hated the miserable woman that looked back at her.

Moments later, a strong and assertive woman emerged. With a clear mind, she returned to her seat and replayed the video.

It showed a couple getting cozy on a medical college campus. Their books and the white gowns were scattered around them as their friends watched them from far. They ran around the campus, sang and danced, walked while holding hands, kissed and rolled over the lawns in an embrace, with old superhit love songs playing in the background. Suddenly the woman stopped. Staring at the man as though repelled, she said aggressively, "Enough now. You are not my friend anymore. I have to focus on my studies." The words 'Purima Chatt' repeatedly flashed near the woman's face. In the next frame, the woman, looking older, canvasses for votes in a dense neighbourhood. The caption read: *My next toy is a parliamentary seat! Ooh-la-la!* The video ended with the message: *Can you trust her with a serious public office?!* in big, bold letters, with music suiting a horror movie playing.

Purnima recognised the video for what it was. They had dug into her past for details of her short-lived romance with Anil Hazarika, another long-forgotten phase of her life. Speculating who would have leaked information on her age-old relationship, Anil was the first person she ruled out; he was too sweet a guy to turn so nasty, that too after so many years. After all, she had never done any harm to him.

She understood it was meaningless to swim against the tide. Minutes later, she accepted the templates for her speech with a few modifications.

Driving home that night, she pondered whether Robin was an active sponsor or a submissive collaborator in his party's smear campaign. He was breaking the agreement either way. She understood why he had chosen not to talk to her.

Radha forwarded another WhatsApp post to her when she was about to sleep. She seethed in rage after watching the video. She reached for her telephone handset.

30

Robin was not savvy with social media. Despite having accounts on all the popular platforms, he rarely visited them. However, Robin endeavoured to increase his presence after joining the electoral fray. His first and last engagements each day were with social media—make a few posts, 'like' as many as he could, write a tweet or two—in essence, do whatever possible to stay current in cyberspace.

Friday morning was no different. The first WhatsApp message was from Suresh Ahluwalia: *I warned you before, didn't I? See the video below. Don't get ragged, get ready for more! And, of course, prepare for a determined reprisal. Best.*

He could not believe anyone could upload such an offensive video for any reason, let alone for an electoral contest. In complete denial, he watched the video clip again. Abruptly getting up from the chair, he took a few deep breaths and paced around the room. As his fury weathered to disgust, he gathered himself and, with a steely face, he watched the video again through a politician's eyes. He was ready to hit back hard with the gloves off.

Two paramedics carried a heavily pregnant young woman on a stretcher to an ambulance parked in front of her house. From the stretcher, she begged her husband—in a formal suit with a briefcase in hand—not to leave her alone. The man gave his wife a stern look and drove away in a fancy car without looking back even once. The ambulance sped away in the opposite direction with the woman. In the next frame, the man smiled and shook hands with a group of formally dressed people in a posh environment. A caption read: *Ruben Gar—a dynamic businessman.* A hospital scene followed with the woman lying dead with a stillborn baby, people wailing around her. The subsequent frame, split into two, showed both the previous two frames side-by-side. The caption asked: *Will you trust such a man?!*

The opposition was willing to stoop to any level to defame him in front of voters, even if it meant cooking up stories and twisting facts. He was sure that his party would not sit idle. They certainly would hit back with worse reprisals. The gloves were off on either side. He and Purnima were now mere pawns in the hands of two powerful political parties who were out to do anything to win the election. With their personal détente made redundant by irrepressible external forces, their dream for a happy future was also in tatters. Weighing his options, he saw precious little that he could do to stop this madness. He could neither run far away from this madness nor avoid his numerous political engagements in the coming days. At the same time, he no more had the conviction to fight a battle he did not believe in anymore.

When Radha had picked up Purnima's call the previous night, she realised her friend was enraged. "What on earth is this, Radha? From where did you get this nonsense? It must have been on millions of phones before reaching you and me! Earlier today, I saw another such rubbish post on me; I forwarded it to you. Now, this incredibly filthy clip targeting Robin *da*! I did not agree to such cheap and dirty tricks when I agreed to contest the elections!"

"Purnima, relax, my friend. It is election time. You better get ready for worse. This campaign is not in your or Robin Garg's hands anymore. You can't control, you can't react, you can't quit! So, play on, dear. You signed up for contesting an election; now accept all the perks that come with it."

"Oh, that's great! You've been a great help, Radha. I am glad I called," said Purnima sarcastically and disconnected. Radha knew

Purnima was best left alone, that another call would follow early in the morning.

After seeing the video, it was Purnima's turn to stay away from Robin. She would find it difficult to have an honest conversation with him.

Later that morning, Robin received the video Purnima had seen the previous afternoon. It was clear that the main protagonists had only limited roles in the now all-out war. Any effort to change its course was futile.

The day brought many new surprises for both of them. With every new social media shock, their immunity grew exponentially. Nothing flustered them anymore.

Twitter was set ablaze with hashtags read and retweeted thousands of times:

Robin left on a business trip and let his heavily pregnant wife die! And you want to trust this man? Don't make a mistake, make the right choice. Your future is in your hands!

Family is everything. After destroying her own family within a year of marriage, she has now set out to 'protect' the interests of your family! Stop Purnima.

Did you know, caught partying with drugs and prostitutes, Robin was put behind bars? Such a man in the Parliament? No! Make the right choice. Your future is in your hands!

A few months of intense in-campus romance, and then she suddenly dumps her lover, gets married to a colleague, and dumps him too in months! Can you trust such a person to be a member of Parliament? Stop Purnima before she dumps you!

WhatsApp and Instagram carried these hostile posts. In one video posted on Instagram, the boss took a young intern out for dinner. After extra-friendly innuendo and unwelcome physical advances, he invited her to his apartment for a post-dinner coffee. The intern politely said no. The boss was angry and offended. The next day, he revealed several mistakes in her work and humiliated her in public. She resigned and walked out of the office like a person just freed from jail. There were no dialogues. The caption 'Ruben Gar' kept flashing near the boss. Another caption—*True story as told by the victim*—flashed at the bottom throughout the video. In the end, the final caption read: *My vote for this man? NEVER!*

After their objections fell on deaf ears, Purnima and Robin decided to boycott social media personally for the remaining days of canvassing. They made up their mind to maintain civility in what they controlled—their direct interactions with the media and the electorate.

However, they had not spoken to each other as yet.

In a further twist, *The Third Eye* released a cover page article on Saturday morning:

The independent candidate for the West Delhi by-election continues to challenge us with many unanswered questions. As we dig in deeper, the mystery only deepens!

The most likely scenario, as we infer till now, presents a story murkier than we had initially suspected. We carried out extensive investigations on various fronts—personal funds for campaign expenses, analysis of the campaign trail so far with focused scrutiny of the pockets of concentration and the areas missed out, a careful review of the speeches and the promotional material—and collected a large amount of data. Our experts have analysed them and correlated various perspectives to create a logical model. Our conclusions below are a result of this scientific approach.

We conclude that the independent candidate is fielded and financed by the NPP to cut into the UNDP votes. This covert move significantly reduces the probability of a UNDP win. It is not a baseless claim but the result of an elaborate modelling exercise on a real database.

The article then explained the method of data collection, the modelling technique, and predicted likely scenarios.

Shazia was understandably very disturbed after reading the report. She was aware that the investigation was precariously close to a reveal-all of her deal with NPP and it was now only a matter of time. She deeply regretted accepting the offer and cursed herself for the urge to take revenge for something that happened in her teenage years. She felt dizzy. When the recurring pain on her left side persisted, she cut short her campaign for the day and returned home. Though restricted to her bed for the rest of the evening, she did not share her distress with Mohammed. He had warned her enough. Now she wanted to run far away from the mess she had created for herself, but she knew it was too late. Scared of a reprimand yet again, she hid the chest pain from her husband and suffered alone in the bedroom. Mohammed chose not to disturb his overworked wife in her well-deserved repose. His wife hoped the pain would go away soon, the way it had in recent instances. The dull ache indeed disappeared after another hour. When she woke up after a sound sleep, she believed that the pain was nothing but the result of overwork and anxiety. She set out on her campaign schedule on time.

Harsh Malhotra fumed while reading *The Third Eye* report; it confirmed his suspicion that the nomination of an independent candidate was nothing but NPP's deceptive strategy to steal his party's votes. He pulled out the NPP press release in response to their first report. They had tried to deflect suspicion towards UNDP rather than going on the defensive for their disgraceful act. He believed such reprehensible political tactics must not go unchallenged.

Looking for additional ammunition in his armour, he got in touch with Arvind Balakrishnan and requested his help in campaigning for at least two days.

"Thanks for asking me, Dr Malhotra," said Arvind. "I will keep my promise. But I'm not sure what you expect me to do or say. Besides, I must make something clear. I have forgotten the bitter past and I do not want to be deeply involved in this political slugfest. So, I shall be brief in whatever interaction you plan for me."

"Please come over tomorrow. You may plan your return for the day after tomorrow. Please leave the rest to me."

He asked Aditi Kasbekar to fly to the capital on an overnight visit. Consistent with her stand, she resisted the idea of physically joining the campaign. However, he succeeded in obtaining her permission to record a telephone interview with her for replay during canvassing as necessary.

He called his most proficient spokesperson, explained Aditi's background along with a brief on the intended plan, and asked him to record an interview with her. Subsequently, he called for a press conference at four o'clock on Sunday afternoon.

Meanwhile, Suresh Ahluwalia had a closed-door meeting with his senior advisers and called for their press conference. It was a coincidence that both conferences were scheduled at the same time.

The media bosses struggled on Sunday afternoon to send reporters to two important events at the same time. With the battle getting more intense and hostile with each passing day and given the intrigue interwoven around the nomination of the independent candidate, they knew that the press meets would be explosive.

Harsh Malhotra took the lead in the UNDP's press conference.

"Ladies and gentlemen, our party has always stood for clean politics. We talk about our achievements, our plans for the future, our strengths, and our dreams. But this ruling party does not love a fair game. They know they have no chance of winning a fair game. So, they have unleashed all their dirty tricks on us. To start with, they have fielded an independent candidate, at their expenses, whose only job is to take away some of the voters they know would never support their divisive and retrograde policies."

He expounded on UNDP's clean campaign strategy, their achievements over the years, their secular credentials and the development plans for the West Delhi constituency. At the end of his speech, he said, "Let me introduce to you Mr. Arvind Balakrishnan, a successful businessman from a very reputed family in Bangalore. He was, at one time, close friends with both Purnima Bhatt and the independent candidate. I request him to say a few words to you."

Arvind, noticeably overwhelmed by the attention, cleared his throat and spoke slowly, "Ladies and gentlemen. I am not a great public speaker. I have given interviews related to my business but have never addressed so many eminent journalists at once. Also, I have never made any comments that could have political connotations. So, please bear with me. I will be brief and will be happy to take questions later if any.

"Purnima Bhatt and Shazia Hameed were the closest of friends in our class. One would rarely see one without the other for six years, whether in school or in other public places. I had special relationships with both of them. Shazia was in our school from before. Purnima joined in the later years. They had a bitter fight in one of our social gatherings over things that I do not wish to get into. There was a huge misunderstanding between them. As a matter of fact, Purnima was innocent. It was all a figment of Shazia's imagination.

"After that, we have never met. I'm not sure whether they have met again at any time. But one thing is clear. Shazia firmly believed that Purnima was a treacherous, scheming villain, and she lost her rosy plot only due to Purnima's manipulations. That is completely untrue. I know it for sure. While Purnima tried her best to rationalise Shazia's strange behaviour, Shazia blamed Purnima for everything and looked for revenge. Having been very close to both, I have reasons to believe that the independent candidate Shazia Hameed is standing in this election for one reason only—to prevent Purnima Bhatt from winning. She is not in the fray to win; certainly, she does not think she has even a remote chance to win. Who supports her politically and who finances her campaign are areas where I have my guesses—just the way any intelligent person would have. I have no comments to make on them. Thank you everyone."

Harsh Malhotra spoke, "Now, I want to play a recorded interview with a fine lady from Bangalore. She talks about her brief acquaintance with the NPP candidate. Please listen carefully."

Aditi Kasbekar's interview, smartly conducted by the interviewer with leading questions that painted Robin Garg as a predator of hapless young trainees, was replayed to a stunned group of journalists.

The last question in the interview was: "So, how would you summarise your views on Robin Garg, strictly based on your own experience, and do you believe he is fit for the role of a member of Parliament?"

She replied, "Well, strictly based on my *own* experience, I can say that he is pretentious, dishonest, and a male chauvinist. He is a business leader who mentally and physically exploits persons of the opposite sex using his position of control, someone who harassed young employees just months after his wife's sudden demise, and someone who is not trustworthy. As to the second part of your question, I think you can answer that yourself based on my answer to the first part."

The press conference continued with few more briefings followed by a question-answer session.

A few kilometres away from the UNDP office, NPP was conducting its own press conference. Suresh Ahluwalia made the introductory comments. "Ladies and gentlemen, thanks for coming to this meet-the-press programme. You are the fourth pillar of our democracy. Your role has never been more important than what it is right now. The opposition has not yet been able to get over the thrashing they got from the National Party of Patriots in the last national elections, so much so that they are ready to go to any extent to win this by-election to stay relevant in national politics. They know very well that we win elections because our policies enjoy solid support from the electorate. We shall win this by-election because we have fielded a candidate with impeccable character—a man well-known for the remarkable work done for the poor and unprivileged children in our country. Knowing well that they cannot beat us by maintaining a decent and democratic campaign, they have let loose an unprecedented barrage of personal attacks on our candidate, inventing skeletons in his cupboard that do not exist. We shall make a few presentations to you this afternoon before we take your questions. Incidentally, a kind doctor has travelled a long distance to help us bring out the truth. Let's have a few words from him to start."

Anil Hazarika nervously took the microphone. After seconds of hesitation, he said, "Good afternoon, ladies and gentlemen! I do not have a personal interest in this election. I do not belong to a political party. In fact, I have no interest in politics at all. However, I believe in democracy and our democratic rights. So, I consider it my solemn duty to share with the public what I know about a candidate, so that they can make informed decisions. After all, our future rests in the hands of the members of Parliament.

"I have known Dr Purnima very closely."

He went on to talk about his tumultuous on-campus affair with Purnima, how they had met, the intensity of their romance, and the heartbreak of their sudden separation. It was an emotional speech quite impressive for a man not used to public speaking. He ended the talk with a powerful message. "So, it is natural that I am concerned. A woman capable of an impulsive switch from passionate love to total indifference, who can change her priorities in a hurry, one who tramples on other's feelings without care—is she fit for a responsible public position for five long years? I leave it to the voters to decide."

This was followed by more briefs from senior party officials and a lengthy question-answer session which kept the reporters busy for over an hour.

Later that evening, all the national television channels repeatedly telecast the details of the press conferences. The allotted airtime and the tone of the newscast varied depending on a channel's allegiance to the first or second party.

After watching Arvind Balakrishnan receive prime time television slots, Shazia released a press statement. It said: *Very disappointed to see one of my close school friends come on national prime time with such baseless insinuations against me. As I said before, our friendship is a historical fact. But these distorted stories, driven by political agendas that I do not understand, are false. The statements given by my old schoolmate in the press conference are fabrications of his motivated imagination. I vehemently deny them and regret that such stories are contrived and narrated to national media for political gains. I wish to retain my propriety and not join such deplorable acts. My opponents are uncomfortable with the rapport I am building with the voters. They are scared to see the prospects of my win increase by the day. So, they are up to various tricks to defame me. I am confident that the voters shall give them a befitting response.*

The entire city talked about the latest developments on the battle for the West Delhi parliamentary seat, with reactions ranging from keen interest to total disdain. Meanwhile, two love-struck individuals sank deeper into misery and helplessness as they watched their promising future hurtle recklessly towards a premature death. Accepting the bizarre situation as a *fait accompli*, they nervously waited for polling day and prayed for a chance to reset their strained relationship. Neither of them had the nerve to call.

31

With only days left for the polls, Purnima gave up hopes of receiving a call from Robin Garg. They had had regular late-night chats before things had gotten out of hand. She was desperate for a heart-to-heart talk with him, to clarify that she had nothing to do with the junk thrown at him, and to urge him not to lose focus on their life beyond the elections. However, she did not initiate the call, holding on to her pride, as she believed she deserved the courtesy of a return call.

The wait ended on Monday morning. Robin sounded disturbed. Without bothering with small talk, he said, "Purnima, this is my last call on this number. Please, destroy this particular SIM soon after I disconnect. I will discard mine as well. If anyone asks you about these telephone numbers, by any chance, deny any knowledge without even a second's hesitation. Read last night's post in *The Third Eye*, the damned e-paper, and you will get answers to the questions you have in your mind right now.

"We need to meet and talk urgently—dinner at my house tomorrow night. I don't want to involve even your best friend in this meeting during this peak campaign phase. You will have a white-Honda Amaze waiting for you two houses away from yours, to the right, at nine. The last four digits of the car's number plate will be 3679. Please note this down—white Honda Amaze 3679 outside the gate to the right. Disguise yourself well while coming out of your apartment block. This whole thing has to be carried out in complete secrecy. I am suggesting my house since anywhere else would entail higher risks. No one should see you coming here. I would think both of us are under some form of surveillance, so take adequate precautions. Is that clear? See you tomorrow. No calls till then. I got to go. Bye."

Robin put the phone down without waiting for a response from Purnima.

Hearing these ominous words, Purnima froze. She felt she was part of a thriller with little control over what was happening and no idea what was in store going forward. She sat down, and poured a glass of water from the jar on the nearby table. She destroyed the SIM card without the faintest clue why and opened her laptop to check out the latest *The Third Eye* report:

West Delhi By-election Story Gets Messier

As if the shady story of the surprise independent candidate was not enough, the by-election for the West Delhi parliamentary constituency has challenged us with a new mystery. This jaw-dropping story, potentially with sweeping consequences, is unprecedented; we have never reported such a thing in years of intense coverage of Indian politics.

Notwithstanding our rich experience in covering numerous state and national elections for many years, we have been truly tested by this particular contest. Amongst plenty of variables in typical election scenarios, we find one thing consistent—the candidates in the fray, usually sworn adversaries, get at each other's throats to win the election. But not this time! We are not even sure who are friends and who are adversaries in this contest!

We broke the news to you about the close friendship between the two doctors in the fray. Though we are supposed to believe the conflicting stories dished out, we are not clear whom to believe. We continue our struggle to navigate through the diverse claims to get to the truth. Meanwhile, a new stunning scoop!

We suspect there is some hidden relationship and understanding between the main contestants as well!

We have noticed that the two leading contestants have been restrained in their references to each other in all the public engagements.

In contrast with the respective parties' social media campaigns, the candidates never attack each other. In fact, they tactfully dodge all questions in this regard. This is far from the usual aggression we are used to for many years now.

A few days back, one of our reporters had discovered, by sheer coincidence, that Robin Garg bought two SIM cards from Dwarka, Sector 6 market—one in the name of his houseboy and the other for his driver. We found it strange that a busy man like him—businessman, social worker, parliamentary election candidate—found time to personally go to a retailer to buy SIMs for domestic helpers. Curious, our colleague used his close relationship with the retailer to note the SIM numbers.

Our investigative team took a deep dive. We now know that the helpers never got their hands on these SIMs. We called the numbers to find that one was with Robin Garg and the other with Dr Purnima Bhatt. Robin Garg picked up our call only for the first time, but that was enough for us to recognise his voice. Dr Bhatt picked up twice. On the second call, we pointedly asked if it was her. She said, "Wrong number," and never picked calls after that.

We called both the numbers again from different telephones at different times; no one answered though both the connections were live at the time of writing this report. There are too many coincidences in this story to be ignored. The NPP candidate buys a SIM for the UNDP candidate! This is weird! Are they in regular direct touch away from the public eye?

Our question: is there a mysterious relationship or secret understanding between the two prime candidates for this seat? From a larger perspective, is there some understanding between these two parties? In that case, this election campaign is nothing but a big drama staged to fool the electorate with the result already decided through backdoor political deals. We have enough evidence to ask this question but not enough to articulate an answer. We shall not rest till we find out more. Stay tuned.

Purnima did not know where to hide her face. She remembered the two calls she had received. The situation was clearly getting out of hand. Before she could fully recover from the shock, she received a call from Harsh Malhotra to discuss *The Third Eye* report. Around the same time, Robin received a harried call from Suresh Ahluwalia. Both the calls were short and precise.

Later in the day, both NPP and UNDP issued separate press releases to reject *The Third Eye* report as the shabby work of an overzealous reporter. They expressed concern that vested interests were at work to hijack the elections and confuse the electorate with stories designed to create suspicion and dismay. They appealed to the voters not to pay attention to divisive forces and urged them to turn up in large numbers to vote.

The parties advised the candidates to direct anyone enquiring about the latest report to their official communique and refrain from additional comments or rejoinders.

Meanwhile, the publication put the residences of Purnima and Robin under surveillance during the evening hours scouting for further evidence of any relationship between them.

Purnima performed her campaign duties for the two days like a robot, not falling short in doing what was expected of her but devoid of the motivation and urgency of a candidate whose electoral fate would be sealed in a few days. She informed her campaign command centre that she was not available for any engagements after seven on Tuesday evening. No one complained; they understood that everyone needed a break at some stage. She reached home a few minutes before eight on Tuesday evening with just an hour to get ready to leave for dinner with Robin.

She changed her hairstyle to something that she had never tried before. The free-flowing layers till the shoulders gave way for a floral ringlet bun. She picked up a dull brown saree that she had never worn before due to its uninspiring colour, one she could not discard easily since it was a gift from a close relative. She chose to wear a flat-heeled sandal in another first. Armed with a black stole, she was an entirely different woman. It was nearly impossible for anyone to recognise her and certainly not from the rear.

Before walking out of her building at five minutes to nine, she took care to apply her best perfume. Despising her appearance after all the efforts to disguise herself, she believed a classy fragrance was her only hope for redemption this evening. The driver of the white Honda Amaze opened the door for her. After a courteous greeting, he drove towards Africa Avenue.

Some time back, Robin Garg drove out of his house in a black SUV with his driver. A reporter from *The Third Eye*, smoking a cigarette less than fifty metres away, observed the car with the utmost attention. He saw two passengers inside the car though it wasn't possible to identify the people through the tinted windows.

Robin got off in a bylane around the corner, walked to the backside of his house, and went back in through a small service gate. The driver sped away. He had specific instructions from his boss. The reporter waited for the car to return.

Another reporter had parked his car about a hundred metres to the left of Purnima's house. He followed the Honda keeping a safe distance. The reporter called Tim Jacob saying, "A lady has just left the house in a white Honda. She was alone. The driver of the car opened the door for her and drove away. She did not look like the doctor to me, though. I am behind their car. Should I follow them or return to my position?"

Tim Jacob thundered, "You expected her to come out alone at this time of the night in her usual look? I am sure it is her. Follow them and let me know exactly where she goes. Keep me informed all through."

"Okay, got it, sir."

Purnima was surprised that the driver did not drive to the Inner Ring Road to turn right for Dwarka. Instead, he took a U-turn and headed to R.K. Puram Sector 1. Minutes later, he parked the car by the roadside near a busy vegetable market. From a distance of about fifty metres, the reporter kept a close watch—the driver and the lady went to buy vegetables. Committed to his assignment, he did not take his eye off the target sedan even for a moment. However, they did not return to their car after nearly an hour. The reporter was surprised that an election candidate was spending so much time in a shabby vegetable market.

Tim Jacob, surprised by the lack of further information from his colleague, called the reporter. "What happened? I thought you were supposed to keep me informed regularly. Where are you now?"

"Same place, sir. They aren't done buying vegetables as yet."

"What? It's going to be an hour. A parliamentary election candidate is personally buying vegetables for an hour, days before polling day! Something is wrong there. If you don't see them in the next ten minutes, inform me and go home."

By the time the disappointed reporter started his drive home, Purnima had already entered Dwarka. Earlier, she had followed the driver's instructions, like an obedient child, to walk with him to the vegetable market, engage in a bargain for a kilo of tomatoes, and return in minutes to a black colour SUV parked a few vehicles ahead of the Honda Amaze. They drove away quickly through R.K. Puram to join Rao Tularam Marg, and then went on to Dwarka Road via NH 48. The watchman of house number twenty-nine welcomed them with a salute. He directed the driver to park the vehicle in the empty slot in the garage.

The Third Eye informant noted that the two persons soon returned to the house. He cursed his fate for the boring assignment. There had been absolutely nothing to report.

Purnima appreciated the well-illuminated and beautifully-maintained lawns as she walked into the veranda. Robin opened the door with a warm welcome, but not before Purnima had a good look at the name plaque—Ritu and Robin.

"This is an absolute honour, dear Purnima, you are so very welcome to this house. For a while, please forget everything and enjoy this visit, just as I will. We shall have dinner and then discuss business. Till then, just chill, please. The furtive nature of this visit somehow enhances the romance of having you home for the first time. I hope you feel the same!"

"Thank you, Robin; so kind of you! Sure, let's chill first; I need some chilling indeed! I think we both deserve it after the mess we go through every day!"

"By the way, I must say you look very different with this new hairdo and the dress. I am sure not many would recognise you from a distance. However, you look as attractive as ever!" said Robin.

"You still have a way with words just like you did back then!" blushed Purnima.

Robin walked Purnima through the right side of the hall to the small extension. On the way, she stopped to appreciate the centre table. "Oh, I love silver artefacts. These are exquisite!" She also had a close look at the Persian wall carpet.

They sat in the extension area for a while. While Robin took his usual place, he asked Purnima to sit in the right-hand chair, the forbidden one. The houseboy who brought water for them could not believe what he was seeing.

"So, it is late for dinner, I know. But we shall still find some time for a drink. I will have my scotch. You?"

"Do you have some wine?"

"Sure, I do. What kind of wine do you like? Dry, fruity, medium-bodied?"

"Wow! I don't think I'm proficient enough to technically specify my choice with such finesse. I can only tell you that I prefer something on the sweeter side."

"All right, that's what most ladies do."

"Ha-ha, how many ladies have you been serving wine lately?" asked Purnima with a naughty smile.

"Well, I can only say: far fewer than I would have wanted to." Both laughed. Robin left her alone to get the drinks.

She looked around the room and loved the way the interiors had been designed and maintained. The choice of size, shape, and colour was impressive. She observed the elegant crystal chandelier; it went so well with the sofa set below. There was definitely some thoughtful planning behind every little thing in the hall. She marvelled that it was a house built and maintained by Robin on his own!

Robin returned with a glass of Lombardo Sweet Marsala that he had personally brought from Sicily and a measure of Caol Ila with four cubes of ice for himself.

Purnima took a sip from her glass and said, "This is nice! Thanks. I am so tense and upset, Robin, by what is happening these days. Really, I have been on the brink!"

Robin bent forward to give her hand a soft touch and said, "As I said before, business only after dinner. For now, let us be in our own world—a world that we control, a world that means more to us than anything else, a world where all these politicians and politics do not exist.

"Since we met last, whenever routine stuff did not cloud my mind, I thought of you... and of our lovely Bangalore days! Tell me, are you in touch with some of our old friends there? Have you ever gone back to Austin Town, your school, Brigade Road, MG Road *et al.*?"

"Before we get to anything else, Robin, please tell me how have you managed to retain over the years this unique art of subtle flirting. In fact, it is now more refined, mellowed and searching!" said Purnima with a smile that exposed her dimples. Robin didn't fail to notice the sparkle in her pretty eyes.

Robin laughed and said, "What do you mean?"

"Oh. Come on! As if you do not know!" She continued after a brief pause, "All right, you asked about Bangalore and my friends there. No, I haven't been there in a very long time; I think not since I joined my medical studies. My parents settled down in Baroda after retirement and most of my friends moved out of Bangalore over time. In any case, why would I go there? You had already left!" she laughed.

Robin quipped, "I can see that it's a payback time!" Both had a hearty laugh.

Purnima said, "You have a lovely lawn with exquisite flowerbeds. Your gardener must be an expert. I'm going to come here once during the day, when all this is over, to have a good look around."

"You are so welcome, anytime!"

"By the way, I see that you admire Claude Monet," said Purnima, walking closer to the distinguished painting on the wall. "It is beautiful! I love his *Impression, Sunrise* as well. Truly a masterpiece! I am inspired by the Impressionist Movement, in general."

Robin responded with his inimitable naughty smile, "Thank God, these great artists didn't get to see you. They would have ditched nature to rush back to their studios to make *your* portraits!"

"Come on, Robin! If you wish to be nice to me, tell me something believable!" Both of them burst out laughing. They held hands and looked into each other's eyes. With radiating smiles on their faces, they hugged each other. The spontaneity of the embrace, delicate and caring, surprised them as did the sudden adrenalin rush in their bodies!

With happiness radiating through the house for a change, the domestic helpers whispered, happy to share their boss's joy—something they had never witnessed before.

Purnima was treated to a delicious spread of choice north Indian delicacies, followed by a handsome serving of *malai kulfi*. Purnima was surprised that Robin still remembered her favourites—tandoori chicken, okra, and to top it all *malai kulfi*. "You are incredible, Robin! I can see that you served all my favourites. It's been such a long time, yet you remembered!"

"I am glad you enjoyed dinner. Now let's get on with business. I will give you a choice. We can sit on those sofas and chat. It may not be very private since these people will be around to finish their errands, or we can go to my small study at one end of this floor. That will be private, but I am not sure if you will be comfortable."

"Let's go to your study."

They sat face to face in the small cosy room to the right of the dining hall. The room was stuffy with its large bookshelf, a music system, and a study table laden with various electronic gadgets.

"This is a comfy place. Do you use it often?"

"Yes, I do. I am here when I do some serious work, and I am also here when I do absolutely nothing!" said Robin, laughing.

"Before we talk about anything else, please unravel this secret operation that you have choreographed this evening—vegetable market, change of car—what was that all about?"

"Purnima, you have read the latest report on *The Third Eye*. I had a hunch that you will be followed the moment you get out of your house late in the evening, even in disguise. Maybe, maybe not; I didn't want to take a chance. If they track you to my house, you can guess how it will play out! I have played some tricks here as well to mislead likely snoopers. Anyway, before we move on, keep this new SIM. I have a new one too. It is not easy for anyone to trace these back to us. I will give you a call tomorrow morning on your new number just like last time. Thereafter, please do *not* receive calls on this SIM from anyone except me under any circumstances."

Purnima took the package from Robin and thanked him.

After minutes of silence, when neither of them wanted to be the first to open up, Robin took the initiative. "We need to face this new reality, Purnima. This election campaign is getting out of hand. I have heard and read the kind of trash your party is throwing at me. First, I was sure you were not involved in any of this garbage and believed they were entirely out of your control. But with time, I am no longer so sure. You have yourself spoken about me in your speeches, raising doubts on my character, my commitment, in fact questioning whether I am an honourable man!"

Purnima tried to stop him. "Robin, I..."

"No, please, let me speak now. Do you or your bosses have any idea how deeply I was in love with my wife? The stories you are spreading on social media hurt me so much that I feel like running away from everything. But then, the next moment, I get an urge to take revenge by winning this election. It is true that I went for an unavoidable business visit to the United States for four days. The baby was due a week after my scheduled return. Her pregnancy had been absolutely smooth. Ritu insisted that I take the trip. Her water broke when I was in the US, and then—communal riots, blocked traffic—it was too late when my father-in-law reached the hospital with her. I lost everything I had—my entire world. And, you guys are telling the electorate that I had left her in an ambulance to celebrate a business deal. So unfair and insensitive!"

Robin was too emotional to continue. He looked the other way and closed his eyelids to prevent embarrassing tears from rolling down his cheeks. The break allowed Purnima to speak, "I understand, Robin. But this is not my doing. I have no idea from where this social media stuff is coming. Someone else writes my speeches, and what you get to hear is a much mellowed-down version of what they insist I say. What am I to do?"

"What are you to do? Just don't give in. Tell them that you shall not be a part of such baseless smear campaigns. You are the candidate after all," replied Robin firmly.

Purnima quickly rebutted, "That way, Robin, your party has not been saintly either. Haven't you seen the social media campaigns against me? I hear that you have leveraged my broken marriage in your speeches. I have overlooked them, thinking you are as helpless as I am. Shouldn't I be as upset as you are?"

Robin regained his poise and said, "No, the scale is not the same. I agree that some level of a negative campaign, a few critical references to the opposition candidate, a few stupid but funny memes on either side have become a part of modern-day politics, and you and I can do nothing about it. But UNDP is crossing all limits. I am under a lot of pressure from my campaign advisers to go all out to attack you personally. I believe they have collected new ammunition against you after digging deep into your past, including into your much-touted philanthropy.

"My party has attacked your capacity to hold together a family and portrayed you as a whimsical person at worst. Am I not right? My speeches did have subtle references to you once in a while under party directives. Look at yours. They are trying to prove I am a characterless person, that I have always been so—drugs, womanising, and what not! I have not conducted myself this way ever in my life. Each of these atrocious allegations can be proven to be untrue. But we have decided not to do this. Instead, we plan to counterattack. Our party is now preparing to beat you at your own game. This is going to be very nasty from now on, Purnima. That's why I wanted to have an open chat with you to find a way to save the situation. If the next few days' campaigns roll out as planned, we may find it impossible to be a part of this double act—fighting like bitter rivals in public and maintaining a close relation in private, with dreams of a beautiful future together. With this kind of bitterness, we shall carry the poison till the end of our lives. Our dreams will perish!

"Imagine a big rally one of these days, and you repeat the rubbish concocted by a disgruntled intern, the audience cheers your speech, they go back home convinced that I am a demon terrorising hapless young girls looking for sexual favours! Whether I win or not, do you think I will be able to forgive you? You think our relationship would continue to bloom thereon?"

"Robin—"

"How would you feel if I dish out exaggerated details on how you dumped a poor classmate after promising him the moon? How would it be if I go all out to prove to the electorate that you are a whimsical, characterless and untrustworthy woman? Believe me, Purnima. I *know* that none of these have an iota of truth. But the way this campaign is progressing, we shall end up demonising each other in this manner in public rallies. Social media untruths will get darker. We are nothing but powerless pawns in this fight-until-death battle between the two most powerful political parties in the country."

Purnima got up from her chair and looked out of the window. She pulled the curtain a little and looked at the beautiful flowers alongside the lawns outside. Looking further away, she could not see beyond the Giant Thujas. It was pitch-dark.

Robin walked up to her and stood very close, so close that he felt her deep breath. He pulled the curtain all the way and opened the window, put his right arm on Purnima's shoulder, and pointed to a bed of flowers outside. "Do you see those lovely roses? Rose was Ritu's all-time favourite. This flower has been a part of my life ever since I met her. Do you remember the chair you sat in earlier this evening? No one else has ever sat in it before. It was forbidden, meant only for Ritu. When I feel lonely or need to make a difficult choice in life, I sit in front of that chair, and in my way, talk to her, seek her advice. And, you and your party tell people that I have neglected her to death?"

Purnima broke down and cried. Robin turned and took her in his arms, patted her back, and held her tight without a word. She hid her face on his shoulders and cried till his shirt was wet with tears. Feeling the dampness on her chin, she said sheepishly, "Silly me! I have wet your shirt!" Raising her head, she looked at Robin's eyes and said, "I am in a mess, am I not, Robin?" In her attempts to laugh away the tears, she was hysterical.

Robin held her face with both his hands. Searching her eyes, he said, "Oh, Purnima, we both are in a mess. Destiny brought us here. We need to find a way out. Don't cry. You break my heart when you do."

Robin lowered his face and let his nose gently rub hers, from left to right and back, and smiled. Noticing a hesitant smile on Purnima's lips, he repeated the move, and then again. Purnima looked down with a shy smile. He observed her—blushing red and wet with fresh tears—a perplexing blend of love, apprehension, excitement and restraint. He lowered his face and raised Purnima's chin. Their lips touched in a soft kiss; he held on to her face and let his thumbs stroke her cheeks. Her lips quivered, disengaged for a fleeting moment, and returned. This time, he pressed his lips hard and released his tongue to explore. She closed her eyes and opened the doors to delight.

Driven by a sudden urge for restraint, she forced herself out of Robin's hands and looked at the other side. Robin said, "It's okay. It's okay, Purnima." As if his reassuring words cast a spell on her, she whirled around and fell into Robin's open arms. They kissed each other passionately, their tongues wildly exploring the depths of pleasure. Holding each other in a tight embrace, they sensed both spontaneity in their intimacy and oneness—a rare preserve only for a couple deeply in love. Riding on those mesmeric moments, they hurriedly walked up to Robin's bedroom.

Lost in a heaven of their own, far from the madding world of politics, they made love, free of all inhibitions, till they came together in one voice, as one soul and one body!

About an hour later, Purnima shuffled on the soft pillow to get closer to Robin. Taking utmost care not to wake him up, she stroked his forehead. Robin opened his eyes with a smile. As he tenderly placed his hand on her cheeks, she asked with a trembling voice, "Now what, Robin?"

32

Aditi Kasbekar was thrilled with the nationwide publicity given to her interview. Most national television channels reported her statements, and newspapers gave her headline after headline. Thereafter, journalists scrutinised her claims and found that the avowals on her job, the rough professional treatment, and the resignation were accurate but could not verify what had transpired between her and Robin Garg in their private moments. They pursued her for interviews. As intended, she stood by her statements but refused to give any interviews in person. They pleaded and tempted her with handsome rewards; a few tried to coerce her. She gave in to none. Meanwhile, her confidence soared as she felt important enough to be in a position to influence a national election.

Harsh Malhotra, a veteran with remarkable perception, watched her closely. As per the feedback he had received, her recorded interview had made a significant impact on the electorate. It was reasonable to believe that her physical presence could be the nail in the coffin for the ruling party candidate. He was keen to use Aditi as a star campaigner for his party as the battle went to its decisive phase. Sensing that the time was ripe for a tactical try, he personally requested Aditi to join their Delhi campaign for a brief period with the promise of a plum post in the Karnataka unit of the party if they succeeded in retaining the prestigious seat. Spurred by her ambitions, she took the bait and agreed to join for the last two days of the campaign. Suitable arrangements were made for her travel and stay in the capital for three days. However, her role as a star campaigner remained a closely held secret. Knowing Purnima's aversion to personal attacks on opposition candidates, they decided not to inform her about Aditi beforehand.

Suresh Ahluwalia had no trouble in convincing Anil Hazarika to join the campaign for the last two days. Unhappy with his lieutenants' failure to find potent material to disparage the UNDP candidate, he went out of his way to make the best of whatever he had. He instructed his social media managers to flood cyberspace with relentless posts on whatever rabble-rousing leads they had. He even suggested that they fabricate bogus stories, if necessary, to create doubts about Purnima Bhatt's personal and professional integrity.

Durjoy Kumar's frustration knew no bounds when he realised that the Delhi president had been hoodwinking him in recent strategy meetings. He regularly attended all high-level party meetings, but the ground action often turned out to be different from the decisions in these meetings. Still smarting from the humiliating denial of a ticket, he could not take any further shame from the party leadership. He became more vocal and less diplomatic about his reservations on the official candidate. His supporters' covert non-cooperation slowly morphed into something that looked more like an open rebellion. There were reports of physical fights between party workers and Kumar's supporters in certain localities. The press exploited the situation to project severe infighting within the NPP. Alarmed with the disturbing developments, the party leadership yet had limited options. They ruled out any direct action against Durjoy Kumar since the party did not want to give him an opportunity to play the victim. It could decisively turn his sympathisers and undecided voters away from the party.

Suresh Ahluwalia rested his hopes on the independent candidate who continued to gain substantial purchase with the voters. She delivered a surprisingly impressive performance throughout the canvassing period. Besides, many observers, including influential media personnel, construed the UNDP's press briefing with Arvind Balakrishnan as their desperate bullying of the independent candidate. The sympathy brought Shazia additional support at the cost of the UNDP candidate. The community factor also worked well since she succeeded in galvanising minority votes.

Shazia was happy to note that her efforts with the electorate were reaping good dividends. For a person who had not joined the fray with political ambitions, reports on making impressive progress with the voters were immensely gratifying. Yet, there was no palpable excitement in her. The unusually demanding schedule was playing havoc with her already-poor general health. Further, the nagging fear of an imminent media revelation on her financial deal with NPP drove her to paranoia. She could not sleep well. With eyes wide open late into the night, she looked at her husband sleeping peacefully by her side and wished she could share her discomfort with him without being punished by an irritating 'I-told-you-so' discourse. Wiping tears, she had an uncomfortable sense of sinking into utter despair.

When her phone rang early on Wednesday morning, she was in two minds whether to accept a call from an unknown number. Ultimately, she did pick up the phone and greeted the caller without enthusiasm.

"Yes, please."

"Hi, Shazia. Sorry, this may be too early for you to receive a call. But I guess any time is a good time for an old buddy to call."

"Who is this please? Sorry, I don't recall your voice."

"Well, I am not surprised. I'm sure my voice is very different from what it used to be nearly three decades back. How have you been?"

"Err, are you…?"

"Hold your breath, it's your old friend Purnima."

"What? Is that *really* you, Purnima?"

"Yes, it's me."

"I can't believe this! Hello! How have you been?"

"I am good. Well, you know all about the politics going on. I am calling as your old school friend. I think we carried our bitterness with us for too long. Despite the awful campaign these days, and irrespective of the results of this election, I believe we should end our hostility now. Can we meet late this evening? It will become impossible after a few more days of this madness. I am suggesting late because by then we can finish all our public commitments. Say yes, please. We really should meet now."

Shazia, not knowing how to react to the strangest of all strange happenings in her life lately, took some time to respond. "That does not seem to be a great idea with only a few days left for the election. As it is, the rumour machines are working overtime. Where and when did you have in mind?"

"If you agree, I shall work out the logistics and revert to you before lunchtime. It has to be, and shall be, absolutely confidential."

"Not easy to say no after you took the initiative to call. It is the first time you are reaching out to me since we met last at the farmhouse. For old times' sake, I say yes!"

"That's great! You will hear from me again before noon. Thanks a ton. I better let you go for now. Bye."

Purnima got busy with planning this vital rendezvous; she was to throw the dice in the gamble of her life.

Clueless about what prompted Purnima to reach out this way after ages, Shazia tried hard to find a motive behind the call. There was no convincing explanation. The irrationality of such a call and its dubious timing perturbed her. Yet, she was by then too weak and jittery to brood over the unknown. Having accepted the request, she decided to take it at its face value and go with the flow. A few minutes before noon, she received instructions from Purnima.

The previous night, Purnima returned home from Robin's house at three in the morning. She could not remember when she had been as confused, worried, and happy at the same time. It was a wild and tender night at once. In the black SUV on her way back home, Robin's lengthy answer to her short question kept echoing in her mind.

She had asked, "Now what, Robin?"

"What now? It is plain and simple. We have something beautiful between the two of us, as we have just experienced. We are witnessing the spring of our lives after a long and dreary winter. We must protect it with all our might. Like I said earlier, if we allow this campaign to run its course as planned, we won't be able to protect ourselves from the effects of relentless public denigration. We have to take charge of the situation as far as we are personally concerned. Whether one loses or wins, a seat in the Parliament is for five years at most. We must not sacrifice the promise of lifelong happiness at the altar of five years of public life.

"The second-best scenario is that we firmly put our foot down against any personal slander. We shall refuse to say anything personally defamatory against the opposing candidates. We shall also do our best to reduce social media attacks. If any one of us loses the election for not defaming the opposition candidate personally, so be it. There will be a lot of protest, cajoling, persuasion, and threats from the party leadership. We shall not budge. The party may suffer then, but they should suffer. This is not how democratic elections should be conducted, in any case. However, I am not sure how much we can succeed since we have limited direct influence in that sphere. Nevertheless, we shall do our bit to the fullest.

"After the results are out, we shall celebrate irrespective of who wins. This way, we can have our future the way we want it. We shall subsequently decide whether to stay in politics or not. Of course, we shall never file nomination papers against each other ever again. Does this make any sense to you?"

Purnima replied, "Sure, it does. But you said this is the second best. What is the *best* scenario?"

"To hope and pray that this election gets cancelled."

"Did you say cancelled? How is that possible? Is there a way we can influence that? That will be so good!"

"It is possible. But there is not much we can do to influence such a scenario. How badly I wish this whole thing gets cancelled. Life shall be so much better!"

Robin thought for a while and continued, "The Election Commission can cancel an election under certain exceptional circumstances—proven instances of corrupt practices, death of a candidate after ballot papers have been printed, etc. It is rare but not unprecedented. It is entirely the prerogative of the Election Commission. There are instances when they have cancelled elections in specific constituencies for ostensibly weak reasons. And elsewhere, they did not do so even under compelling circumstances. We have an independent Election Commission, and we must trust them to make the right decisions. So, you pray for something to happen so that the Commission decides to cancel this election. In that case, they will have to start the entire process again at a later date. This option is like a dream at this time. Let us focus on the second option." He continued after a pause, "I believe we can do that and secure what is more important to both of us, our future together."

A question had resonated in her ears ever since—could anything be done to force cancellation of the current election? That seemed like an ideal escape from this baffling maze.

I am not rich enough to set up a large-scale vote-for-money scam under the nose of the election observers. That option is a no-go. Death of a candidate? What good is it if one of us dies and the election gets cancelled?

Useless. What about Shazia? If she dies, the election gets cancelled. Oh God, let Shazia die tomorrow… this is the only way out.

The more she thought, Shazia's death, weird as it was, seemed the only route towards bliss with the man she always loved.

The next moment, she hated herself for being selfish, cruel and violent, and tried to exorcise these bizarre thoughts from her unsettled mind. However, these thoughts would not go away. As she tossed around in bed in yet another battle for sleep, they constantly troubled her.

Shazia has, after all, craved revenge on me all her life; that's what I got in return for my absolute loyalty in years of friendship. She has been ruthless, scheming to hurt me. Now she has set out to humiliate me on the national stage. She was never my friend at all.

In an attempt to vindicate herself, she argued—*What is wrong in seeking my own happiness? Shazia is the worst example of a selfish and manipulative human being! I have no doubt at all that she struck a deal with NPP for a handsome reward when she agreed to stand as an independent candidate just to steal my votes. The Third Eye report says so. I am well aware of her love for expensive things; she is certainly vulnerable to pecuniary temptations. How is it wrong if I act in my own interest? After all, I am not planning to kill her myself.*

Having found some justification for her wild thoughts, she let them gain strength within her and began to deliberate if she could bring about Shazia's death.

Purnima knew that Shazia's heart was not in good condition. Some time ago, the same friend from Indradhanush had told her in one of their casual chats, "Do you remember I told you about one of my colleagues, Shazia, who had undergone angioplasty? Sad that her heart condition has further deteriorated despite all the attention she has been receiving at the hospital. Her heart remains quite weak. I get so worried thinking about this. A perfectly healthy woman suddenly turns so vulnerable. I don't know what's in store for us. You are also a busy doctor with so many commitments. Please do take care of yourself."

Purnima wondered if there was anything she could do to precipitate a drastic deterioration in her ailment—something that could lead to a fatal attack.

She found herself in an intense battle between her heart and conscience. Irrespective of who won the election, Robin and she would never find love and peace in their life together. An active political life for either one of them would invariably hurt their relationship. She wanted this election cancelled; nothing less would do. For this, Shazia had to go.

The tug of war between a woman ready to do anything for love and someone who had knowingly never hurt others continued till love won decisively. If she could somehow give her a dose of the formulation next evening, Shazia might not be able to complete her canvassing schedule on the following day. Then, the election would get annulled. She and Robin would be free to live their lives the way they wanted!

She could barely wait for the morning to break. Early in the morning, she called Shazia to set up a late evening get-together.

33

When Shazia wore her mother's *abaya*—preserved for years as memorabilia—she could barely recognise herself. She had never worn the black overall before. Mohammed Hameed was surprised to see his wife in the new look. All he got was a mysterious smile from her in response to his curiosity. He decided to not pursue it.

Purnima had called her with instructions - "Nine in the evening at the Crowne Plaza, Okhla. I suggest that place because it is nearer to your residence. I'm conscious that you have a family and it may not be convenient for you to travel far in the night. Once you enter the hotel lobby, ask for the general manager, and someone will escort you to a private meeting room. I shall be there before time. Please be as discreet as possible as we do not want to be noticed by anyone. Wear an *abaya* if you have it; I shall also wear something suitable. So, see you then, my friend."

Purnima cancelled her engagements after seven in the evening. Reaching home as early as possible, she wore faded tight-fitting black jeans, a body-hugging pink cardigan, and a matching scarf to cover most of her hair. Her driver could barely recognise her. On the way to Crowne Plaza, she stopped by at her regular chemist's shop in Green Park Extension to buy a drug. The chemist had known Purnima for many years. Though the medicine was not in their stock, he quickly sourced it from a nearby pharmacy.

She made herself comfortable at a private meeting room at one corner of the hotel's ground floor fifteen minutes before nine. Her close friendship with the hotel owner came in handy—she could set up the meeting in confidence without having to answer too many questions. Waiting for Shazia to arrive, she ordered an espresso; she needed the caffeine to calm her nerves.

The concierge escorted Shazia to the room at five minutes past the hour. Purnima got up to greet her with a warmth reminiscent of their schooldays. "Oh, Shazia! So nice to see you after all these years. Come on in! Thanks for accepting my invite."

Shazia, nervous about walking into a meeting shrouded in mystery, gave her an unenthusiastic smile and said, "Same here, Purnima. Good that you took the initiative after all these years."

"First things first, what will you drink?"

"Some water and a cappuccino will be great."

After ordering two cappuccinos, Purnima said, "Shazia, when I think how our relationship has gone from best friends to challengers in a national election, I wonder—did it have to be like this? I so badly want you to know, actually hope you know by now, that I did nothing to come in between you and Arvind. In fact, I argued with him until the very last minute to not misjudge you and end your beautiful relationship."

Shazia interrupted, "These are all in the past, Purnima. What I think does *not* matter anymore. You, I, Arvind, all of us have moved on with our lives. We have grown up despising each other ever since that night. We have had our successes and failures, happiness and sorrow. Indulging in a rear-view analysis at this stage of our lives has no meaning. We can't reclaim our youth by revisiting the rights and wrongs of our teenage years. So, there is no point in talking about our fight at this time."

Reminiscing over their childhood and school anecdotes, they returned to their teenage years in Bangalore. The cappuccinos came. Shazia drank half a glass of water and excused herself to go to the restroom. Purnima took a bite of the complementary cookie with a rushed sip of her coffee. She was very nervous. There was only a minute's window to act—it was now or never.

She opened her handbag and searched for the drug. The coffee was hot, so it would not take much time to dissolve the formulation. As she picked it up with an indecisive hand, she found herself once again engaged in a fight with her alter ego. A part of her saw justice in every act that promised her the man she loved. After all, the planned action was not a homicide since the drug would only increase the chances of a fatal heart failure for a sick person, and would not guarantee death on its own. It also comforted her that it was not wrong to retaliate against a true enemy, someone who was out to hurt her at any cost. But what if she got caught for this act after Shazia's death? The law would never spare her. She would have to spend the rest of her life behind bars. *A doctor saves lives, not play a part in ending one! On the other hand, Robin will be devastated. Will he ever be able to forgive me?* Then, again: *I mustn't reason too much and retract for fear of the unknown. Do this now. It is my best chance for happiness. Shazia is my enemy. She stands between me and my bliss.*

The intense battle between the two continued till one of them prevailed.

Shazia returned to her seat. "Sorry, what were we talking about?"

Purnima looked pale and frazzled. Shazia asked, "What happened to you? You look so worried!"

Purnima replied, forcing a smile on her face, "Nothing. We discussed our past for too long, I guess. We have been stupid to live for so long with awful memories of just one night, forgetting the beauty of our friendship for six years. Let us leave the past behind. Can we move on and try to revive our friendship, at least now? Can we attempt to wash our sins and enjoy a bond for the years left to us?"

"We can, and we should. I will never have a clear view of what had happened among the three of us in the last few months of school. At the same time, I know it is time to move on. Giving you the benefit of the doubt, I am ready to start afresh. But this election is turning very nasty."

Purnima interrupted to say, "Let me talk about that."

In an attempt to frame her words appropriately, Purnima drew a blank. She intended to hit Shazia where she knew it would hurt the most. She wanted to scare and confuse Shazia as much as possible with the hope that she wilted under pressure. Bending forward to rest her elbows on the table, she spoke in a heavy voice, "Shazia, listen, I know you too well to believe that you are doing this out of love for politics or public service. On the other hand, all this running around for votes cannot be merely to take some revenge on me. You are not the kind of person to throw your money and time after a lost cause. I have been following *The Third Eye* investigations closely; I am sure you are doing so too. They hinted that one of the national parties put you up to cut into the other party's votes. That explains a lot. I know UNDP has not done this. So, many others and I, know for a fact, that you are a proxy for NPP. That explains the money spent on electioneering. It is *their* money. But even then, it is very much unlike you to spend so much time and energy only for the convenience of a political party. The condition of your heart is far from satisfactory; I am well aware. There must be something big for you here. I do not know how much money they have promised you, but one thing is sure—those investigative journalists are damn good, and I believe they are very close to cracking this wide open. If money could buy an apolitical person like you, lesser money would buy an NPP strategist who will expose the entire arrangement. Imagine your societal standing, your image before friends and relatives, after it gets reported that a political party bought you to serve their petty tricks.

"I know it is too late for you to run away from this. As your friend, I strongly advise that, in the next few remaining days of campaigning, slow down your activities, stop the rhetoric, and refrain from any personal attack on me. I shall do that as well, I promise. Even if I lose this election, I shall not throw dirt on my opponents, on both opponents, not just you. If you do that, it doesn't matter who wins this election, we would have started a new chapter in our lives."

Shazia looked like a shadow of herself. Whitish and shrunk, she stuttered, "Do you know *The Third Eye* reporters? Can you do anything to stop them from writing about me? I had no idea that this would cause so much heartburn for me. Please, can you help me, Purnima?"

Purnima's conviction was validated—there was indeed a financial deal between NPP and Shazia. She felt disgusted, but also pity for the beseeching eyes in front of her, a far cry from the marauding young girl who had blasted her years back.

She replied, "There is precious little I can do about others. But I can assure you that I shall never mention your financial deal to anyone as long as you do not attack me personally in your speeches and campaigns. You keep your part of the bargain, and we shall be friends again irrespective of who wins. I hope I have been clear in what I have said. Thank you so much for accepting my invite and so good to see you again. I think you better go back to your family; they may be worried if I hold you here any longer."

"Sure, Purnima. Bye. Take care."

"*You* take care of yourself! I believe you have difficult days ahead."

They left the meeting room one at a time, Shazia first and Purnima after a gap of ten minutes. Driving back home, Shazia was a wreck. She saw an unendurable disgrace coming her way like a powerful hurricane. She wished death would come to rescue her from inevitable public mortification. Walking into her house, she did not say a word to anyone and locked herself up in the bathroom. A shower later, she refused dinner and joined her husband in bed but chose not to tell him about the dull ache on the left side of her body yet again. She felt weak and dizzy. A little later, sensing her heart palpitate, she wondered if she should alert her husband. After a dose of aspirin, the symptoms subsided. Once again, waking up fresh in the morning after a good night's sleep, she did not think it necessary to talk to her husband about her brief discomfort the previous night. She convinced herself that it was because of a bout of acidity due to skipping dinner last night.

Purnima, for a change, was humming her favourite song on her way back home. Her driver was pleasantly surprised to find his boss relaxed for the first time in weeks. She had a shower followed by a peaceful dinner.

Earlier that morning, she was given a new draft for her speeches. She was happy that the team did not react sharply to her firm rebuff to any personal disparagement of the opposition. The campaign manager agreed to respect her wishes. He also insisted that they would do whatever was required on their part to win the election and that Purnima must not interfere in that. She understood that some callous defamatory campaign was to unfold in the days ahead. Helpless, she did not respond.

She looked forward to the days ahead, nevertheless. Having played her hand, she believed the coming days would usher in a new spring in her life.

Robin Garg was not as lucky to find peace. His qualms about his budding relationship with Purnima were proven to be baseless after their intimate time last night. Purnima agreed to his proposal for a complete taboo on personal attacks during the campaign.

Everything seemed to be in order. Yet he was restless, unable to get over his sixth sense that the campaign would still get too dirty for their delicate relationship to withstand.

He also knew that, despite their agreement to celebrate a win either way, it would not be easy for him to do so. How would he handle defeat at the hands of a political greenhorn he once treated like a little girl? Would he be able to forget everything and start living with her while she became a high-profile public figure? That was far from certain. He recognised that the only event that could ensure a happy future with Purnima was the cancellation of the by-election. He lost sleep over what he could do to create a situation for the Election Commission to do precisely that.

He knew that a cancellation of the poll—the ideal scenario in this case—was very rare and only done under extraordinary circumstances. In this three-cornered contest, the death of just any candidate would not help. Robin Garg knew enough about politics to be aware that, as per a Supreme Court judgement passed a few years ago, the deceased candidate had to be from a recognised political party for calling off an election. So, either he or Purnima had to die for the election to be called off! The independent candidate's death would certainly be ignored by the Commission. Thoughts of orchestrating large-scale bribe-for-vote scams came to his mind. But he was not sure of his ability to pull off such a feat in a short time. Without a firm plan of action in hand, he did not want dawn to break. The sun was, in any case, still a few hours away.

Half an hour later, in a frenzy of inspired ideas, he made two calls to two of his most trusted friends in the business community. They were very wealthy and connected. Both of them agreed to have a breakfast meeting with Robin at nine o'clock in the morning.

Robin slept well for the rest of the night.

Early in the morning, he called his campaign manager to assert that he would not attack any of the candidates personally henceforth. Looking at the ease with which the manager accepted his stand, in sharp contrast to the party's persistent efforts earlier to convince him that personal slander was unavoidable to win elections, Robin knew that the party was up to some new tricks. He believed the campaign team would intensify vilification of Purnima to make up for what he would not do.

34

West Delhi was a beehive of activity on Thursday as the polling day closed in. Both the national parties planned for big evening rallies to build up momentum. The NPP's largest public meeting to date was to take place in Dwarka. The UNDP, meanwhile, set up their show of strength in Janakpuri. The independent candidate focused on smaller community caucuses in Uttam Nagar, Hari Nagar, and Madipur.

The Third Eye senior team met in Tim Jacob's house early Thursday morning to review the progress of their investigations. Frustrated with the lack of any significant headway and well-aware that time was running out, Tim was not in the best of moods while addressing his colleagues. "This is a poor reflection on our investigative capabilities. You very well know the kind of scams we have dug up in recent years. On this occasion, we *know* there is a shady deal between one of the leading parties, most probably the NPP, and the independent candidate. We *know* there must be a bounty for the doctor who came from nowhere to fight this election. She is also proven to be a childhood buddy of the UNDP candidate. Further, my intuition says there is definitely a personal relationship or an understanding between the two principal candidates; my suspicion points more to a close relationship. This election is turning out to be a spectacle staged for the public eye with the result fixed somewhere else. And the most brilliant investigative journalists in this country are going around in circles like a set of clowns lost in a maze!

"I am going to release a short piece this morning to precipitate things, to stir them up if you please, with the hope that some of these actors will react, and in the process, reveal the truth behind this spectacle. Have a look, and give your inputs, but I need your feedback right here. We do not have time on our side."

He circulated a brief note. Everyone reviewed the report. Despite reservations about its assumptive nature, they agreed that it was their best bet given the circumstances. Everyone concurred that the release would significantly raise their stakes in the controversy. As a team, they accepted the collective risk and dispersed since there was nothing else on the agenda for the meeting.

Meanwhile, both parties lined up a galaxy of speakers to address the crowds at the Thursday evening rallies. UNDP campaign managers were excited to have Aditi Kasbekar as their trump card for the Janakpuri rally. From the time she had landed at Indira Gandhi International Airport, she was kept undercover. Harsh Malhotra personally reviewed her speech and gave her additional tips on political oratory. Arvind Balakrishnan was asked to rehearse an aggressive speech, with a sharp focus on Shazia's teenage years, to hit her hard and neutralise her recent gains. However, Arvind was not willing to be too aggressive. He didn't want his long-forgotten teenage relationship with Shazia to come under the spotlight. Besides, he was not a party to this election and he had no axe to grind. Malhotra understood and asked Arvind to do his best.

The NPP planned to introduce Anil Hazarika at the Dwarka rally. Since he was not a natural public communicator, he had to train extensively. They wanted his speech to paint a damaging portrayal of his erstwhile girlfriend. But Anil was not their star speaker. Suresh Ahluwalia was happy to pull out his closely guarded and potentially explosive trump card—the embittered husband! While approaching Satish Bhatt to address a public rally, he had never expected the reclusive doctor to agree. However, to his pleasant surprise, the doctor agreed with the condition that no one else must refer to him and his marriage with Purnima in the same rally. Robin Garg, like his UNDP opponent, was in the dark about any of the guest speakers. The party did not want to risk it. His abomination for negative campaigning was well-established by then.

Shazia did not have anything grand planned for the last days of canvassing. Her block-level meetings had been doing well to enthuse voters. So, it was logical for her campaign team to stay the course. Her first engagement was in Uttam Nagar at eleven in the morning.

However, experiencing considerable unease while getting out of her house for the meeting, she asked Srikant Tiwari if she could skip the first engagement and start the day from Hari Nagar early in the afternoon. Srikant Tiwari did not like the idea. UNDP was well ahead of NPP in Uttam Nagar assembly constituency; Shazia needed to improve her vote share at the cost of the UNDP candidate. Not left with a choice, she overlooked her discomfort, took some additional medicine on her own, and set out for the meeting. Fortunately, her condition improved by the time she reached the locality. She and her team had successful interactions with the voters in two separate engagements within the same assembly constituency. It was evident that many undecided voters' opinions swung in her favour. Delighted with the brilliant feedback, Harish Gupta called to congratulate her and acknowledged that the Uttam Nagar meetings were her finest yet. He believed that her spectacular performance in the last phase of the campaign would significantly boost NPP in the by-election.

Around mid-day, *The Third Eye* fired their latest salvo—this time, they did not spare any of the three candidates:

The polling day for the West Delhi parliamentary by-election is just around the corner. We have made remarkable progress in unearthing the mysteries behind this extraordinary election drama. The more we learn, the more we know that the national parties are certainly taking the electorate for a ride. It seems an election drama is unfolding with a fixed end-game. In our years of covering various elections, we have never seen or suspected anything like this before. We have seen a lot: conspiracies, cheap tricks, corruption, intimidation, violence, slandering, and what have you! But never have we had serious doubts about the sanctity of the entire election process.

Consider this: both the national parties nominate political novices as their candidates for this prestigious seat, snubbing claims from other seasoned and deserving candidates. An independent candidate springs up from nowhere to spend her time and money on a contest she knows she cannot win. She turns out to be a close friend of the UNDP candidate. Then, hold your breath—we strongly suspect the NPP candidate has a secret relationship with the UNDP candidate. We would have loved to go a few steps more to claim that the candidates share a romantic relationship going back many years. But we are not claiming that yet, pending more investigations. If you think this claim is appalling and irresponsible, listen to their recent speeches carefully. They never attack each other on any forum. Listen to their public rallies, search their policy statements and poll promises, their interviews, and multiple town hall meets; you will never hear of any adverse references to their prime opponent. It is unreal! If you sensed flavours of mild criticism in the early days of their campaign, even those have disappeared now. Have you ever seen anything like that in a national election? To top that, let us not forget the mysterious case of the two SIM cards we wrote about in our earlier report. Those SIM cards were disconnected from the network soon after that report was published. Some coincidence that!

So, our take—there shall be no real loser in this contest as far as the main two political parties are concerned. They and their candidates will celebrate the result irrespective of who wins the election, since they had it all figured out well before the contest started! The independent candidate will lose and go home with a big purse, estimated anything between fifty lakhs to a crore on top of all campaign expenses, as per the deal struck with one of the parties. We do not wish to insult your intellect by going further to name the party that has commissioned the independent candidate to cut into their opponent's votes. It is now all too obvious for anyone who is following this campaign.

The above is based on well-researched conjecture pending further validation. Our investigations continue. Hopefully, we shall return soon. The story is likely to be the same, this time with impeccable validation. Stay tuned.

Harsh Malhotra read the report while reviewing arrangements for the Janakpuri rally. He cursed the publication and asked his team to ignore the piece. Though Purnima did not get a chance to read the report, the state president briefed her. He asked her to laugh the article off as a work of imaginative journalism and to offer no further comments. However, she was tense. She had a tough time appearing relaxed in her public engagements. It was clear that nothing was beyond the suspecting reporters' prying eyes. The only comfort was that it did not matter much to her anymore. She was by now in bliss in a different world away from the unfolding electoral drama.

Suresh Ahluwalia, directing the Dwarka arrangements personally, had no time to look at any press report. The rally was very important for their campaign. However, his party president instructed him to urgently go through *The Third Eye* report well before the rally to prepare for uncomfortable questions during his interactions with the public during the event. Suresh was furious after reading the column. More than the fear of a catastrophic exposé, he thought it unfair of the publication to put out such damaging reports based on suspicions and wanted to warn Tim Jacob of the consequences of spreading such sinister insinuations. But the master politician soon eschewed such thoughts since he knew such responses risked interpretation as defensive posturing.

That was the last thing his party could afford. He briefed Robin Garg and guided him to suitable evasive answers if necessary.

Robin Garg was angry with the reporter for unearthing a truth he thought he did well to hide. He was relieved that his party president ridiculed the report as another instance of the fourth estate's populist sensationalism. He managed to put on his best act to stay composed, helped by the fact that he had risen above election-related anxieties by now. Having engineered a few innovative and potentially decisive moves, he set his sights on his future. The election and its result did not matter anymore.

After the romantic night with Purnima, Robin yearned for a countermand of the election. He wanted to create a situation that forced the Election Commission to act conclusively to retain the sanctity of the election process and its high reputation. In a very productive breakfast meeting on Wednesday morning, Robin explained the circumstances to his business friends and shared his predicament. They understood and sympathised with him. Given complete faith in their friendship, neither the business magnates nor Robin had concerns about absolute confidentiality. And, given the liquid resources at their disposal, the funds required for the planned operation were not an issue. The tycoons, indebted to Robin for his invaluable support in their trying times, committed to doing their utmost to change the course of this election and help Robin out of his impasse.

Shazia was a few minutes away from the Hari Nagar venue when Srikant Tiwari showed her *The Third Eye* article on his mobile phone. She read it with rapt attention. Giving the phone back to him, she held on to the front seat with her left hand and looked out of the car's window. As her head sagged a little, a visibly pale and exhausted Shazia leaned on the windowpane and massaged her left arm.

Srikant Tiwari was alarmed. "Shazia, are you okay? Do you want some water?" He opened a small bottle of mineral water and offered it without waiting for an answer. "Please take a sip." Shazia drank some water and slumped to her left. She responded, "Don't worry. This is just heartburn. It's not the first time; it must be acidity. I shall be fine. I will just shut my eyes till we reach the venue. You relax too."

The audience in Hari Nagar was ready to receive her after they heard two local community leaders speak in support of her candidature. Shazia took to the stage to hearty applause. There were a few shouts of 'Dr Shazia zindabad' and 'Vote for Shazia Hameed'. She smiled and waved at the crowd. When she raised her hand, they turned quiet and waited for her to speak. Shazia had learned the art of befriending and cosying up to the audience with surprising ease. Striking the right chord with the audience, she paced her speeches right till they hit dramatic climaxes. The people laughed, cheered, clapped, and chanted her name as she spoke. Srikant could not resist the temptation to call his boss. He conveyed that both Uttam Nagar and Hari Nagar—SJP strongholds predicted to favour UNDP—would now vote for Shazia thanks to her stellar performances. With a large chunk of definite UNDP votes switching to Shazia—precisely the purpose of fielding the independent candidate—an NPP win looked imminent.

Later in the evening, after the local area activists' fiery speeches and the entertainers' performances, Harsh Malhotra got ready to introduce Aditi Kasbekar to the audience. That was when the party's district president whispered something in his ears. He was stunned. Storming out of the stage, he called his senior team to one corner, issued some instructions, and drove away to the party office. Everyone was surprised to see the president hurriedly walk off the stage. However, there was no chance to ask any questions. The show had to continue.

The rally continued as per schedule. Purnima was upset to see Aditi Kasbekar and Arvind Balakrishnan participate in the rally and attack the opposition candidates without any restraint. She stayed away from them but delivered a good speech on the merits of her candidature.

The NPP rally got delayed for some time. The party's district president chatted with their star campaigner for the evening, Satish Bhatt, while Anil Hazarika sat some distance away. Robin Garg reached the venue but stayed away from all the guest speakers. Suresh Ahluwalia was to get there any time.

Ten minutes short of the rally venue, Suresh Ahluwalia received a phone call. He responded, "What? Say that again. Are you sure? Confirmed? Damn it!" He asked the driver to turn the car and head to their party headquarters. He informed Robin that he would be missing the rally for something very urgent. He enquired, "Suresh *ji*, what happened? Something serious?"

Suresh Ahluwalia said, "Nothing much, you need not worry, please go right ahead with the rally. This one has to be very successful. Give your absolute best." He disconnected and took out a handkerchief to wipe his face.

Meanwhile, Mohammed Hameed rushed out of Indradhanush Speciality Hospital in a big hurry. The sight of the characteristically poised senior doctor running through the corridors shocked everyone. After an extremely busy day since morning, he had barely taken a few sips of his coffee when the call came from Deen Dayal Upadhyay Hospital asking him to reach there as quickly as possible. Mohammed had so far distanced himself from his wife's activities in her new political avatar. He believed the whole effort was puerile and self-defeating but failed to convince her to stay away. He worried about her health all the time. Now that his worst fears came true, he cursed himself for not prohibiting Shazia from joining the senseless campaign. *The unrelenting campaign trail was a death warrant for Shazia! Hell, why didn't I stop her!*

By the time he reached the hospital's emergency section, it was too late!

Earlier, Shazia, delivering the speech of her life to an adoring Hari Nagar audience, fainted and collapsed suddenly. Clutching the left side of her chest, she cried out in extreme discomfort. Srikant Tiwari and his colleagues rushed her backstage. She was short of breath and did not respond to any questions. After making futile attempts to make her drink some water, they drove her to the nearby Deen Dayal Upadhyay Hospital. A panel of doctors worked hard in the emergency ward to save her life, but to no avail.

Mohammed held on to Shazia's hand as his eyes frantically searched her face for some signs of life. None whatsoever! As he delicately stroked her hair, teardrops rolled out of his moist eyes. He wiped them off with a hankie and looked around. He had things to do! The first one would be to call his father.

Later, Shazia was declared dead by the hospital management in an official bulletin.

35

Shazia's mortal remains were brought to her house, which was packed with grieving family members and well-wishers. Everyone was in utter shock. A few had their share of guilt as well. While Mohammed strongly opposed his wife's political gamble, others in the family, particularly Begum Mumtaz, enthusiastically supported Shazia's enterprise and believed her daughter-in-law had a decent chance of making it to the Parliament. Nasser Suleiman Hameed put his weight behind the campaign through his distinguished power network. Begum Mumtaz personally joined a few campaign trails. The support from her in-laws significantly boosted Shazia's prospects since they were well-connected and influential in the constituency. They weren't aware of Shazia's recent health concerns because she never discussed these with anyone—at times, not even with her husband. Both now felt they should have done better.

Alok Oberoi, Nasser's ex-colleague said, "So sorry about this, Nasser *ji*. She was doing so well with the public. Going by the press reports on her chemistry with the electorate, no one could say she was new to politics. I don't want to add to your pain. But I cannot hide from you what's in my mind. Is it completely out of place to doubt some foul play in this? She seemed strong and in high spirits! Surely, someone will benefit from her exit from the scene."

Nasser sighed and replied in a restrained voice. "I don't want to get there, Alok *ji*. It would be a lie if I say the thought didn't cross my mind at all. But any such talks shall mean taking on the mighty political establishment. That is a world well beyond mine.

Too much muck out there. Besides, in all likelihood, my daughter-in-law has had a natural death. She was a heart patient. The stress may have been the culprit. Let go! Our lovely daughter-in-law shall never come back, irrespective of what we do now!"

Conspiracy theories thrive on the grapevine. In this case, the whispers died quickly due to lack of any support from Shazia's family. Begum Mumtaz cursed herself for supporting an adventure that ultimately took her daughter-in-law's life. Mohammed barely talked to anyone.

The state presidents of both NPP and UNDP skipped important rallies and returned to their headquarters to take stock of the situation. The UNDP rally had concluded as scheduled. However, as the sad news spread like wildfire, NPP's rally was cut short as a mark of respect for the departed soul.

The election process headed to its logical end. Meanwhile, more drama unfolded. Late Thursday night, five persons were caught on camera distributing cash to people in Najafgarh against pledges to vote for NPP. Similar incidents were reported and recorded in Madipur and Matiala. The party workers were disbursing amounts varying from two thousand to three thousand rupees to each family, asking the adult members to vote for their party. They promised similar amounts of money again once their candidate won the election. It was not possible to identify them since their faces were covered. In separate video interviews taken at random, the voters confirmed that they had received cash from the party. A group of responsible citizens who crusaded against such nefarious activities lodged complaints with the Election Commission with the recorded evidence and urged them to take suitable action.

Early next morning, two vans laden with money were apprehended by cops, one in Vikaspuri and the other in Dwarka, along with UNDP campaign material. The documents seized included a comprehensive cash distribution plan and confirmed that the bulk of cash had already changed hands. The drivers managed to escape. As per FIRs lodged in the Daryaganj police station, the vans were stolen from an Old Delhi locality the previous evening.

Further, various parts of the constituency reported incidents of widespread alcohol distribution among the voters. The Election Commission received twenty-six complaints of coercion by armed hooligans to vote for either of the parties in different West Delhi localities. People had received threats of dire consequences if their candidate did not get their votes. With the press giving premium coverage to these incidents, there was no doubt in anyone's mind that both national parties had indulged in undemocratic practices to win this election.

With only two days left for polling day, the Election Commission held an emergency meeting on Friday afternoon to take stock of the latest developments. They reviewed the overwhelming evidence of extensive corrupt and undemocratic practices by the leading political parties to influence voters. They also noted that the independent candidate died of a heart attack while campaigning.

One of the election commissioners commented, "In a three-cornered contest, the death of a candidate, even though she was an independent, shall have significant adverse effects on the electorate and the voting process. On top of it, all these reports on corrupt practices are proven beyond any doubt! It seems impossible to hold a free and fair election under such conditions. We should immediately annul this election."

"I don't quite agree to this," said another. "The rules are pretty clear. Death of an independent candidate cannot trigger annulment of an election process. The election must proceed as scheduled, and only if the deceased independent candidate wins, the process has to be repeated under certain clearly laid out rules."

"What about all the serious irregularities in campaigning from either side?" Shot back the commissioner who had spoken earlier. "We cannot remain like ostriches! We have to investigate these incidents thoroughly and punish the guilty parties. We need time. Let us cancel this and call for a new election."

The arguments continued. The Chief Election Commissioner heard everyone but didn't say a word. It wasn't an easy decision to make. Their pronouncement tonight would have far-reaching consequences. They went through all the reports and evidence once again and got into an intense discussion. There must be a firm decision tonight.

Purnima was on the edge. Shazia's demise brought her mixed emotions. She had wanted her dead, but when it happened, she questioned whether her happiness was worth the life of a childhood chum. She repented the wild moments of weakness when she had considered catalysing her death. The shame of stooping so low made her sick and despondent. Having understood by now that the expiry of an independent candidate did not oblige the Election Commission to revoke an election process she realised her intentions had not only been heinous but also fundamentally flawed. She had been moments away from a blunder that could lead to only one result—lifelong regret for a pointless crime. Furthermore, the uncertainty around the election took a heavy toll on her. In case the Commission decided to go ahead with the scheduled process, one of them would be declared a winner! And, then what?

Oh, God, please ensure the Commission cancels this election. I don't want either of us to lose. This is a zero-sum game. One shall win at the cost of the other. How will Robin and I reconcile to this messy politics without jeopardising our happiness? Given the two parties' intensely contradictory ideologies, it would be a challenge to live happily under the same roof even if we do our utmost to avoid bringing work home.

No, I will not let anything come in the way of Robin and me as a happy couple. I have waited for this for decades; I'm not going to let go, come what may! If I win the contest, I shall resign and leave politics soon after we get married. I'll ask Robin to quit as well. But will he agree? Will he allow me to do so? Oh, Robin, why didn't you come back into my life a few months earlier?

She pulled her hair to get some relief from a throbbing headache. Well aware that a chat with Robin might calm her nerves, she opted to give herself some more time to sort out her own mental mess.

She picked up the handbag she had carried to the Crowne Plaza Hotel on Wednesday night and slipped her hand inside. After a few seconds' search, she pulled the drug out, still in its original pack. She stared at the formulation till her vision blurred with tears. She looked up, thanking the heavens for guiding her to make the right decision in those tense moments at the hotel. She would go to the chemist next afternoon along with the cash receipt. The chemist knew her very well. He would surely take the drug back without any objections.

Robin Garg was disturbed as well. He was sorry about Shazia's death and wished she had not joined the hostile world of parliamentary elections with poor heart conditions—it was a futile loss of life. However, Robin did not know her well enough to get hurt. He had no particular feelings for her. If anything at all, Robin harboured some resentment against Shazia for being unreasonably rude to Purnima. Hence, he could get over Shazia's death as an unfortunate event. He hoped it would influence the Election Commission's decision to cancel the election.

He wanted to talk with Purnima to share her grief but thought it wise to give her time to get over the trauma of losing a close classmate in this way. He could wait to call after the Commission's decision on the poll. The time would be ripe for their new beginning! Robin was confident that this election would get cancelled. He marvelled at the efficient work his friends had done at such a short notice. *The authorities cannot overlook such widespread violation of the code of conduct by either party. This election is doomed. Purnima and I shall quit politics, get married and find happiness that has long eluded us.*

But what if the Election Commission decides to go ahead with this process! If she wins, will I be able to take this embarrassing loss in my stride?

I will. Purnima is my love. I shall let her play her politics, take pride in her success and stand by her in all her efforts. But both of us cannot remain in politics. Besides contradictory ideologies, the intolerable bitterness and rivalry between the two camps shall only intensify in the years ahead. I shall quit the party and concentrate on my work.

What if I win? What if I get this golden chance to play my role in bringing about the changes I wish to see in my country. No one forced me to fight this election. I joined politics for a purpose. I worked hard to get this ticket, unlike Purnima. Will I be able to let the fruits of my labour go waste by resigning from the Parliament for happiness at home? No, that may be a tough call. I shall have to ask Purnima to give a wide berth to politics. Will she? Wouldn't that be an unfair demand on someone struggling to accept a humiliating defeat? Good heavens, I don't want to have to choose between my political beliefs and personal happiness. If there is an election in the coming days, I hope and pray that I lose!

Please, let there be an annulment. No elections, no winner, no loser, just a happily married couple!

He called his friends with whom he had had the breakfast meeting on Wednesday morning to thank them for their superb work. Irrespective of the Election Commission's ultimate decision, they had done a great job. The friends agreed to meet in two weeks to settle accounts and celebrate their success.

Durjoy Kumar welcomed the latest developments. He knew that the Commission had been discussing the latest developments in an emergency meeting and hoped the polling would get revoked. That would be a far better deal than what he had bargained for. With fresh nominations, there would be a new battle to fight. He would lobby Manoj Seth directly for the ticket, not the state president; it was abundantly clear who called the shots. Meanwhile, even if the election happened on schedule, Robin Garg's chances would significantly reduce due to an overwhelming wave of sympathy votes for the deceased candidate.

A few minutes past midnight, the Chief Election Commissioner presented a summary of their discussions with his take on the issue. "We have heard arguments for and against an annulment of the present process, and must say this is not a straightforward decision to arrive at. I believe we need to play by the book at all times. Our decision tonight shall be scrutinised threadbare by all and sundry, looking for gaps to criticise the Commission. The independent candidate's death can have no effect on the election process. The rules are quite clear on this. It is not for us to assess what effect it may or may not have on the electorate. As for the irregularities, very serious as they are, I am not convinced that they are so widespread as to advocate countermanding of the entire process. West Delhi is a large constituency. The unlawful activities occurred in certain pockets. I wouldn't term them as isolated instances since we have reports from many areas, but not wide enough to convince me that the whole constituency has been affected by such irregularities."

"Hence, I am of the opinion that the polling must proceed on schedule. Meanwhile, let us postpone counting of votes by one week. So, instead of counting the votes on the third day after polling, let us do this on the tenth day. That will give us adequate time to review reports from all the booths with extra care. If we find significant irregularities, we shall then take a call accordingly."

The Election Commission reached a unanimous decision and released necessary briefs to the media.

36

Purnima was back home when she received the news from Harsh Malhotra. Her worst fears came true; the voting was on schedule! Disappointed and nervous about the days ahead, she lost no time to call Robin using their private communication lines. Busy! *Must be a network error. Robin is not supposed to use this number for any other call!* A few seconds later, she dialled the number again. Still busy!

Robin received the news in the midst of a high-level meeting in the party headquarters to review their booth management strategy. He immediately excused himself and went out of the room to call Purnima. Though shocked and unnerved himself, his immediate concern was for Purnima. He was surprised to find Purnima's number engaged. *She is not supposed to use this line to make or receive calls. How come it is engaged!* He dialled again. Same result! *Is she calling me at the same time? That's the only possible explanation. Let me give a minute's break!*

Robin's phone rang. He picked up at the first ring. "Hello, Purnima! We must have been dialling each other's number at the same time. It *is* bad news! Things haven't worked out the way we wanted."

"I am so upset, Robin," said Purnima in a choked voice, "we *have* to go through this ordeal now. Please, tell me there's a way out of this mess. I don't want to lose *us* at any cost!"

Robin knew he had to take charge. "No, we shall never lose us, dear Purnima. We have come a long way now. The politics, this election and the results are fait accompli for us. We *cannot*

258

do anything about it. But what we *can* do is ensure that our future shapes the way *we* desire. I don't have a clear plan in hand right now. But I know, irrespective of who wins this election, our love will rise above everything else. Let us maintain a status quo till the polling closes. After that, we shall be free from all these political constraints. We shall walk together in public, letting the people infer whatever they wish. Is that okay?"

"Okay, Robin. We must meet soon after the polling day to work out our plans."

"Done! Let's now go back to our current role-plays! We are the sworn adversaries in an all-important by-election! As I said before, once the polling is over, we shall not hesitate to be seen together. It's our life. We shall live it the way we want."

"Is that possible at all, Robin? What about our party leaders, the media, the voters?" exclaimed Purnima.

"It *is* possible! Not easy, but that's how it will be. After polling, the fate of the candidates as well the electorate gets sealed inside the ballot boxes. We do not have to care anymore for what others say or do."

Robin continued after a pause, "Tell you what, I think both of us owe a visit to Shazia's house. Let's do this together this Tuesday. Is that okay?"

Purnima could barely believe what she just heard. Nevertheless, she promptly agreed, "Okay, Robin. Let's do it."

"Love you, Purnima!"

"Love you too, Robin."

Both took comfort from the fact that there was no further campaigning left.

Suresh Ahluwalia and Harish Gupta visited Shazia's house on Sunday to pay condolences on their party's behalf. Harsh Malhotra followed them later the same day with Jamal Ahmed. Rising above his aversion to politics, Mohammed Hameed gracefully received the high-profile guests. He ensured the visits were as brief as possible.

After the due courtesies, both leaders were quickly back at their work. With voting to start early the next day, they had a lot of organisational issues on their agenda with no time to brood over the past.

Voting was very slow on Monday morning. It picked up pace as the day progressed. By the time the booths closed, sixty-three percent polling was reported. There were no reports of untoward incidents or irregularities except a few minor skirmishes among polling agents in a handful of booths.

On Tuesday evening, Robin and Purnima went together to Shazia's house to offer their condolences. The ubiquitous press reporters did not miss this intriguing sight. When the candidates returned to their car after spending time with the bereaved family, the waiting reporters descended on them from all sides. Unperturbed, the duo stopped for a while and waved at the newspersons. There was no need for disguise anymore; gone were the days of fretting over public opinion or running away from stalking journalists. A few reporters aggressively threw questions at them with colourful microphones at the end of their stretched-out hands.

"Mr Garg, Miss Bhatt, do you have any comments on *The Third Eye* reports on your relationship?"

"Mr Garg, are you two together? Is it true that this election was all stage-managed?"

"Miss Bhatt, any comments on your friend Shazia's sudden demise? She was doing very well with the electorate!"

"Excuse me, how long have you two been together? Are you getting married soon?"

Robin and Purnima replied to each question with smiles, not a word! They hurried into their car and drove straight to Purnima's house for dinner together without bothering to search the rear-view mirror for the paparazzi. They were like free birds just released from iron cages; no more compulsions to hide their friendship from anyone. The drive to Safdarjung Enclave seemed not so long as they joked, laughed, and crooned as the car stereo played popular Hindi movie scores from the nineties.

Riding on their newfound wings, Robin and Purnima reviewed their options for the immediate future. Elections were just over. The counting was more than a week away. They wouldn't miss this week for the world! After a relaxed dinner, they selected ten beautiful countries that offered on-arrival visas for Indian nationals and drew a lot to pick their destination for a holiday together. Once the place got firmed up, Robin completed the travel plans. No compromises! This holiday, their first together, had to be the finest! There would be not a word of politics till they returned from this holiday. Seven days of seclusion, away from everything and everyone. Just the two of them with decades of missed opportunities to catch up on! They would fly out of New Delhi on Wednesday evening and return to the city a day before counting day. Party instructions were unequivocal. The candidates must be in town on the special day.

As Robin walked out of the apartment, Purnima's moist eyes adoringly followed him till he disappeared into the night. She felt like a spellbound teenager again, torn between a painful void and rosy promises, like she did in Austin Town in her adolescent years.

Robin also felt twenty years younger. Purnima possessed his mind all through the drive back to his house. Walking up to the veranda, Robin stared at the nameplate for a while. For a second, he thought it read 'Purnima and Robin!'

Gently shaking his head in disbelief, he smiled.

37

Purnima frantically looked at her watch. The check-in counter was to close in fifteen minutes, and Robin was still nowhere to be seen. She did well to avoid unwanted public attention and reached the airline counter an hour ago, dot on the time agreed with Robin. They had decided to meet directly at the airport to avoid additional travelling through the busy New Delhi streets. Now in Robin's absence, Purnima struggled to ignore all kinds of negative thoughts shrouding her mind.

Five minutes later, Robin came to her, gasping for breath, "So sorry to keep you waiting, Purnima. I came here more than twenty minutes ago, but two journalists and a couple of bystanders just wouldn't let me enter the airport. They asked me all sorts of questions, ignoring my pleas that I may miss my flight. I couldn't be rude because I didn't want to give them a chance to write some nonsense about me in their publication. Finally, I had no choice but to abruptly run away from them! Did you face such problems?"

"No, I didn't," replied Purnima. "I had my dupatta wrapped around my head. Maybe that helped. Anyway, let's rush to the counter. Don't want to get stuck without our boarding passes!"

After checking in, they could bypass a long queue at the security, thanks to the kind passengers who let them get ahead. Since there was no time to go to the lounge, they walked up to the gate and waited for the boarding announcements.

After the seat belt sign was off, Robin held Purnima's hand and said, "Here we go, Purnima. Now, we are free birds!"

"Yes, we are, Robin. And, we are off on our first holiday together. Crazy as it may sound, this election has done us good!

In normal course, our relationship would not have developed so quickly. It's been only a few weeks since we rediscovered each other!"

"Yes, indeed! Just a few weeks, and so much has happened!"

"It's all because of me, right?" Squeezing Robin's hand, she said with a smile, "Come on, say it, it's all because of me."

Robin leaned towards Purnima, rested his head on her shoulder, and repeated softly, "It's all because of you, Purnima. There's no question about it."

"The only sad thing in this incredible drama is poor Shazia, I feel so sorry for her. Wish she were alive. I know it is not true, but I don't know why, I am unable to absolve myself of any responsibility for her death. We were great friends once upon a time."

"You shouldn't think that way, Purnima. Isn't it obvious that Shazia was bent upon punishing you for a crime that you never committed? She played a dangerous game and she paid for it with her life. Come on, let's not talk of death in these beautiful moments."

Robin turned his head on Purnima's shoulder and planted a soft kiss on her neck. "You are a beautiful person, my love! We have a lot to give to each other. We have lost our younger years, but surely, we have the rest of our lives to be in each other arms."

Purnima moved closer till her breasts touched Robin's arms and her cheek rested gently on his head. Robin shuffled a bit in his seat. The delicate touch of her firm breasts took his breath away for a moment. He pushed in closer. Purnima ran her long fingers through Robin's hair as he closed his eyes in utter delight.

Both of them savoured the intimate moments in silence, before Robin whispered, "My dear Purnima, at thirty-five thousand feet above sea level, on board this beautiful large bird, I want to ask you something. May I?"

"Sure, Robin, go ahead," replied Purnima in a shaky voice.

"Will you marry me?"

She turned to Robin, gently lifted his head a little with both her hands, searched his eyes, and said, "Yes, Robin, yes! Probably I have waited all my life for this very moment! I am yours!"

Two days later, on a misty cold morning, Robin and Purnima drove along a meandering, picturesque Georgian highway towards the Russian border. On the way, they walked up to the famous Gergeti Trinity Church on the banks of the Chkheri. After looking around the historic fourteenth-century church, they sat on a bench overlooking Mount Kazbek and held each other. Cloudy sky, hanging haze, freezing temperature, a soft drizzle—the romantic ensemble woke up the young lovers in them. They passionately kissed and explored each other like two youngsters enjoying their precious privacy. Time stood still as a thousand blooming daffodils, melodic mountain streams, and chorusing birds were at their best in this Georgian rhapsody.

With their scheduled return to the political hotbed still a few days away, they drove around Georgia's beautiful countryside with excitement usually seen in newly-wed couples in their late twenties. They walked around Tbilisi trying out local delicacies like Khachapuri, Khinkali and Lobio with choice Georgian wines, sat by the beautiful Kura River to get a majestic view of the city, took a wine tasting tour of the Kakheti region and spent a few days in the beautiful Black Sea resort of Batumi.

As their flight took off from the Tbilisi International Airport, they realised it marked not only the end of a glorious holiday but also the beginning of challenging days ahead. Lost in their thoughts, they held each other's hands in silence. Soon, one of them would be declared a winner, the other a loser. Victory processions, sweets, garlands and a stream of congratulatory messages for one while empty party office, disappointment, frustration, insinuations, and consolatory words for the other. With a gentle squeeze on his grip, Robin smiled at Purnima as she searched his eyes for reassurance. They told each other in unspoken words—*Now, our love is all that matters till death do us part!*

Robin and Purnima did well to avoid unwanted public attention at the airport and reached home on schedule. The next day, they woke up to a chirpy morning, full of confidence. The counting of votes would start in less than two hours.

LIST OF SELECT CHARACTERS
(ALPHABETICALLY)

Aditi Kasbekar:	Robin's ex-colleague who worked with him as an intern
Ajay Chowdhury:	Chairman of Topaz Investigative Services – country's top detective agency
Anil Hazarika:	Purnima's batch mate at the medical college
Arvind Balakrishnan:	A businessman and Shazia's boyfriend in high school years
Bhupinder Gupta:	An NPP politician and aspirant for the party ticket for the by-election
Durjoy Kumar:	A veteran NPP politician and ex-member of Parliament, aspiring for the ticket for the by-election
Harish Gupta:	A senior NPP functionary and the party president's confidante
Harsh Malhotra:	President of the Delhi unit of the UNDP, the main opposition party in the Parliament
Jamal Ahmed:	A UNDP senior functionary, confidante of the party district president
Manoj Seth:	The national president of the NPP, the country's ruling political party – a powerful politician known for his wiliness and command

Mohammed Hameed:	Shazia's husband, a doctor
Mumtaz Hameed:	Mohammed Hameed's mother, and a social worker
Nasser Suleiman Hameed:	Mohammed Hameed's father, and a retired Supreme Court judge.
Pradeep Raina:	A senior executive at the Topaz Investigative Services
Praveen Lakhotia:	An office helper at the NPP national headquarters
Purnima Bhatt:	The novel's protagonist, in her late thirties. A popular doctor, and philanthropist
Radha Saluja:	Purnima's best friend, a journalist
Raman Srivastava:	A senior NPP functionary
Robin Garg:	The novel's protagonist, in his late forties – a prosperous businessman, social worker, and the co-founder of a successful NGO
Ritu:	Robin's wife. Co-founder of the NGO, Ritu's World
Satish Bhatt:	A doctor, and Purnima's ex-husband
Shazia Sultana Hameed:	Purnima's erstwhile childhood buddy
Srikant Tiwari:	A junior NPP functionary
Sunil Sharma:	A general secretary of the UNDP
Suresh Ahluwalia:	President of the Delhi unit of the NPP, the ruling party in the Parliament.
Tim Jacob:	The Chief Editor of a widely-read online publication – The Third Eye.

ABOUT THE AUTHOR

Jayanta Gopal Borpujari is an electronics engineer from BITS Pilani and an MBA from Edinburgh Business School. He has published columns on contemporary political issues and musings based on street-level experiences in eminent publications like *The Asia Times*, *The Indian Express*, *Times of Oman*, *The Assam Tribune*, and *DailyO*. A few of these are in his blog http://pensivereflex.blogspot.com/.

His debut novel *Beyond the Blinding Sun*, sold worldwide, has earned rave reviews. It deals with the sensitive subject of the exploitation of immigrant labourers.

He is an avid golfer and a passionate music enthusiast.

Ballots and Betrayals is his second novel. He can be reached via email at borpujari@outlook.com. His social media handles are X (Twitter): @borpu2 and Instagram: @jayantaborpujari